D0801881

Treating Adolescent Substance Abuse

Related Titles of Interest

Preventing Relapse in the Addictions: A Biopsychosocial Approach
Emil J. Chiauzzi
ISBN: 0-205-14303-2

Rational-Emotive Therapy with Alcoholics and Substance Abusers
Albert Ellis, John F. McInerney, Raymond DiGiuseppe, and Raymond J. Yeager
ISBN: 0-205-14434-9

Cognitive-Behavioral Procedures with Children and Adolescents: A Practical Guide
A. J Finch, Jr., W. Michael Nelson III, and Edith S. Ott
ISBN: 0-205-13435-1

Helping People Change: A Textbook of Methods, Fourth Edition
Frederick H. Kanfer and Arnold P. Goldstein (Editors)
ISBN: 0-205-14382-2 Paper ISBN: 0-205-14383-0 Cloth

Handbook of Differential Treatments for Addictions
Luciano L'Abate, Jack E. Farrar, and Daniel A. Serritella (Editors)
ISBN: 0-205-13237-5

Handbook of Alcoholism Treatment Approaches: Effective Alternatives
Reid K. Hester and William R. Miller (Editors)
ISBN: 0-205-14390-3

Preventing Substance Abuse Among Children and Adolescents
Jean E. Rhodes and Leonard A. Jason
ISBN: 0-205-14463-2

Treating Adolescent Substance Abuse

Understanding the Fundamental Elements

George R. Ross
Psychologist and Chemical Dependency Counselor

Allyn and Bacon
Boston • London • Toronto • Sydney • Tokyo • Singapore

A Division of Simon & Schuster, Inc.
160 Gould Street
Needham Heights, Massachusetts 02194

Library of Congress Cataloging-in-Publication Data

Ross, George R.
Treating adolescent substance abuse: understanding the fundamental elements / George R. Ross.
p. cm.
Includes bibliographical references and indexes.
ISBN 0-205-15255-4
1. Teenagers--Substance use. 2. Substance abuse--Treatment.
I. Title.
RJ506.D78R67 1993
616.86'00835--dc20 93-11215
CIP

Printed in the United States of America

10 9 8 7 6 5 4 3 2 97 96 95 94

This book is dedicated to the countless millions of adolescents nationwide who still suffer from the dreaded disease of chemical dependency.

About the Author

George R. Ross, Ph.D., is nationally recognized as a leader in the field of teenage substance abuse. Since 1978 he has worked with nearly one thousand chemically dependent youth and their families. He has given several workshops on this topic; appeared on a national radio program, "Focus on the Family," with noted psychologist Dr. James C. Dobson; and was an invited participant at the White House Conference for a Drug Free America. He is the founding director of Life, Inc., Kids Helping Kids, Inc., and Possibilities Unlimited, Inc., all substance abuse programs for teenagers.

Dr. Ross has completed training in reality therapy with William Glasser, M.D., and in rational behavioral therapy with Maxie C. Maultsby, Jr., M.D. He is an experienced teacher having taught at both the high school and college level. Dr. Ross is also a licensed psychologist and certified chemical dependency counselor. Currently, Dr. Ross operates a private counseling practice and consulting business in Lexington, Kentucky.

Contents

Foreword

George Ross has written a wonderful book to help therapists do a better job of treating teenagers addicted to alcohol and other drugs. Here is a thoughtful review of the latest psychological research into chemical dependence, especially the cognitive-behavioral approach to this cunning, baffling, and powerful disease. Here is a new synthesis of research and experience for the practitioner. This book is given life and force by the 15 years of hard work Dr. Ross has done as a nationally recognized treatment program leader in the field of adolescent substance abuse.

Dr. Ross offers eight fundamental elements for the treatment of adolescent substance abusers. They create a solid foundation for a successful clinical approach to adolescent addicts and to their families. He offers important new insights into the personalities of adolescent substance abusers and useful ways to use these insights to help troubled youth. His techniques for making a diagnosis and of negotiating the continuum of care are creative and understandable. His insights into the vital role of the counselor in this process are refreshingly candid.

For me, however, the most valuable part of the book is the skillful way Dr. Ross integrates the twelve-step program and the disease concept of addiction into every facet of his work. These mutual-aid programs, a modern miracle, cannot be understood without an appreciation of the spiritual impoverishment that is at the heart of addiction or of the spiritual renewal that is the soul of recovery. Dr. Ross gets this message right. He communicates it to his readers with marvelous clarity and commendable simplicity.

Addiction is a malignant disease of the whole self and ultimately of the family and the community. Addiction is not self-curing. Left alone, addiction only gets worse, leading to total degradation, to prison, and, ultimately, to death. The sad truth is that too few people today understand the stakes in the battle for the youth of our country. Too few people understand that addiction cuts like a deadly scythe through adolescence in North America, mowing down 10% or more of our youth, some for a few years, many for their lifetimes. Addiction hides behind the facade of "normal" teenage drinking and drug "experimentation." North America needs to wake up to the realization that drinking and drug use are neither normal nor safe for youth, and that communities, families, and youth need to team up to help kids grow up free of the use of chemicals to get high. We need to redefine getting high as what it truly is: "brain poisoning." We need to recognize that addiction is the most potent of all forms of environmental pollution.

George Ross's book is a giant step forward for everyone who wants to understand teenage addiction and wants to know what to do about it. Here are the practical nuts-and-bolts needed to help addicted teenagers and their families get well. The disease of addiction is desperate and degrading. The recovery from addiction is joyous and wonderful. This book celebrates that transformation, from the desperation of addiction to the serenity of recovery. Here is a road map for therapists and others out of chemical dependence and into robust good health, not only physical good health but also mental and spiritual good health.

Although much has been written about teenage drug addiction over the past 30 years, there have been few books written about the diagnosis and treatment of adolescent substance abusers. None, to my knowledge, have placed the treatment of adolescent addiction into a comprehensive framework that includes the latest psychological research and the twelve-step program. None, that is, until this new book filled that serious gap. Now counselors and program managers can find in one convenient and readable book the answers to their questions and a workable strategy to help addicted kids get, and stay, well.

Robert L. DuPont, M.D.
Former Director of the
National Institute of Drug Abuse

Robert L. DuPont, M. D. is the founding director of the National Institute on Drug Abuse (NIDA) and served in this capacity under Presidents Nixon, Ford, and Carter. He is the author of the informative book, *Getting Tough on Gateway Drugs: A Guide for the Family* and soon will have two new books published entitled: *The Selfish Brain: Coping with Chemical Dependence* and *A Bridge to Recovery: An Introduction to 12-Step Programs.*

Preface

Treating Adolescent Substance Abuse: Understanding the Fundamental Elements is a book written to introduce practitioners in the field of chemical dependency and related professions to eight fundamental elements for treating adolescent substance abuse. These elements were derived from an examination of the literature, talks with numerous professionals in the field, information gathered at several workshops and conferences, and most importantly, this writer's experience from having diagnosed and treated nearly one thousand teenage substance abusers and their families over the past 15 years.

The intent of this book is to provide the practitioner with a comprehensive overview of these eight fundamental elements. In doing so, the practitioner is introduced to (1) a sound rationale for conceptualizing the problem of chemical dependency, (2) a framework for addressing the problem (3) a list of defined goals and objectives for confronting chemical dependency, and (4) field-tested treatment strategies for helping teenage substance abusers and their families overcome the problem.

In this book, the practitioner is also introduced to a cognitive-behavioral explanation of the disease of chemical dependency. *Chemical dependency* is defined as a disease of attitudes leading to the use and abuse of mind-altering substances (e.g., alcohol, marijuana, cocaine) culminating in physical deterioration of the body, emotional instability, and spiritual bankruptcy. Chemical dependency is viewed as a progressive disease with four distinct stages: (1) initial usage, (2) problem usage, (3) psychological addiction, and (4) physiological addiction. It also involves the formation of a distinct self-defeating self-talk that, left unchallenged, will form the foundation of a distinct personality and cognitive structure that will ultimately lead to an untimely death of the chemically dependent teenager.

In addition, this book also presents several treatment strategies that have proved useful in the intervention and treatment of adolescent substance abusers and their families. These strategies are described within a framework of a defined treatment rationale that outlines a process of recovery and clearly states goals and objectives.

In this book, the time-proven steps of Alcoholics Anonymous are introduced, and spiritual concepts such as prayer, meditation, and higher power are integrated with cognitive-behavioral techniques. It is shown how these combined strategies are useful in helping the chemically dependent adolescent identify and change self-defeating thinking. In addition, the importance of developing quality assessment and intervention procedures for chemically dependent adolescents is stressed. The need is also emphasized to provide them a continuum of treatment options that are implemented by a caring and competent staff in an environment that is palpable, efficacious, and efficient.

In the first chapter, eight fundamental elements of an effective treatment program are introduced. The fundamental elements include (1) a clearly defined rationale for diagnosis and treatment, (2) screening, assessment, and diagnostic procedures, (3) a continuum of care, (4) a healthy treatment environment, (5) treatment strategies, (6) family involvement, (7) a competent staff, and (8) efficacy and efficiency of treatment.

In the second chapter, a cognitive-behavioral model of emotion and behavior is introduced, and the importance of self-talk in the formation of personality is discussed. The emerging personality of a teenage substance abuser is also presented, and the attitudes underlying the personality structure of a chemically dependent adolescent are delineated.

In chapter 3, a multi-method approach to assessment is introduced that includes (1) drug screening, (2) a signs and symptoms checklist, (3) psychosocial assessment and family interviews, (4) parental evaluation, (5) interviewing the teenage substance abuser, (6) medical examination, (7) psychological/psychiatric evaluation, and (8) clinical observations. Three diagnostic dimensions used to formulate a diagnosis of an adolescent substance abuser are also explained. These three dimensions are (1) degree of dependency, (2) mental state of the teenager, and (3) mental state of the parents.

In chapter 4, treatment options and the treatment environment are discussed. Treatment options range from outpatient treatment to intensive day treatment. Hospitalization is recommended under restricted conditons. Three important aspects of a healthy treatment environment are also introduced. They include treatment climate, staffing patterns, and supportive services.

In chapters 5 and 6, four distinct plateaus of recovery are presented: (1) admitting, (2) submitting, (3)committing, and (4) transmitting. Thirty treatment strategies are also introduced that have been useful in helping adolescent substance abusers develop healthier cognitive structures, enabling them to reach these four plateaus. Techniques are also outlined that teach adolescent substance abusers how to be more *aware and honest with themselves,* how to more *effectively manage their feelings,* and how to *change self-defeating emotions and behavior.* In addition, techniques are also presented that show chemically dependent youth how to *identify self-defeating self-talk, change it, and keep it from reoccurring.*

In chapter 7, the core attitudes of a co-dependent enabling parent are examined. Thirty treatment strategies that have proved useful in helping parents and other family members overcome co-dependent enabling tendencies are also presented. Methods for helping parents develop more effective communication and interaction patterns with their family are also discussed.

In chapter 8, the attributes and requisite skills of an effective chemical dependency counselor are outlined. Attributes include (1) character strengths, (2) confidentiality, (3) timing and tact, (4) listenership, (5) objectivity and discernment, (6) empathy and understanding, (7) honesty, (8) genuine interest and love, and (9) patience and perseverance. Skills include (1) basic counseling skills, (2) cognitive-behavioral therapy skills, (3) chemical dependency counseling skills including a working knowledge of the steps and principles of Alcoholics Anonymous (AA), (4) knowledge of developmental theories, (5) knowledge of family systems theories, (6) knowledge of other counseling theories, especially gestalt, reality, and actualizing therapies, (7) cognitive-behavioral one-on-one counseling, and (8) cognitive-behavioral group counseling.

In chapter 9, issues of efficacy and efficiency of treatment are examined. The current "state-of-the-art" of adolescent treatment programs and the adequacy of methodologies available to assess their effectiveness are reviewed. In addition, four types of evalution are introduced: context, input, process, and product. Measurable outcome variables for adolescent treatment programs are also discussed.

In chapter 10, a model treatment program for treating adolescent substance abuse is introduced within the context of the eight fundamental elements.

Studying this book will expose the beginning student and the experienced professional to eight fundamental elements for treating chemically dependent adolescents and to a comprehensive overview of how to diagnose and treat adolescent chemical dependency. Building on this understanding, the professional can then use this book as a practical guide to diagnose and treat adolescent substance abusers and their families in a more efficacious and efficient manner.

This book is intended to be used as a practitioner's guide, a college text, and as a resource book for professionals interested in the treatment of adolescent substance abuse and related disorders. The theories and techniques discussed in this book can also be applied to adult substance abusers, to other forms of addiction, and to oppositional defiant and conduct disorders.

This book will appeal to a variety of readers including psychologists; psychiatrists; family practitioners; pediatricians; social workers; nurses; family, mental health, guidance, and chemical dependency counselors; ministers; teachers; and students. Adolescents and adults in recovery, and their family members, may also find this book beneficial.

A special thank you is extended to Ellsworth Mason, Karen Doyle, Mark Simpson, Dave McAdams, and Edythe Lach for their help in proofreading this book, to Brian Murphy for helping prepare the figures. Thank you to Daniel Serritella, marriage and family therapy consultant, Jonesboro GA, for his suggestions on how to organize and present more clearly the material outlined in this book.

A very special thank you is extended to my wife, Glenda, for her encouragement and support while writing this book.

List of Figures

1

Fundamental Elements of Effective Treatment

When this writer first became involved in the treatment of adolescent substance abuse in 1978, few programs existed for treatment, little was known about the subject, training programs were sparse, the majority of chemically dependent adolescents were being diagnosed and treated as mentally ill, and a limited information base was available on how to diagnose and treat adolescent substance abuse. Information that was available mostly focused on the diagnosis and treatment of adult alcoholics or hard-core adult heroin addicts. In addition, a pervasive political and social climate existed condoning experimentation with mind-altering drugs. Cocaine and marijuana were perceived as "safe recreational drugs."

Fortunately, much has changed since 1978. A proliferaton of research has been published dispelling the notion of "safe drug usage." Marijuana and cocaine are no longer considered safe recreational drugs. Much has also been written about diagnosing and treating teenage substance abuse.

However, current review of the literature on the diagnosis and treatment of adolescent substance abuse revealed few, if any resources that specifically outlined the fundamental elements of an effective treatment program for adolescent substance abusers. Although many fundamental elements could be found sprinkled throughout the literature, no one source was available that attempted to incorporate these elements into a comprehensive approach. Resources were not found that included a comprehensive overview of the subject that (1) incorporated a sound rationale for conceptualizing the problem, (2) outlined a framework for addressing the problem, (3) listed defined goals and objectives for confronting the problem, and (4) furnished field-tested strategies for helping teenage substance abusers and their families overcome the problem. This book is written to provide such an extensive coverage.

In this overview chapter, eight fundamental elements of an effective treatment program for adolescent substance abusers are outlined. They were derived from an examination of the literature, talks with numerous professionals in the field, information gathered at several workshops and conferences, and most importantly, this writer's experience from having diagnosed and treated nearly one thousand teenage substance abusers and their families over the past 15 years.

Fundamental Elements

The U.S. Department of Health and Human Services Office for Treatment Improvement (OTI) for alcohol, drug abuse, and mental health recommends that programs developed for treating alcohol and substance abuse include the following elements: (1) *program structure and administration* that encompasses joint cooperation with other agencies, an oversight body or advisory board, cross-training of corrections and substance abuse staff, ongoing program evaluation, staff training, employee incentive measures and professional development, and (2) *clinical interventions and other services* that include same day intake services, medical care, counseling for HIV-positive/AIDS patients, pharmacotherapeutic interventions, urine testing, basic substance abuse counseling and psychological counseling, health education and prevention, life skills education, educational training and remediation, justice system liaison, other support systems, and ongoing intervention and treatment (OTI, 1992).

Treatment programs for adolescent substance abusers must encompass more than "program structure and administration...and clinical intervention and other services." A treatment program for adolescent substance abusers must also include at least eight fundamental elements if effective intervention strategies and treatment services are to be provided. These fundamental elements include (1) a sound rationale for diagnosis and treatment, (2) appropriate screening, assessment, and diagnostic procedures, (3) a continuum of care, (4) a healthy treatment environment, (5) effective treatment strategies, (6) active family involvement, (7) competent staff, and (8) efficacy and efficiency of treatment.

Rationale for Diagnosis and Treatment

The first fundamental element of an effective treatment program for adolescent substance abusers is a sound rationale for diagnosis and treatment. Nay and Ross (1993, p. 317) explain:

> *Efficacious assessment tools and intervention schemes emerge only from a sound conceptual framework...from a sound conceptualization of the variables that instigate and maintain drug use...a conceptual model for better understanding the phenomenon of adolescent substance abuse and, more importantly, with a sound framework for intervention.*

Only from a sound rationale can assessment strategies and clearly defined treatment goals and objectives be formulated. A sound *assessment strategy* determines the need for treatment and generates appropriate intervention procedures. *Treatment goals and objectives* establish the outcome expectancies for the adolescent substance abuser and his or her family, determine the types of treatment strategies employed, and provide the clinical staff with a standard to gauge the ongoing effectiveness of the treatment methodologies used.

Assessment strategies and treatment goals and objectives stemming from a sound rationale provide the cornerstones for developing and implementing effective intervention and treatment plans. As one wise person once remarked, "If you don't know where you are going then any road will get you there.

In chapter 2, the reader will be introduced to a conceptual model from which sound assessment strategies and treatment goals and objectives can be derived. The conceptual model also serves as a reference point to help understand and explain various procedures used to treat adolescent substance abusers.

Screening, Assessment, and Diagnostic Procedures

The second fundamental element of an effective treatment program for adolescent substance abusers entails the development and employment of sound screening, assessment, and diagnostic procedures. Nay and Ross (1993, p. 317) explain:

> *A variety of events may compel a reasonably well-adjusted youth from a functional family to initiate drug use.... Given the myriad of possible combinations of person and life factors that may combine to influence a child's use of chemicals, a thorough assessment must be performed.*

A thorough assessment will adopt a multi-method clinical approach (Nay, 1979) that includes (1) drug screening, (2) a review of signs and symptoms, (3) psychosocial assessment including family interviews, (4) parental evaluation, (5) interviewing the suspected adolescent substance abuser, (6) medical examination, (7) psychological and psychiatric evaluation, and (8) clinical observations.

In chapter 3, an outline of a multi-method approach for conducting assessment will be presented in light of the emerging personality and cognitive structure of an adolescent substance abuser. Critical factors needed to derive an appropriate diagnosis will also be reviewed.

Continuum of Care

The third fundamental element of an effective treatment program for adolescent substance abusers involves the deployment of an intervention strategy that offers a continuum of care. Such care can range from outpatient individual and group counseling for adolescents at stage one of the disease to temporary hospitalization for teenagers who have become physiologically addicted.

In chapter 4, various types of treatment options available for the treatment of adolescent substance abuse will be examined.

Treatment Environment

The fourth fundamental element of an effective treatment program for adolescent substance abusers involves a healthy treatment environment (King, 1988, Nay & Ross, 1993; Stanton, 1979; Voth, 1980). In the later part of chapter 4, three important aspects of the treatment environment will be discussed. They include treatment climate, staffing patterns, and types of supportive services.

Treatment Strategies

The fifth fundamental element of an effective treatment program for adolescent substance abusers involves treatment strategies. What treatment strategies will be used in treating the chemically dependent adolescent, and what is the rationale for their usage?

For example, should treatment include the use of antipsychotic and antidepressant medications? What kinds of therapeutic approaches work most effectively? What kinds of therapeutic relationships need to be established? Should therapy be conducted in groups or individually?

In chapters 5 and 6, some of these issues will be addressed. Several treatment strategies effective in helping adolescent substance abusers combat their chemical dependency will also be outlined.

Family Involvement

The sixth fundamental element of an effective treatment program for adolescent substance abusers entails active family involvement, especially on the part of the parents. Selekman and Todd (1991, pp. 8–9) explain:

> *Although many traditional drug abuse programs for adolescent substance abusers stress the importance of family therapy as a major component, it is questionable how important this modality is in actual practice.... Outmoded belief systems and problem-maintaining patterns of interaction were left untouched while the adolescent was in the hospital or residential treatment program.... Considering the impact on the families to which adolescents return, it is no surprise to us that close to 56 percent of the adolescent substance abusers who receive inpatient treatment resume chemical use following discharge.*

In chapter 7, the importance of active family involvement will be discussed. Treatment strategies that have been effective in helping family members of chemically dependent adolescents overcome co-dependent enabling behaviors and develop healthier communication and family interaction patterns will also be detailed.

Developing Competent Staff

The seventh fundamental element of an effective program for adolescent substance abusers focuses on developing competent clinical staff (George, 1990; G. W. Lawson, Ellis, & Rivers, 1984; Ross, 1991). In chapter 8, two aspects of this important element will be addressed: the counseling attributes desired and the counseling skills needed to treat chemically dependent youth and their families.

Efficacy and Efficiency of Treatment

The eighth fundamental element of an effective treatment program for adolescent substance abusers involves establishing a means to measure the effectiveness, or efficacy, of treatment and to determine its overall cost, or efficiency.

Friedman and Glichman (1986, p. 669) reported, "Very little is known about the actual 'state of the art' of the treatment that is being provided for adolescent substance abusers." Further compounding the problem is the state-of-the-art of the methodology available to evaluate treatment outcome (Sobell, Serge, Sobell, Roy, & Stevens, 1987, p. 113). In summary, the overall state-of-the-art of treatment in the field of adolescent chemical dependency and accompanying methodology for evaluating treatment outcome is, at best, emerging.

In chapter 9, some of the apparent challenges to conducting effective evaluation of program outcomes will be addressed. A conceptual framework for conducting ongoing program evaluation and examining important outcome variables will be introduced.

The last chapter of this book, will present a model program for treating adolescent chemical dependency. The model program incorporates the eight fundamental elements for effective treatment and illustrates their use.

Summary

In this chapter, eight fundamental elements of an effective chemical dependency treatment program for adolescents were outlined. They included (1) a sound rationale for diagnosis and treatment, (2) screening, assessment, and diagnostic procedures, (3) a continuum of care, (4) a healthy treatment environment, (5) effective treatment strategies, (6) active family involvement, (7) competent staff, and (8) efficacy and efficiency of treatment.

2

Emerging Personality and Cognitive Structure of an Adolescent Substance Abuser

Whether the practitioner considers chemical dependency a disease or a behavior disorder, or attributes its cause to genetic factors, environmental, family, and cultural influences, or underlying personality conflicts;[1] clinical evidence clearly suggests that a faulty cognitive structure, or *self-defeating self-talk,* is a critical element in the assessment and treatment of adolescents suffering from the use and abuse of mind-altering substances.[2] In this chapter, a conceptual model is introduced that examines these various influences in light of the emerging personality and cognitive structure of a chemically dependent adolescent.

Chemical Dependency: A Disease of Attitude

Rokeach (1970, p.112) defined an *attitude* as "a relatively enduring organization of beliefs around an object or situation pre-disposing one to respond in some preferential manner." There are two types of attitudes (Ross, 1978) that contribute to the emerging dynamics of a chemically dependent personality

The first, *a priori attitude,* consists of an enduring organization of beliefs around a person's perception or images of the environment. A priori attitudes help a person make sense out of their external experiences, their environment. The second, *a posteriori attitude,* consists of an enduring organization of beliefs around a person's autonomically mediated physiological responses (emotions). A posteriori attitudes help a person make sense out of their internal experiences, their feelings or emotional response to the environment. Formation of these two types of attitudes produces automatic emotional and behavioral responses and eventually results in the formation of distinct personality structures.

Chemical dependency is defined as a disease of attitudes leading to the use and abuse of mind-altering substances (e.g., alcohol, marijuana, cocaine) culminating in physical deterioration of the body, emotional instability, and spiritual bankruptcy. Chemical dependency involves the formation of distinct self-defeating a priori and a posteriori attitudes that, left unchallenged, will form the foundation of a distinct personality and cognitive structure that will ultimately lead to the untimely death of the person adhering to these dysfunctional attitudes.

Nomological Network

A cognitive model of an emotion and behavior[3] contains at least five interrelated but distinguishable elements: (1) perceptions or images, (2) a priori cognitions, (3) autonomically mediated physiological responses, (4) a posteriori cognitions, and (5) behavioral responses.[4] Figure 2-1 depicts this nomological network of the anatomy of an emotion and behavior (Ross, 1978). A person's sensory system transmits certain signals to the brain (neocortex), activating certain learned sets of a priori cognitions (descriptive, evaluative, and prescriptive propositions around percep-

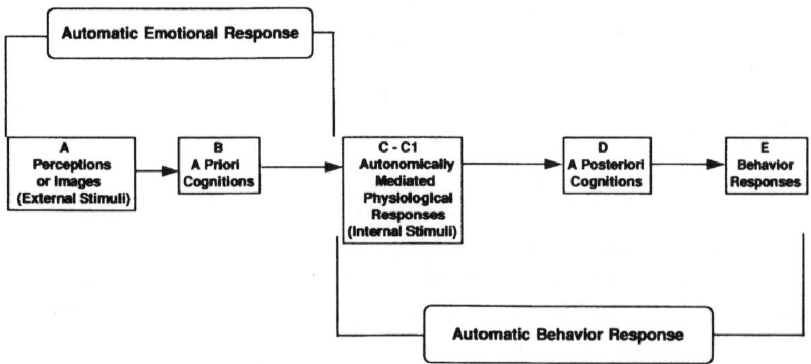

FIGURE 2-1 Nomological Network of the Anatomy of an Emotion and Behavior

tions or images). A priori cognitions in turn activate appropriate autonomically mediated physiological responses congruent with the person's positive, negative, or neutral evaluation of the perceptions or images. The internally experienced physiological changes in turn activate in the brain (neocortex) certain learned sets of a posteriori cognitions that describe and evaluate the physiological experience (emotion) and prescribe how the person should respond behaviorally. The habitual use of certain sets of a priori and a posteriori cognitions results in the formation of specific attitudes. These specific a priori and a posteriori attitudes create automatic emotional and behavioral responses—that is, only an external stimulus (perception or image) or an internal stimulus (physiological response) need be present to elicit certain emotional and behavioral responses.

Figure 2-2 depicts this nomological network in conditioning terms. During phase one, certain a priori cognitions (B) are seen as having been previously paired with punishment or with the withdrawal of a positive reinforcer (refer to Figure 2-2). As a consequence of this pairing, the a priori cognitions (B) act as a conditioned emotional stimulus (CES) that elicits certain emotions (C), the conditioned emotional response (CER).

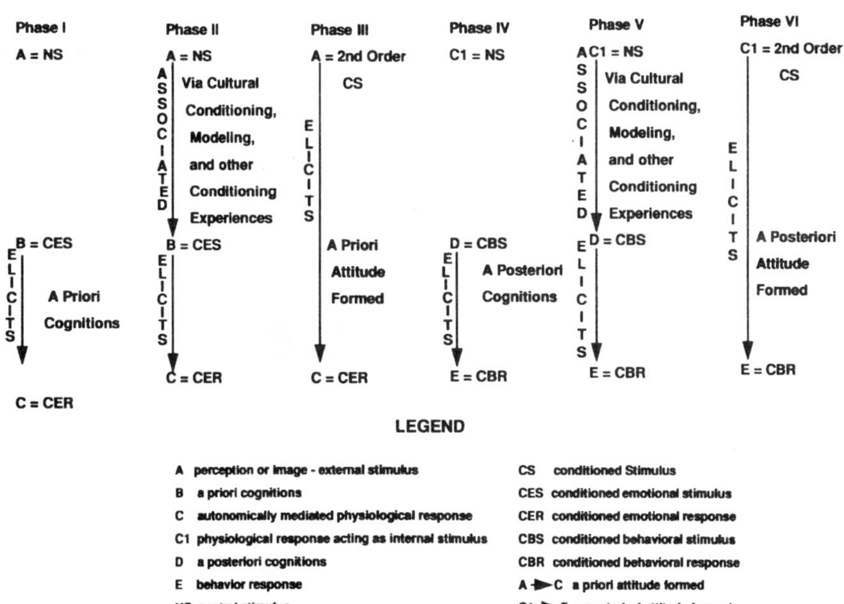

FIGURE 2-2 Nomological Network Describing the Anatomy of an Emotion and Behavior in Conditioning Terms

The external stimulus, the perception or image of oneself or one's environment (A), acts as a neutral stimulus (NS) at this point in the process.

During phase two, a pairing or association between the neutral stimulus (A) and the previously conditioned emotional stimulus (B) occurs via cultural conditioning, modeling, or various other reinforcing consequences or conditioning experiences.

During phase three, the previous neutral stimulus (A) becomes a second-order conditioned emotional stimulus capable of eliciting the conditioned emotional response (C). In other words, the continued or habitual use of certain a priori cognitions (B) in the presence of certain perceptions or images (A) has resulted in the formation of an a priori attitude

During phase four, certain a posteriori cognitions (D) are seen as having been previously paired with punishment or the removal of a positive reinforcer. As a consequence of this pairing, the a posteriori cognitions (D) act as conditioned behavioral stimuli (CBS) that elicit certain behaviors (E), the conditioned behavioral responses (CBR). The internal stimulus, the autonomically mediated physiological response (C-1), acts as a neutral stimulus (NS) at this point in the process.

During phase five, a pairing or association between the neutral stimulus (C-1) and the previously conditioned behavioral stimulus (D) occurs via cultural conditioning, modeling, or various other reinforcing consequences or conditioning experiences.

During phase six, the previous neutral stimulus (C-1) becomes a second-order conditioned behavioral stimulus capable of eliciting the conditioned behavioral response (E). In other words, the continued or habitual use of certain a posteriori cognitions (D) in the presence of certain autonomically mediated physiological responses (C-1) has resulted in the formation of an a posteriori attitude.

Cognitive Structure

Viewing the anatomy of an emotion and behavior in this manner results in an alternative explanation to the long debated argument as to whether physiological changes (emotions) precede thoughts or whether thoughts precede physiological changes. Earlier theorists had failed to clearly distinguish the difference between a priori and a posteriori cognitions, between conscious thoughts preceding experienced physiological changes (emotions) and conscious thoughts proceeding experienced physiological changes. Acceptance of this explanation of the anatomy of an emotion and behavior also enables the research efforts of several theorists to be synthesized into a more comprehensive explanation. As Schacter (1967, p. 124) explained in describing the emotion fear:

> *Cognitive or situational factors trigger physiological processes, and the triggering stimulus usually imposes the label we attach to our feelings. We see the threatening object, this perception—cognition initiates a state of sympathetic arousal and the joint cognitive—physiological experience is labeled fear.*

Viewing the anatomy of an emotion and behavior in this manner also helps clarify Meichenbaum's (1977, p. 123) notion of "cognitive structure...that organizing aspect of thinking that seems to monitor and direct the strategy, route, and choice of thoughts...a kind of executive process which holds the blueprints of thinking and which determines when to interrupt, change, or continue thought." This explanation helps redefine the function of a person's cognitive structure as one of managing emotional and behavioral responses, and its role as one of describing and evaluating external and internal stimuli.

Figure 2-3 depicts this revised notion of Meichenbaum's concept of a cognitive structure. The cognitive structure contains two separate but interrelated cognitions: a priori and a posteriori. The a priori cognitions contain descriptive evaluative and prescriptive propositions (beliefs) around a person's perceptions and images (external stimuli). The a poste-

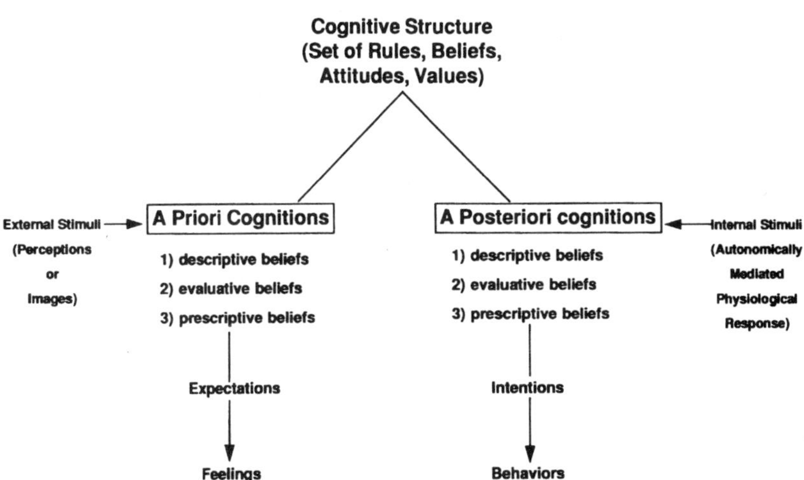

FIGURE 2-3 Two Dimensions of a Person's Cognitive Structure

riori cognitions contain descriptive evaluative and prescriptive propositions (beliefs) around a person's autonomically mediated physiological responses (internal stimuli). Therefore, a priori cognitions serve as rules for defining and evaluating external stimuli within a framework of expectations about the external stimuli, thereby activating positive, negative, or neutral affect toward the stimuli. The a posteriori cognitions, in contrast, form a network of rules that serve to label and evaluate the experienced affect (internal stimuli) as well as prescribing how one should act or respond (intentions) to the aroused affect.

As explained previously, both a priori and a posteriori cognitions become automatic with continued use. Therefore, a statement such as "She made me angry and therefore I hit her" summarizes two distinct types of rules that have been well learned, stem from an overall cognitive structure of rules, and are applied a priori and a posteriori. Application of the a priori rules leads to a state of emotion, and application of the a posteriori rules leads to a state of action. Thus, "she" did not make the person angry; rather, it was a set of conditioned a priori cognitions about "she" that caused the emotional response. Likewise, "she" did not cause the behavioral response; it was a direct result of a set of conditioned a posteriori cognitions that had been learned while experiencing the emotion of anger.

Significance

Understanding this cognitive-behavioral explanation of an anatomy of an emotion and behavior becomes critical when attempting to diagnose and treat chemically dependent youth. It is imperative that the diagnosis and treatment of chemically dependent adolescents take into consideration their cognitive structure. More specifically, the clinician must be attuned to how these adolescent substance abusers have habitually applied a well-rehearsed set of a priori and a posteriori cognitions. The clinician must learn how these adolescents describe their environment, the opinions and judgments they have formed about it, and the kinds of results they expect from it. The clinician also must decipher how these adolescent drug users decide to act on their environment.

Successful diagnosis and treatment involves helping chemically dependent adolescents identify and change the a priori and a posteriori attitudes that constitute a self-defeating personality and cognitive structure and keep chemically dependent youth in a state of intoxication and emotional and behavioral turmoil. Or, as the wisdom of Alcoholics Anonymous would explain, "It's all about learning how to stay sober and obtain sobriety. It's all about learning how to stop drinking and learning how to experience peace of mind."

Emerging Personality and Cognitive Structure

Personality is the habitual application of a set of a priori and a posteriori cognitions that create and maintain a set of predictable emotional and behavioral responses across situations. Simply explained; "Sow a thought, reap an act; sow an act, reap a habit; sow a habit, reap a character; sow a character, reap a destiny" (Swindoll, 1987b, p. 48).

For the chemically dependent teenager, the cognitive structure that creates and maintains a self-defeating personality emerges over time and is directly and indirectly influenced by a variety factors.

Figure 2-4 depicts several factors that contribute to drug use and abuse and to the formation of a self-destructive personality (Nay & Ross, 1993, pp. 320–323).[5]

Chemical use, abuse, and dependency in teenagers emerges when a distinct set of a priori beliefs (B) about the environment (A) results in a multitude of self-defeating emotional responses (C) that in turn activate a

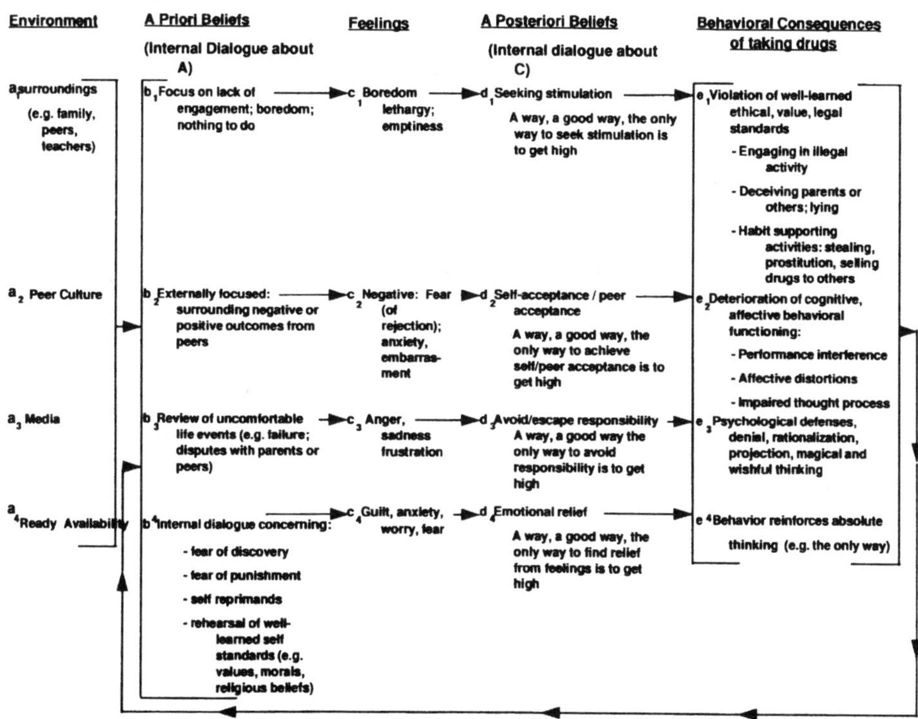

FIGURE 2-4 Factors Contributing to the Emergence of a Chemically Dependent Personality

distinct set of a posteriori beliefs (D). These a posteriori beliefs in turn activate a distinct set of self-defeating behavioral responses (E).

Critical environmental factors (A) influencing a priori beliefs include the teenager's surroundings, especially his or her family (a_1), peer culture (a_2), media (a_3), and the ready availability of drugs (a_4). The beliefs (b_1, b_2, b_3) and subsequent feelings (c_1, c_2, c_3) that emerge from these environmental influences create a distinct mind set (d_1, d_2, d_3,) conducive to drug use, abuse, and, when left unchallenged, habitual drug usage.

Over time, the behavior (E) of taking drugs reinforces a set of a posteriori beliefs that states "a way" to seek stimulation (d_1), gain self-acceptance and peer acceptance (d_2), and avoid/escape responsibility (d_3), is to take mind-altering chemicals. With repeated drug usage, the teenager eventually develops an erroneous obsessive thinking pattern that states a "good way," and eventually the "only way," to seek stimulation, gain self-acceptance and peer acceptance, and to avoid/escape responsibility is to get high. As the drug usage continues, the teenager's life becomes more unmanageable, and a sense of powerlessness or loss of control fueled by this erroneous obsession intensifies. Behavioral consequences including the violation of well-learned ethical, value, and legal standards (e_1); deterioration of cognitive, affective, and behavioral functioning (e_2); and the emergence of psychological defenses (e_3) become more pronounced.

As the addictive personality develops, an added set of a priori beliefs (b_4) concerning the fear of discovery and possible punishment emerges. This additional internal dialogue significantly increases the anxiety level of the teenage user, creating an increased demand for emotional relief (d_4). The obsession becomes greater at this point as the temporary emotional relief produced by the use of drugs reinforces the erroneous a posteriori belief that "the only way" to find relief) from unpleasant feelings is to get high.

As this addictive process (A-B-C-D-E) repeats itself over and over again, a distinct personality pattern and cognitive structure emerge that ultimately dictate the destiny of the teenage drug user. This emerging cognitive structure will maintain a caldron of emotional pain and self-defeating behavior patterns culminating in physical deterioration of the body, emotional instability, and spiritual bankruptcy.

Psychological/Physiological Addiction

The emerging cognitive structure of the teenage substance abuser's personality can be divided into four distinct interrelated layers. The first and outer most layer is called *psychological/physiological addiction*. This layer of the cognitive structure contains the erroneous belief that the "only way" to manage life is to get high. This obsession (psychological addiction) is often reinforced by a bodily craving (physiological addiction). The homeostasis, or equilibrium, of the body chemistry has adapted to the foreign drug or combination of drugs being taken.

Figure 2-5 depicts the psychological/physiological layer of the emerging personality and cognitive structure.

Denial of Feelings and Actions

The second layer of this cognitive structure, *denial of feelings and actions,* is made up of five distinct a priori beliefs. These beliefs create a direct avoidance of any honest examination of the consequences of continued

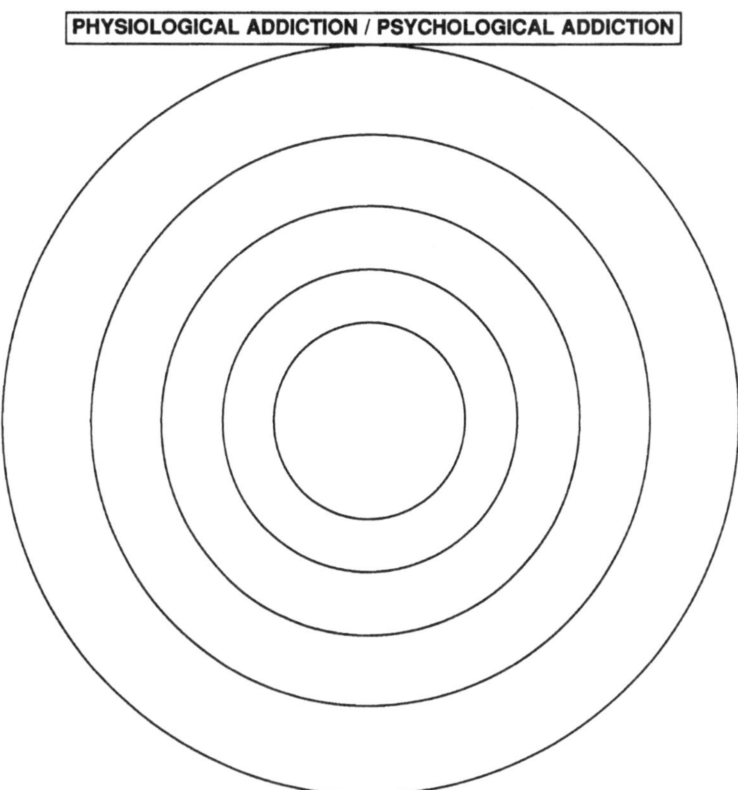

FIGURE 2-5 Psychological/Physiological Layer of the Emerging Personality and Cognitive Structure

drug usage. These a priori beliefs include (1) denial, (2) rationalizations, (3) projection, (4) wishful thinking, and (5) magical thinking.

Figure 2-6 depicts the denial layer of the emerging personality and cognitive structure.

Denial is characterized by an outright nonacceptance of any confrontation that openly and honestly portrays the factual consequences of drug usage. Denial is reinforced by a set of *rationalizations,* excuses that justify the drug usage. It is not uncommon to hear the teenage drug user explain; "I'm not really doing all that bad especially when compared to.... Besides, everybody gets high now and again." Denial and rationalizations are usually accompanied by *projection,* that is, blaming everyone else for

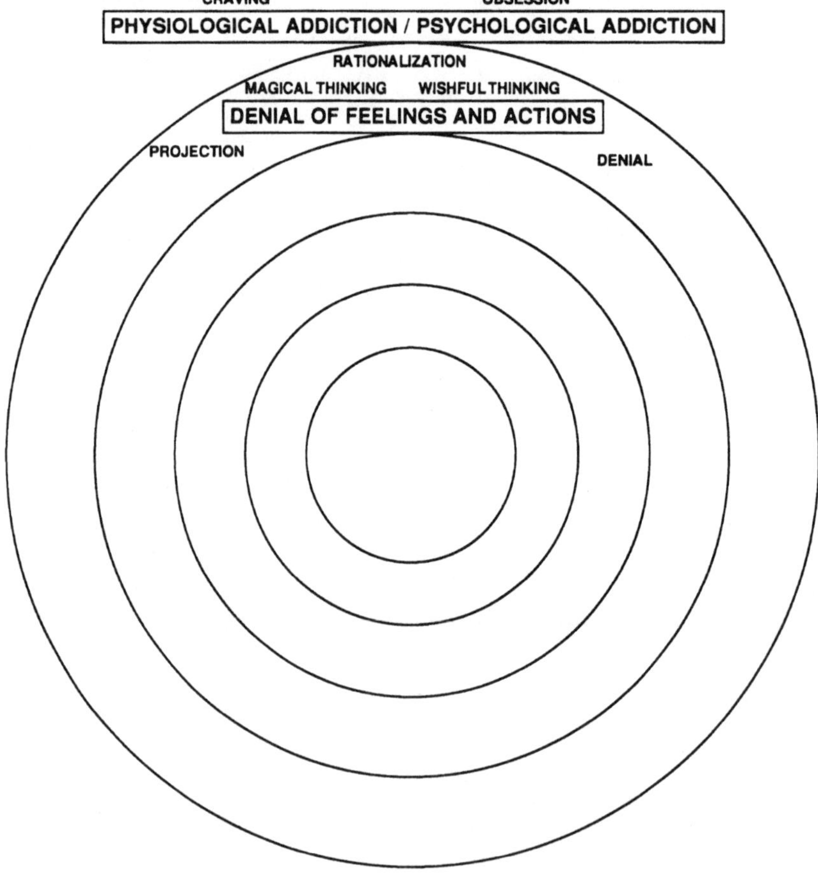

FIGURE 2-6 Denial Layer of the Emerging Personality and Cognitive Structure

current circumstances and difficulties. *Wishful and magical thinking* further compound the problem. The teenage user becomes convinced that the drug usage can stop anytime, with little effort, and without anybody else's help. It is also believed that continued drug usage will not cause any physiological, psychological, or spiritual harm now or in the future. The teenager explains; "If you all would just leave me alone...get off my back.... Look, I can stop anytime I want, and besides I'm doing just fine. It's all of you who have the problem. Besides, it's my life and I have a right to do with it what I want." Collectively, these erroneous a priori beliefs create a rose-colored emotional response that severely deceives the user into believing that all is quite well with self and the world.

Refusal

Refusal, the third layer of the cognitive structure, encompasses a distinct set of a posteriori beliefs that significantly interfere with the abusing teenager's willingness to ask for and accept help for a drug problem. These a posteriori beliefs include indifference, self-sufficiency, self-righteousness, defiance, rejection, and belligerence. Figure 2-7 depicts this layer of the emerging personality and cognitive structure.

Indifference takes the form of an "I don't care attitude." *Self-sufficiency* emphasizes that "I can get off the drugs myself." *Self-righteousness* politely explains that "I already know how to get off drugs." The *defiant* attitude rudely informs you that "no one can make me stop using drugs." The attitude of *rejection* pitifully explains that "I can't do it...I'm really not worth it." The *belligerent* attitude will fight every attempt offered to help the teenager to stop using the drugs: "It's my life and no one is going to tell me what I can and cannot do."

Individually and collectively, these a posteriori beliefs of refusal keep the drug-using teenagers from acting in their best interest and accepting much needed help. These beliefs also reinforce the a priori beliefs of denial.

Self-Destructive Attitudes

At the core of the cognitive structure of the teenage substance abuser is a deeply ingrained set of self-destructive a priori cognitions that may have been developing prior to drug usage, but definitely emerge as a result of sustained drug usage. This fourth inner layer of the personality, *self-destructive attitudes*, consists of five distinct a priori beliefs. These beliefs create and sustain a set of emotional and behavioral responses best characterized as selfishness and hate. Figure 2-8 depicts this layer of the emerging personality and cognitive structure.

The first self-destructive attitude is *damnation of self.* Whenever something goes wrong, or the teenager makes a mistake, the immediate conclusion is "It must be all my fault." The second self-destructive attitude is the *damnation of others.*—"If it's not my fault, then it must be everybody else's fault." The third self-destructive attitude, the *tyranny of shoulds,* demands that reality be different than it is: "This should not be happening to me." The fourth self-destructive attitude, *awfulizing,* views the situation as being awful, terrible, or insurmountable.—"It's just awful that I made this mistake." The first four attitudes usually occur simultaneously

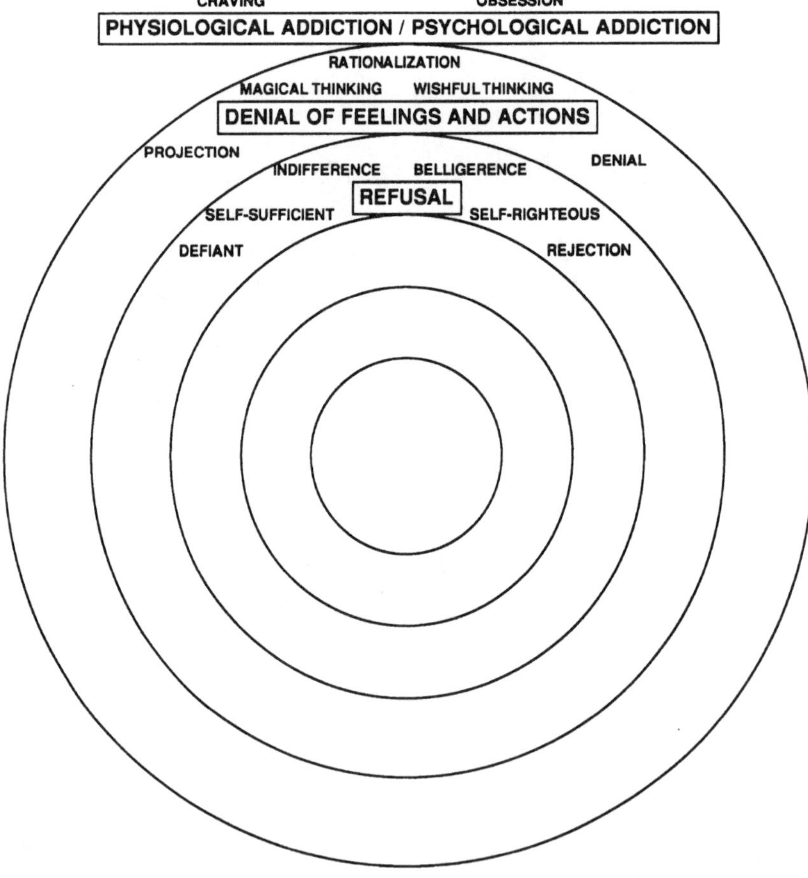

FIGURE 2-7 Refusal Layer of the Emerging Personality and Cognitive Structure

and are followed eventually by the fifth self-destructive attitude, *I can't stand it-itis.*—"I just can't take it any longer. Screw it all." At this point the teenage abuser usually says, "The hell with it all." and goes and gets high.

This inner layer of self-destructive attitudes creates a major challenge for the teenager in recovery. Using these thought patterns as a means to cope with an ever-changing environment, the recovering teenager experiences grave difficulties in emitting loving and sharing behaviors. In addition, these beliefs foster a set of unpleasant emotions (e.g., resentment, self-pity, worry) that were previously diminished by the act of getting high, thereby making the teenager vulnerable to relapse.

The first three layers of the "druggie" personality create an obsession of wanting to get high, maintain a state of denial, and sustain an illusion

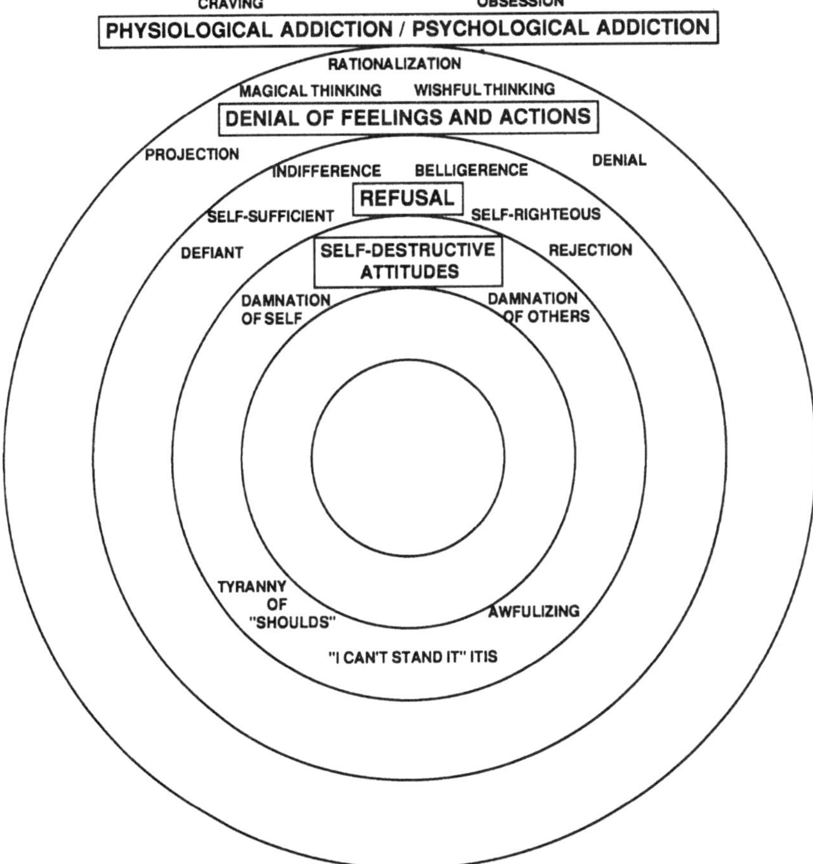

FIGURE 2-8 Layer of Self-Destructive Attitudes

of safety resulting in a refusal to ask for, seek, or accept help. This fourth layer of self-destructive attitudes, in contrast, maintains a set of self-defeating emotional and behavioral responses (i.e., character defects) that significantly impairs and at times handicaps the recovering teenager from achieving maximum mental and emotional health. These self-destructive attitudes create a serious dilemma for the recovering teenager: "How can I feel good now that I'm no longer getting high?"

Caldron of Emotional Pain

At the innermost center of the personality of the drug-abusing teenager lies a caldron of emotional pain. Resentment, anger, loneliness, self-pity, hurt, despair, fear, isolation, guilt, worry, and shame fill this caldron. If indiscriminately unleashed, they could lead to the untimely death of the drug-abusing teenager.

Because of this caldron of emotional pain, teenagers undergoing treatment for chemical dependency are both vulnerable and explosive.

Figure 2-9 depicts all four layers of the emerging personality and cognitive structure along with the caldron of emotional pain.

Collectively, the outer layers of the personality—the physiological/psychological layer, the denial and refusal layer, and the self-destructive attitudes—feed the caldron of emotional pain. Ironically, they also serve to protect the teenage substance abuser from experiencing the full impact of the emotional pain. Chances are great that a drug-abusing teenager would commit suicide if he or she experienced the full intensity of this pain. Unfortunately, these outer layers also shield the teenage substance user from those who would attempt to challenge or stop the self-defeating behavior. Nakken (1988, pp. 28–35) explains:

> *Addiction starts to create the very thing that the person is trying to avoid—pain. In creating pain, the process also creates the need for an addictive relationship. The addict seeks refuge from the pain of addiction by moving further into the addiction process.... Slowly over time, addictive logic develops into a belief system—a delusional system from which the person's life will be directed. The person will fight this and delay it as long as possible, but eventually the delusional system and the addictive personality take over control.*

The delusional system over time, Nakken further explains, "becomes more complex" with "a quality of rigidity," as if "a wall was surrounding the person." This wall serves to keep "the addict's focus and energies directed inward" and to "keep away people who would endanger the addictive relationship."

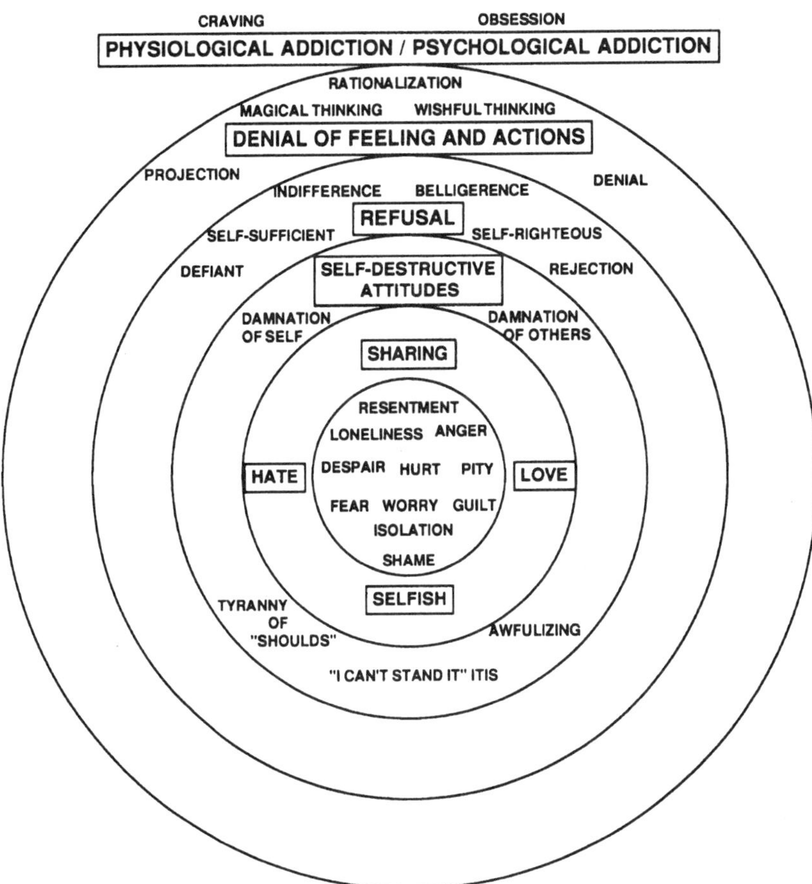

FIGURE 2-9 Caldron of Emotional Pain

Summary

In this chapter, a rationale for diagnosing and treating adolescent chemical dependency was presented.

Chemical dependency was defined as a disease of attitudes leading to the use and abuse of mind-altering substances (e.g., alcohol, marijuana, cocaine) culminating in physical deterioration of the body, emotional instability, and spiritual bankruptcy.

Attitudes were defined as "a relatively enduring organization of beliefs around an object or situation predisposing one to respond in some preferential manner." A nomological network explaining the formation of attitudes was depicted. A person's cognitive structure was viewed as containing two types of cognitions, a priori and a posteriori. A priori cognitions help a person make sense out of their external experiences, their environment. A posteriori cognitions help a person make sense out of their internal experiences, their feelings, their emotional response to the environment.

Personality was explained as the habitual application of a set of a priori and a posteriori cognitions that creates and maintains a set of predictable emotional and behavioral responses across situations.

The emerging personality of an adolescent substance abuser was depicted as an evolving cognitive structure that contained four distinct interrelated layers: (1) psychological/physiological, (2) denial of feelings and actions, (3) refusal, and (4) self-destructive attitudes. At the core of the emerging personality was a caldron of emotional pain.

Understanding and appreciating the emerging personality and cognitive structure of an adolescent drug abuser are instrumental in recognizing and diagnosing the teenage drug user and are essential in developing and implementing a treatment regimen sufficient to counter the disease's effects.

Endnotes

1. See for example, Donovan and Marlatt (1988), Fowles (1988), George (1990), Isralowitz and Singer (1983), G. G. Lawson and A. W.Lawson (1992), Marlatt and Gordon (1985), W. R. Miller and Hester (1980), Snyder (1993), Vaillant (1983).
2. See for example, Beck and Emery (1977), Donovan and Marlatt (1988), Ellis, McInerney, DiGiuseppe, and Yeager (1988), Marlatt and Gordon (1985), Maultsby (1978), McCourt and Glantz (1980), Nakken (1988), Nay and Ross (1993), Rothschild (1986), Twerski (1990), Wilson (1987).
3. The nomological network outlined is written in technical language. For those readers prefering a less technical presentation, please refer to Chapter 5, the ABCDEs of emotion and behavior.
4. See for example, Arnold (1970), Beck (1976), Ellis (1962), Kelly (1955), Lazarus (1966), Maultsby (1975), Meichenbaum (1977), Mischel (1973), Mowrer (1960), Peters (1970), Schacter (1967, 1971), Spielberger (1970).
5. The figure and narrative that follows is adapted from W. Robert Nay and George R. Ross, Cognitive-behavioral intervention for adolescent substance abuse, in A. J. Finch, et al., *Cognitive behavioral procedures with children and adolescents*, Allyn & Bacon, © 1993. This material is reprinted with the permission of Allyn & Bacon.

3

Diagnosing Adolescent Substance Abuse

Diagnosis of an adolescent substance abuser requires an accurate recognition of the signs and symptoms, a determination of the degree and extent of drug usage, and the identification of any medical and psychological problems resulting from or present prior to the drug usage. In addition, careful review of psychosocial factors, the degree of parental denial and enabling patterns, and the mental state and drug history of parents is also required. Combined, each of these dimensions will significantly assist the practitioner in developing and implementing a sound effective treatment. A multi-method approach (Nay, 1979) that includes drug screening, a review of the signs and symptoms, psychosocial assessment including family interviews, parental evaluation, an interview with the teenager, medical examination, psychological/psychiatric evaluation, and clinical observations is recommended.

Drug Screening

Drug screening is an important practitioner's tool in determining whether an adolescent is using or abusing drugs. It should be included as part of a thorough diagnostic process. MacKenzie, Cheng, and Haftel (1987) and Wilford (1990) provide excellent explanations on how to use drug screening as an effective diagnostic tool.

Signs and Symptoms Checklist

A review of the signs and symptoms that strongly suggest prolonged drug usage is an essential part of the diagnostic process. Important signs and symptoms to review include the following:

School. Has the teenager's grades declined? Has a negative attitude toward school emerged? Does the teenager skip classes? Has the teenager been suspended or expelled from school? Heavy drug users often drop out of school.

Dishonesty. Has the teenager concealed drug usage, denied usage, or minimized it when discovered? Has the teenager been caught in obvious lies by his or her parents or been caught lying about friends? Drug-using teenagers often resort to cheating in school and forging school excuses.

Personality Changes. Has the teenager changed friends or chosen undesirable friends? Does the teenager use a lot of foul language? Does the teenager tend to be secluded more often, especially wanting to avoid adults? Does the teenager become easily upset and show signs of increased irritability? Does the teenager become easily angered or enraged with little or no provocation? Does the teenager appear lost with no apparent direction in life? Teenagers using drugs become increasingly amotivational as their drug problem becomes more severe.

Sexual Behavior. Does the teenager openly admit to engaging in sexual intercourse? Has the teenager ever had a venereal disease? In the case of female abusers, use of birth control pills, pregnancy, and abortions are quite common. Overall, sexual promiscuity is quite high among teenagers using and abusing drugs.

Physical/Medical Condition. Personal grooming and hygiene may deteriorate. Speech and actions may become detectably slowed. Gait and posture may change. Clothing and hairstyle may become bizarre with themes of rebellion more evident. Younger teenagers may show signs of impaired physical development. In teenage females, menstruation may become less frequent or stop. The teenager may exhibit a lack of vitality with a need for excessive sleep at unusual times. Extreme fatigue and lassitude may result. Eating habits may become altered, and weight loss may occur. Infections of the skin and respiratory tract are common. A chronic cough without apparent infection oftentimes occurs. The teenager may complain of frequent colds and chest pains. Bloodshot eyes and dilated pupils are very common. Bloodshot eyes are often masked by excessive use of eye drops as are the odors of marijuana and alcohol by the excessive use of perfume, shaving lotion, and mouthwash.

Law Breaking. Traffic violations, especially DUIs are common. Vandalism, shoplifting, breaking and entering, and stealing usually occur. Teenagers who have experienced run-ins with juvenile authorities most likely are using drugs. Cigarette and other types of tobacco usage often indicate the usage of drugs.

Family Relationship. Withdrawal from the family is common. The teenage drug abuser may avoid being seen with parents and refuse to participate in family activities. Relationships with other siblings usually deteriorate. Household chores and responsibilities are neglected. The teenager will often accuse parents of hassling or of being mistrusting and attempt to create conflict between the parents. As the disease becomes more severe, verbal feuding is more frequent, and fights often occur between the teenager and the parents.

Some of these indicators might occur as a part of normal adolescence. Clinical experience has indicated, however, that when 50% or more of these signs and symptoms are observed, it strongly indicates the teenager is harmfully involved with drug usage. Even if the drug screening test returns negative and the teenager has never been caught using or being in the possession of drugs, teenagers demonstrating many of these symptoms should be evaluated very carefully.

Some practitioners may also prefer to complement this checklist with the administration of a diagnostic screening instrument to be completed by or in conjunction with the adolescent being assessed. Currently available assessment instruments with established reliability and validity include (1) Addiction Severity Index (ASI), (2) Problem-Oriented Screening Instrument for Teenagers (POSIT), (3) Adolescent Problem Severity Index (APSI), (4) Personal Experience Inventory (PEI), and (5) Adolescent Drug Abuse Diagnosis (ADAD) (National Institute on Drug Abuse [NIDA], 1992, pp. 19–23).

Psychosocial Assessment and Family Interviews

It is extremely important to interview family members of a teenager suspected of drug usage. Interviewing the parents prior to interviewing the teenager is especially helpful. Family and parental interviews help the practitioner begin to formulate the extent of drug usage, determine the degree of dysfunctionality in the family, especially as related to codependency and enabling tendencies, and arm the practitioner with information to catch the user in contradictions and lies.

The interview process provides an excellent opportunity to commence educating the family about the disease of chemical dependency and the challenges of denial. It also provides an opportunity to begin preparing the family on how they can best assist the practitioner in encouraging the teenage drug abuser to seek treatment (i.e., a family intervention). Family interviews should determine and include

1. Any and all evidence of suspected or observed drug usage including the frequency and duration of usage.
2. A review of the signs and symptoms checklist with parents and other appropriate family members.
3. Previous history of any and all professional counseling received by the teenager, the parents, and other family members.
4. Previous and current history of alcohol and drug usage by family members including parents, grandparents, aunts, uncles, cousins, and siblings.
5. Previous history of mental illness by any family members including grandparents.
6. Previous and current work history of the teenager.
7. Legal history of the teenager including current legal problems.
8. The ethnic and socioeconomic background of the teenager, the marital status of the parents, and whether the teenager is the natural or adopted child of the parents.
9. Whether the teenager has ever attempted suicide or has the family heard the teenager express a desire to commit suicide.
10. A complete school history including the last grade completed, current school status, and whether the teenager has ever been diagnosed as having a learning or a mental disability.
11. Incidences and frequency of running away from home.
12. A description by both parents as to how they currently perceive their relationship with child.
13. Any previous medical history of diabetes, epilepsy, seizures, hyperactivity, or pregnancy. Also, when was the last time the child received a complete physical examination.[1]

Parental Evaluation

The following list of questions (Lach, 1991) has proved helpful in determining the extent the parents' lives have been disrupted by their child's drug-using behavior and provides a fairly clear indication of the severity of denial and enabling patterns being demonstrated by the parents. Clinical experience has suggested that the higher the frequency of yes responses, the stronger is the parent's denial and enabling pattern. The questions include

1. Do you and your spouse frequently disagree or argue about your child's behavior?
2. Do you often worry about your child's problems?
3. Do you find yourself trying to cover up or make excuses for your child's behavior?

4. Do you feel frustrated because no matter how hard you try, nothing seems to change your child's behavior?
5. Do you feel relieved when your child leaves the house?
6. Do you feel angry with or have a general dislike for your child?
7. Are you afraid that you may have become a failure as a parent?
8. Have you tried to change your behavior in hope that it would cause a change in your child's behavior?
9. Do you give money to your child without your spouse's knowledge?
10. Do you have a growing fear that your child has become out of control?
11. Do you have a fear that your child might injure himself or herself or others?
12. Do you find yourself frequently bargaining with your child in an attempt to change his or her behavior?
13. Do you feel heart-sick because you have had to compromise your own values or lower your expectations concerning your child?
14. Do you find yourself desiring to spend less time at home to avoid conflicts with your child?

Discussing these questions with the parents will help the practitioner determine the degree to which feelings of guilt, shame, and embarrassment are hindering the parents from getting help for their child. Their responses will also help the practitioner determine their mental state and the degree to which the parents will need therapy prior to any intervention with their child. For example, very distraught parents will require significant emotional support prior to and during any intervention and especially during the early stages of treatment. They will tend to vacillate back and forth as to whether placing their child in treatment is the right decision.

Interviewing a Teenage Substance Abuser

Most adolescents suffering from the disease of chemical dependency find it extremely difficult to be honest with themselves, much less with someone else. Experience has shown, therefore, that effective interviews with suspected drug-using teenagers are best conducted with the practitioner assuming the worst scenario until the suspected user can provide sufficient and convincing evidence to the contrary.

It is helpful for the practitioner to first establish the purpose of the interview. A good opening remark might be "Why do you think your parents have asked you to talk with me today?" This open-ended lead question usually results in a series of responses that can help the practitioner determine to what extent the teenager is willing to be honest, how much others are being blamed for current conditions, and how much deterioration has already occurred in the relationship between the teenager and his or her parents (see Anglin, 1987).

The interview continues with other informational questions such as How old are you? How well did you do in school this last report period? Is this typical of your school performance? How many times did you cut class this past semester? How many days of school did you miss? What did you do when you cut or missed school? How long have you been working? How many and what kind of jobs have you had? How well do you get along with your parents? Who are you closer to, your father or your mother? Why? How do you get along with your brothers and sisters? Have you ever been arrested for any reason? What happened?

These additional questions are relatively nonthreatening and will help the practitioner begin to determine the teenager's degree of honesty. At this point in the interview, the practitioner should explain to the teenager:

> *When I talked with your parents, they expressed many concerns about you and your recent behavior. I can only be helpful if you are willing to be honest with me. All people who come to see me are usually very truthful with me, they tell me what they believe is happening. Very few, however, are honest with me or themselves. Allow me to explain. Suppose I told you I could fly around this room by flapping my arms. Would I be telling you the truth? If I firmly believed it, I would be. Now, if I jumped off a ten-story building, what would happen? Yes, I would fall, but I didn't believe this would happen. Now on the way to the ground I could change my belief and begin to be more honest with myself. But of course, it would then be too late.*

Introducing this analogy often sets the stage for an open and frank discussion about drug usage and other problems the teenager is encountering. It also provides the practitioner with information as to the current mental state of the suspected user (i.e., whether the teenager could understand the analogy).

The next step in the interview is to ascertain from the teenager a history of drug usage. The approach to questioning should assume usage until proven differently. Ask the questions in this manner.

> *How long have you been smoking cigarettes or chewing tobacco? How often do you smoke? When was the first time you drank alcohol? How many times have you drunk since then? How often do you currently*

drink? How much do you drink? How many times have you been drunk? How long have you been smoking pot? When was the first time you smoked pot? How often do you now smoke pot? What other drugs have you used? When was the last time you got high? What drugs did you use?

Most teenagers will be somewhat open with the practitioner if the teenager believes you already know that they have been using tobacco products, alcohol, and marijuana. Note, also, that tobacco products, alcohol, and marijuana are considered "gateway drugs" to more involved and extensive drug usage (Dupont, 1984).

The next critical step in the interview process is to discuss with the teenager whether he or she thinks they might have a problem with drug usage. How the teenager responds to this discussion will indicate the extent the teenager is in denial and will also provide an opening for the practitioner to begin to educate the teenager about the disease of chemical dependency. Asking questions about what the teenager would be willing to do about the problem if he or she were to have one, will assist the practitioner in determining the degree of motivation the teenager has to seek help and will determine to what extent refusal attitudes have developed. During this interview process, the practitioner also needs to play close attention to the mental state of the teenager. Appearance, behavior, affect, perception, intellectual functioning, orientation, insight, judgment, memory, thought content, and stream of thought need to be noted.

In closing the interview, the practitioner needs to set the stage for a return visit to begin outpatient treatment for the teenager, to conduct further assessment, or to intervene with the help of the family to get the teenager in a more intensive treatment setting. One successful way to facilitate this transition is to ask the teenager to summarize what was discussed in the session and then ask the teenager to think further as to how a person would know whether they had a drug problem. Explain to the teenager that this question will be discussed in the next session.

Medical Examination

A thorough medical examination (Wilford, 1990) should be administered by a physician who has background and experience working with chemically dependent adolescents. The physician should examine the youth to determine current health status and especially note any physical complications resulting from or exacerbated by drug usage and conditions that would preclude the youth from receiving certain kinds of treatment interventions.

Psychological/Psychiatric Evaluation

A mental status examination should be conducted at the time of the interview with the adolescent substance abuser. It has been the author's experience to delay additional psychological testing until the effects of the drug usage have had an opportunity to significantly diminish or cease. In some cases this can take several months. If psychological tests are given as part of a routine screening process, interpretation of the results should be made with great caution.

Clinical Observations

Clinical observations may also be required before a final determination of an appropriate diagnosis can be made. These observations should be ongoing, and careful clinical records should be maintained throughout the course of treatment. Usually, initial diagnosis can only determine at best the degree and extent of drug usage. Additional psychological problems are usually confounded by the drug usage, resulting in an unclear picture as to their magnitude and effect.

Forming a Diagnosis

In formulating an initial diagnosis for the chemically dependent adolescent, and subsequently developing and implementing intervention and treatment strategies, three critical dimensions should be reviewed: (1) degree of dependency, (2) mental state of the adolescent, and (3) mental state of the adolescent's parents. In addition, the current physical health of the teenager should be taken into consideration.

Figure 3-1 depicts these three diagnostic dimensions, illustrating 80 possible combinations that could occur.

Determining the Degree of Dependency

Chemical dependency can be viewed as a disease with four stages: (1) initial usage, (2) problem usage, (3) psychological addiction, and (4) physiological addiction. Accurately identifying the stage of the disease to which the adolescent has progressed is critical in determining the type of treatment the teenager should receive. Review of the results from drug screening, the signs and symptoms checklist, the psychosocial assessment, the family interviews, the adolescent interview, the medical exami-

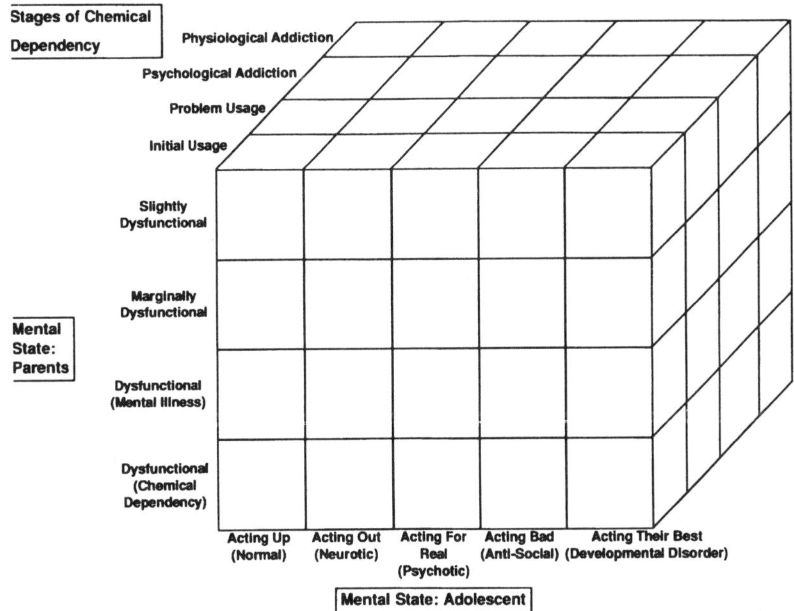

FIGURE 3-1 Three Diagnostic Dimensions Illustrating 80 Possible Combinations

nation, the psychological/psychiatric evaluation, and clinical observations provides a plethora of information for the practitioner to make an appropriate determination as to which level the adolescent has progressed.

Stage one, *initial usage,* is indicated when the evidence clearly shows that the teenager has used alcohol and drugs on a minimal number of occasions (one to five times) and that the usage has not significantly interfered with any aspect of the teenager's life including physical, emotional, and spiritual growth, family relationships, school/work performance, leisure time activities, friendships, sharing with others, and financial responsibility. The cognitive structure (self-talk) at stage one includes the view that alcohol and/or other drugs is *"a way* to alter one's feelings, deal with unpleasantness, or gain acceptance." Review of the facts must clearly show that the usage has not significantly impaired the adolescent's ability to function. At this point in time, the teenager is at risk to progress in the disease. The teenager should be monitored carefully to ensure that usage does not continue. Individual and family therapy on an outpatient basis is indicated.

Stage two, *problem usage,* creates an interesting dilemma for the drug-using adolescent. The cognitive structure (self-talk) at this stage includes a view that "alcohol and other drugs are a *good way* to alter one's feelings, deal with unpleasantness, or gain acceptance." But, at the same time, the teenager begins to experience some negative consequences from using drugs. The using teenager may, for example, begin to show signs of decreased concentration in school, have difficulties disciplining himself to study, or begin to lose interest in extra curricular activities. Irritableness and elevated levels of anxiety may begin to appear. The teenager may begin telling lies, breaking the law, or indulging in sex. At this point, the teenager often realizes that drug usage is contributing to the experienced upheaval and, therefore, may express a strong desire to quit. But, unfortunately at this stage, the usage pattern has usually increased from a few times to a regular pattern, and the teenager has begun to prize the experience of getting high. Some teenagers in recovery have described this point as being between a rock and a hard place: "I know that this stuff is no good for me, but I really like it."

Intervention at this stage of the disease requires an open and honest confrontation with the teenage user as to the nature of the disease and the consequences that will occur if usage does not immediately cease. For a small percentage of drug-using teenagers at this stage, extensive outpatient individual and family therapy may prove successful, if careful guidelines are established, randomized drug screening is implemented, and the attitudes of denial and refusal are minimal. If all drug usage does not immediately cease, and the presenting dysfunctional behaviors do not begin to improve significantly after a couple months of therapy, more restrictive and intensive treatment is then indicated.

Stage three, *psychological addiction,* is relatively easy for the trained practitioner to diagnose. Most questions on the signs and symptoms checklist will be answered yes, the parents are usually at their wits end, and they usually are desperate about seeking help. The teenage user at this stage is often very open about drug usage and many times will defy you to try to stop the usage. Suicidal ideas are usually present, or attempts at suicide may have already been made. Emotional lability is pronounced, signs of physical deterioration are beginning to show, and denial and refusal attitudes are readily apparent.

The teenage user at this stage of the disease either needs to be hospitalized or enrolled in an intensive outpatient program in a controlled setting where access to any and all mind-altering drugs is cut off and 24-hour monitoring of behavior is provided. The cognitive structure (self-talk) at this stage of this disease has progressed to full-blown obsession: "*The only way* I can manage my life is to get high." The "druggie personality" as described earlier in this chapter has fully emerged.

Stage four of the disease, *physiological addiction*, presents all the symptoms, signs, and complications evidenced in stage three, with the additive factor that the homeostasis, or equilibrium, of the body (i.e., the body's chemistry) has adapted to the presence of the drugs. Physiological withdrawal is necessitated at this stage, and detoxification procedures need to be implemented (see Schuckit, 1984).

Mental State: Teenager

Adolescents being referred for psychiatric or psychological evaluation can be classified into one of five mental state categories. These classifications are (1) acting up, (2) acting out, (3) acting bad, (4) acting for real, and (5) acting their best (Maultsby, 1979).

Acting-up adolescents experience normal power struggle issues with their parents and with others in positions of authority. Although sometimes behaving in disrespectful ways, and occasionally testing the limits of parental and adult control, acting-up teenagers for the most part will conform to reasonable rules and expectations and adjust well to presenting challenges and circumstances.

In contrast, *acting-out* adolescents will experience difficulty in conforming to reasonable rules and expectations and adjusting to presenting challenges and circumstances. Acting-out teenagers will develop self-defeating emotional and behavioral patterns (neuroseis) that significantly interfere with their ability to cope successfully with life's challenges. For example, acting-out adolescents may experience difficulty controlling their temper, experience abnormal levels of anxiety or depression, or create roadblocks to their development of meaningful and healthy friendships. Often, these teenagers are well aware of their self-defeating patterns, but simply do not know how to change them.

Acting-bad adolescents experience extreme difficulty in complying with established rules and expectations and may or may not cope well with presenting challenges and circumstances. Sometimes referred to as antisocial, these teenagers are rule breakers and seem to experience much delight in pushing the limits of authority. Also labeled oppositionally defiant or conduct disordered adolescents (American Psychiatric Association, 1987, pp. 49–58), these young people usually show a prolonged history of disruptive behavior patterns.

Acting-for-real adolescents are teenagers suffering from severe emotional disturbance. Severe mood disorders such as major depression or a bipolar disorder, psychosis, and schizoaffective disorder would be representative of acting-for-real adolescents. These teenagers experience major difficulties in coping with life's challenges.

Acting-their-best adolescents include that group of teenagers experiencing developmental disorders such as mental retardation (American Psychiatric Association, 1987, pp. 28–49). As the term implies, these teenagers are acting their best, but they are limited in their ability to cope by their developmental disorder.

Drug-abusing teenagers present a major challenge for practitioners attempting to classify drug-using and drug-abusing teenagers as acting up, acting out, acting bad, acting for real, and acting their best. The signs and symptoms exhibited often mimic all five classifications. Ries, Batran, and Shuckit (1980, p. 18) explain:

> *Patients who abuse drugs and those who seek treatment for depression or other functional complaints are frequently a diagnostic dilemma.... Abuse of drugs is associated with a variety of psychopathologies... suicidal depression...high levels of anxiety, and a variety of psychotic behavior, which at any time can be identical to the cross-sectional symptomology of schizophrenia. These drug-induced states can last from hours to days or even months.*

Polydrug abusers, explains Meyer (1983, p. 59), "could be described as psychotics without the loss or reality contact. That is, they show deterioration of behavior in a wide variety of arenas...affect is generally flat, or when emotion is manifest, it is quite labile."

Therefore, in formulating a diagnosis for a drug-abusing teenager, it is important to allow ample time for the effects of drug usage to diminish before attaching any diagnostic label to the behaviors being observed. Most chemically dependent teenagers who have been heavily involved in the use of drugs will exhibit signs and symptoms of acting out, acting bad, and acting for real and occasionally will present themselves in the extreme, appearing acting up one moment and acting their best the next moment.

Elevated levels of depression, anxiety, anger, and suicidal and delusional thinking are quite common for addictive teenagers in the earlier and, sometimes, in the later stages of recovery. In general, teenagers recovering from chemical dependency do suffer from an adjustment disorder with mixed emotional features (American Psychiatric Association, 1987, p. 331).

A minimum of 9 to 14 months may be required for the full effects of the drugs to significantly diminish. During this time period, the practitioner is well advised to treat only the substance abuse problem. Carefully noting baseline behavior as indicated by presenting problems, previous history, and clinical observations is also advisable. These observations will help determine whether the teenager is making any long-term improvement. A small percentage of chemically dependent teenagers will eventually need additional treatment for other psychological disorders that were either present prior to the drug usage, brought on by the drug usage, or both.

Mental State: Parents

The mental state of parents of drug-abusing teenagers can usually be classified into one of four categories: (1) slightly dysfunctional, (2) marginally dysfunctional, (3) dysfunctional due to mental illness, or (4) dysfunctional due to chemical dependency.

The *slightly dysfunctional* category describes the type of parent that, for the most part, has developed sound coping strategies and has met the challenges of life in healthy and productive ways. All parents are to some degree or extent dysfunctional. We all seem to carry some kind of childhood baggage into our adult lives. In the case of this group of parents, the degree of dysfunctionality is minimal. However, because of the stress and strain that the chemically dependent adolescent places on the family structure, slightly dysfunctional parents will appear marginally dysfunctional, or worse, during initial interviews and in the early phases of treatment. These parents most probably would not have sought counseling for their family or themselves if their child had not become involved with drug usage.

The *marginally dysfunctional* parents, in contrast, show signs of having developed maladaptive or self-defeating emotional and behavioral responses to life's challenges. Similar to the acting-out teenager, marginally dysfunctional parents may be experiencing difficulties controlling anger, have abnormal levels of anxiety and/or depression, be experiencing discord in their marriage, or suffer from eating disorders or workaholism. Often, this group of parents may have come from a home where one or both of their parents were chemically dependent. These adult children continue to use maladaptive childhood survival strategies to cope with current adult challenges. Sometimes, these parents are recovering alcoholics who are still struggling with the character defects that accompany the disease. Like the slightly dysfunctional parent, their symptoms are much more pronounced when first seen by the practitioner and during the early stages of therapy.

The third category are parents who are *dysfunctional due to mental illness*. They include several diagnostic categories such as mood disorders, personality disorders, and psychotic disorders. Like the two previous categories, parents dysfunctional due to mental illness often appear more disturbed than usual at initial contact and during the early stages of treatment.

The fourth category, *dysfunctional due to chemical dependency,* represents a group of parents who are still active in their use of alcohol and/or other illegal drugs. Often, they are functioning alcoholics or chemical-dependent persons. That is, they are able to maintain employment, but the rest of their lives is in shambles. In most cases, it is very difficult to get this type of parent involved in treatment.

Summary

In this chapter, a multi-method approach to assessment was introduced that included (1) drug screening, (2) a signs and symptoms checklist, (3) psychosocial assessment and family interviews, (4) parental evaluation, (5) interviewing the teenage substance abuser, (6) medical examination, (7) psychological/psychiatric evaluation, and (8) clinical observations.

Three diagnostic dimensions used to formulate a diagnosis of an adolescent substance abuser were explained. These three dimensions are degree of dependency, mental state of the teenager, and mental state of the parents.

Endnote

1. Appendix A contains a prototype of a psychosocial assessment.

4

Intervention, Continuum of Care, and Treatment Environment

In this chapter, intervention options are outlined and treatment environment concerns for intensive inpatient and intensive outpatient treatment programs are addressed.

Intervention and Continuum of Care

Intervention for adolescent substance abusers involves a continuum of care ranging from outpatient individual, group, and family counseling for adolescents at stage one of the disease to temporary hospitalization for teenagers who have become physiologically addicted.[1]

Options

Several different kinds and levels of treatment are available to drug-abusing teenagers and their families (Cassidy, 1992; Henry, 1989; Kids Helping Kids [KHK] 1990; G. G. Lawson & A. W. Lawson, 1992; Nay & Ross, 1993; Wheeler & Malmquist, 1987). Several options include but are not limited to (1) doing nothing, (2) individual and family outpatient treatment, (3) individual and family treatment with AA/Alanon support groups, (4) short-term hospitalization coupled with and followed by individual and family therapy and AA/Alanon support groups, (5) long-term hospitalization coupled with and followed up with therapy at a halfway house and AA/Alanon support groups, and (6) long-term intensive outpatient therapy for the entire family with use of temporary host homes and AA/Alanon support groups.

Each of these options must be considered in relationship to the degree of dependency, the mental state of the teenager, the mental state of the parents, and the current physical health of the teenager. For example, a teenager at stage one of the disease, with signs of acting-up and acting-out behavior, whose parents are only slightly dysfunctional will most likely succeed in an outpatient setting. In sharp contrast, a teenager at stage three of the disease, exhibiting acting-out, acting-bad, and acting-for-real behavior, with dysfunctional parents due to mental illness or chemical dependency would require long-term treatment for the entire family.

In too many cases, either the dysfunctionality of the parents or the strong objections by the teenager to receive help only leaves open the option to do nothing, unless the teenager's drug usage has resulted in entanglements with the juvenile authorities, with treatment being mandated by the courts.

Scenarios

It has been this writer's experience that a high degree of success is evidenced among teenagers whose mental state was acting up or acting out prior to drug usage and/or as a result of drug usage, who had not yet become psychologically addicted to drugs, and who came from homes where the parents' mental state was slightly to marginally dysfunctional. In most cases, both the adolescent and the parents benefited immensely from treatment. Treatment usually consisted of outpatient individual, group, and family therapy and involvement by the family in Alcoholics Anonymous and Alanon.

Also, success was often achieved among teenagers whose mental state was acting up and acting out prior to drug usage and/or as a result of drug usage, who had not yet become addicted psychologically to drugs, and who came from homes where the mental state of the parents was dysfunctional because of mental illness or chemical dependency. Additional support was required, however, for the parents. In addition, the teenagers were also taught strategies to successfully cope with the dysfunctionality of the parents. In many of these cases, the child would often immensely benefit from treatment, but the parents would continue to flounder in their dysfunctionality.

For adolescents whose mental state was acting for real, acting bad, or acting their best prior to drug usage and/or as a result of drug usage, who had not yet become psychologically addicted to drugs, and who came from homes where the parents' mental state was slightly to marginally dysfunctional, often the parents would immensely benefit from treatment but only marginal results were achieved with the teenager. Long-term extensive outpatient treatment was made available for the entire family.

For adolescents whose mental state was acting for real, acting bad, or acting their best prior to drug usage and/or as a result of drug usage, who had not yet become psychologically addicted to drugs, and who came from homes where the mental state of the parents was dysfunctional because of mental illness or chemical dependency, marginal results were achieved for both the teenager and the parents. Long-term extensive outpatient treatment was made available for the entire family.

For teenagers whose mental state was acting up or acting out prior to drug usage and/or as a result of drug usage, who were psychologically or physiologically addicted to drugs, and who came from families where the parents were slightly to marginally dysfunctional, high degrees of success were often evidenced for the teenagers and their parents. Long-term extensive treatment was provided for the entire family.

For teenagers whose mental state was acting up or acting out prior to drug usage and/or as a result of drug usage, who were psychologically or physiologically addicted to drugs, and who came from families where the parents were dysfunctional because of mental illness or chemical dependency, success was often observed with the teenager. Additional and extensive supportive help was provided for the parents, the teenagers were taught strategies to successfully cope with the dysfunctionality of the parents, and the duration of treatment for the entire family was long term and intensive. Marginal results were usually achieved with the parents.

For teenagers whose mental state was acting for real, acting bad, or acting their best prior to drug usage and/or as a result of drug usage, who were psychologically or physiologically addicted to drugs, and who came from homes where the parents' mental state was slightly to marginally dysfunctional, marginal success was evidenced for the teenager, and the parents usually benefited immensely from treatment. The treatment was intensive and long term for the entire family.

For teenagers whose mental state was acting for real, acting bad, or acting their best prior to drug usage and/or as a result of drug usage, who were psychologically or physiologically addicted to drugs, and who came from families where the parents were dysfunctional because of mental illness or chemical dependency, success was usually marginal for both the teenager and the parents. Long-term intensive outpatient treatment for the entire family was provided.

Figure 4-1 summarizes these eight possible treatment scenarios.

It has been this author's experience that as the degree of dependency and psychopathology of the teenager and the degree of dysfunctionality of the parents increases, the more intensive and longer in duration the treatment needs to be. Also, chances for overall success for all the family members decrease as the degree of dependency and psychopathology of the teenager and the degree of dysfunctionality of the parents increases.

Treatment Environment

Effective inpatient and outpatient treatment programs for adolescent substance abusers must address elements of the treatment environment: treatment climate, staffing patterns, and types of supportive services (Ross, 1991; Shulman, 1985; Stanton, 1979; Voth, 1980).

Treatment Climate

Inpatient and intensive outpatient adolescent chemical dependency treatment programs should foster a therapeutic climate that initially assumes complete responsibility for the care of the adolescent to ensure that access to alcohol, other mind-altering chemicals, and tobacco products are removed for a minimum of 45 and in some cases up to 90 days. These programs should address the physical needs of the client including adequate food, clothing, shelter, and medical needs. The treatment climate should be free of all tobacco products and provide a sound nutritional program with minimal use of sugar products.

These programs should employ a staff of professionals and paraprofessionals that exemplify warmth, empathy, discipline, and a positive mental attitude and that have life styles free of alcohol, other mind-altering drugs, and tobacco products. The treatment climate is enhanced by providing the teenager access to positive peer influence, an environment free of any physical abuse or threat, and a set of reasonable rules and regulations that are consistently and fairly enforced and stem from clearly defined expectations. Care must be taken to ensure that the treatment climate does not become either too laissez faire or too authoritarian. Either extreme is detrimental to treatment outcomes.

Scenario	Type of treatment	% Success
acting up or acting out teenager, not psychologically addicted, slightly to marginally dysfunctional parents	outpatient individual, group and family therapy, AA & Alanon	high % success teenager & parents
acting up and acting out teenager, not psychologically addicted, dysfunctional parents due to mental illness or chemical dependency	outpatient individual, group and family therapy, AA & Alanon, additional support for parents, coping strategies for teenager	high % success teenager, marginal % success parents
acting for real, acting bad, or acting their best teenager, not psychologically addicted, slightly to marginally dysfunctional parents	long term extensive outpatient treatment for the family, AA & Alanon	marginal % success teenager, high % success parents
acting for real, acting bad, or acting their best teenager, not psychologically addicted, dysfunctional parents due to mental illness or chemical dependency	long term extensive outpatient treatment for the family, AA & Alanon, added parent support	marginal % success teenager & parents
acting up and acting out teenager, psychologically addicted, slightly to marginally dysfunctional parents	possible short term hospitalization, long term extensive outpatient treatment for the family, AA & Alanon	high % success teenager & parents
acting up and acting out teenager, psychologically addicted, dysfunctional parents due to mental illness or chemical dependency	possible short term hospitalization, long term extensive outpatient treatment for the family, AA & Alanon, added parent support	high % success teenager, marginal % success parents
acting for real, acting bad, or acting their best teenager, psychologically addicted, slightly to marginally dysfunctional parents	possible short term hospitalization, long term extensive outpatient family treatment, AA & Alanon	marginal % success teenager, high % success parents
acting for real, acting bad, or acting their best teenager, psychologically addicted, dysfunctional parents due to mental illness or chemical dependency	possible short term hospitalization, long term extensive outpatient family treatment, AA & Alanon, added parent support	marginal % success teenager & parents

FIGURE 4-1 Summary of Eight Possible Treatment Scenarios

The treatment climate should include individual therapy as well as group therapy sessions that openly and honestly discuss basic cultural values and that consistently confront irrational and dysfunctional patterns of thinking. These programs should provide opportunities to practice newly learned skills within a supportive environment and provide opportunities to make mistakes and learn from them. Individual treatment plans should be maintained with guidelines for periodic review and recommendations for ongoing follow-up treatment.

Staffing Patterns

Effective inpatient and outpatient treatment programs for adolescent substance abusers must also address the issue of administrative structuring and clinical staffing.

Figure 4-2 depicts an example of a recommended administrative structure and pattern of staffing for an intensive day treatment program.

An administrative structuring and staffing pattern should include (1) a governing board of directors or trustees, (2) a clear delineation of clinical and nonclinical functions and roles and their relationship to each other, (3) clearly defined lines of authority, and (4) clearly defined job descriptions.

A chemical dependency treatment program for adolescents needs to incorporate a careful blending of professionals and paraprofessionals into its staff, being careful to ensure that all clinical personnel involved are well trained in the principles and practices of chemical dependency counseling including cognitive-behavioral techniques. In addition, clinical staff mem-

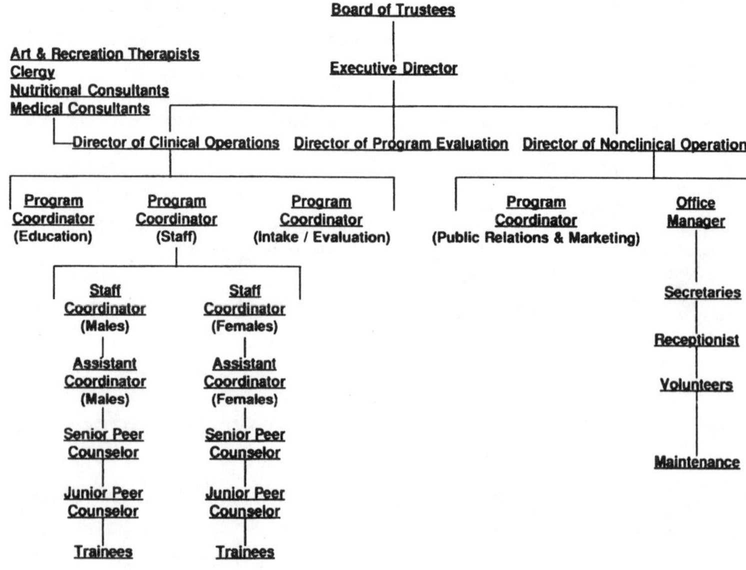

FIGURE 4-2 Administrative Structure and Pattern of Staffing

bers should exemplify life styles free of alcohol, other mind-altering drugs, and tobacco products and should practice, to the best of their ability, the life principles they are teaching to the recovering teenagers.

Professional staffing may include psychiatrists, family practitioners and pediatricians specializing in adolescent medicine, psychiatric nurses, psychologists, social workers, mental health counselors, recreation and art therapists, and clergy.

In addition, it is strongly recommended that staffing include a group of peer counselors consisting of well-trained adolescents who have been in recovery for a minimum of one year. When carefully trained, supervised, and directed by adult professionals, peer staffing has been shown to be an extremely effective means to treat adolescent substance abusers (Covert & Wangberg, 1992; Friedman, Swartz, & Utada, 1989; Hoogerman, Huntley, Griffith, Petermann, & Koch, 1984; Kids Helping Kids, 1990; Nay & Ross, 1993).

Support Services

Effective inpatient and outpatient treatment programs for adolescent substance abusers also need to provide support services. Support services include but are not limited to medical and psychiatric consultation, educational training and remediation, art and recreational therapy, career and job counseling, nutritional counseling, and spiritual counseling. In addition, the treatment program requires mechanisms to handle issues of special concern including (1) dual diagnosis; (2) sexual issues such as pregnancy, abortion, homosexuality, rape, masturbation, and sexual promiscuity; (3) AIDS; (4) child abuse and neglect; (5) homes with alcoholic or drug-abusing parent(s); (6) homes where one or both of the parents are deceased, have experienced a divorce, or the child has been adopted; (7) physical impairments; (8) court-ordered teenagers; (9) the role of God in recovery; and (10) the use of self-help support groups and twelve-step program.

Dual Diagnosis

Chapter 3 stressed that mental state needs to be considered in formulating a diagnosis of an adolescent substance abuser and pointed out that symptomatology of chemical dependency often mimics other psychopathologies such as depressive disorders, anxiety disorders, and schizophrenia. I concluded that careful evaluation was required in making any diagnosis other than chemical dependency and that chemically dependent teenagers should be carefully monitored for several months before concluding they were suffering from other psychopathologies.

Nonetheless, a certain percentage of chemically dependent teenagers suffer from other mental disorders. It can be argued that all recovering teenagers undergoing treatment demonstrate an adjustment disorder with mixed emotional features. They also demonstrate signs and symptoms indicative of oppositional defiant and conduct disorders, anger, depression, and anxiety. However, failure to observe improvement in these various symptoms over time may indicate that the denial and refusal layers of the chemically dependent personality have yet to be penetrated. This failure to improve could also suggest that other psychological disorders may be confounding the recovery process.

It is not uncommon to observe in at least 5% of recovering teenagers other psychological problems that have developed either prior to and/or as a result of drug usage. Borderline personality disorders, schizophrenia, attention deficit hyperactivity disorders, mood disorders, and eating disorders are not uncommon. Almost all chemically dependent adolescents display signs and symptoms of oppositional defiant disorder when first being referred for evaluation, with a significant number displaying signs and symptoms of a conduct disorder group type and solitary aggressive type. As one researcher (Beschner & Friedman, 1985, p. 988) concluded; Teenage substance abusers "tend to be compulsive, dedicated, and multiple drug users who have serious personal problems. Their family, social and psychological problems generally predate their drug usage."

Subsequently, in the advanced stages of treatment, care must be taken to reassess the mental state of the recovering teenager and to provide appropriate concomitant treatment to address other psychological disorders. As one writer (O'Connell, 1988, p. 1) concluded; in treating dually diagnosed addicts, "Successful management of such patients requires specialized knowledge and skills for the chemical dependency counselor."

In addition, during each stage of treatment, the clinical staff needs to carefully evaluate teenagers showing poor progress and to meticulously note clinical observations that could possibly suggest that they are suffering from additional psychopathologies. Psychological and psychiatric consultation is also strongly recommended.

Sexual Issues

Teenagers entering treatment for a problem of chemical dependency bring with them an array of sexual issues unthinkable in a normal population of adolescents. Consequently, these teenages have feelings of shame and guilt that most find extremely difficult to reveal let alone talk about. But such issues as pregnancy, abortion, homosexuality, rape, masturbation, and sexual promiscuity must be talked about openly, compassionately, and frankly if recovery is to occur.

Experience has taught that these issues are best discussed in segregated group therapy sessions (i.e., males and females separated) or in individual counseling sessions. Most teenagers will open up and talk about these issues more readily with a therapist of the same sex.

One method useful in helping recovering teenagers overcome the challenge of revealing past sexual secrets is a technique developed by Ross (1983e). Borrowing from the Hazelden Meditation Series, Each Day a New Beginning (Anonymous, 1982, p. August 22), the following passage was read to a group:

> *Harboring parts of our inner selves, fearing what others would think if they knew, creates the barriers that keep us separate, feeling different, certain of our inadequacies.*
>
> *Secrets are burdens, and they weigh heavily on us, so heavily. Carrying secrets make impossible the attainment of serenity—that which we strive for daily. Abstinence alone is not enough. It must come first, but it's not enough by itself. It can't guarantee we will find the serenity we seek. This program of recovery offers self-assurance, happiness, spiritual well-being, but there's work to be done. Many steps to be taken. And one of these is total self-disclosure. It's risky; it's humbling, and it's necessary.*
>
> *When we tell others who we really are, it opens the door for them to share likewise. And when they do, we become bonded. We accept their imperfections and love them for them. And they love us for ours. Our struggles to be perfect, our self-denigration because we aren't only exaggerates even more the secrets that keep us sick.*
>
> *Our tarnished selves are lovable; secrets are great equalizers when shared.*

After hearing this reading, most teenagers will usually begin to share some of their past sexual secrets. Having recovering teenagers in the group who have already talked about their sexual secrets can also prove helpful, especially when you call on them first as an encouragement for newer group members to relate. Not all of the newer group members will initially respond to this technique, so it is important to repeat the invitation on a regularly scheduled basis. Repeating this group therapy session on a regular basis also provides more advanced group members, who have already related, additional opportunities to report other sexual situations they had forgotten about or failed to address adequately.

AIDS/HIV

The possibility of encountering HIV-positive chemically dependent adolescents is ever increasing, especially given the fact that they are engaging in activities that place them at greater risk to contract the disease. Special care must be taken, therefore, to screen for the disease at the time of intake and on periodic intervals during the course of treatment. Safeguards should also be introduced to educate the staff as well as those participating in the therapeutic community as to measures they need to take to avoid contracting the disease, given the probability that one or more of the group may test HIV positive sometime during the course of treatment (American Medical Society on Alcoholism and Other Drug Dependencies [AMSAODD], 1988). Prevention education should also be introduced during the course of treatment.

Child Abuse and Neglect

It could be argued that all adolescents entering a treatment program for a chemical dependency problem have been victims of child abuse. Not only does the disease of chemical dependency inflict severe and sometimes irreversible physical, emotional, and spiritual damage, but drugs are ultimately introduced by an adult society that is more concerned with making money then it is with the welfare of is young. Setting this larger issue aside, many teenagers entering treatment for chemical dependency have experienced physical, emotional, and sexual abuse and have often inflicted physical, sexual, and emotional abuse on others.

Most states require the mandatory reporting of suspected child abuse and neglect, and changes in federal laws in 1986 were amended to remove any restrictions on compliance. It is therefore imperative that a chemical dependency treatment program for adolescents implement provisions for both the reporting and treatment of abused and neglected recovering teenagers.

Care must be taken, however, to ensure that abuse issues are dealt with in a way that avoids convenient rationalizations and excuses for recovering teenagers to deny and/or ignore the seriousness of their drug problem or to begin blaming others for their choice of using drugs. It is also important to confront the issue of abuse or neglect if the recovering teenager is identified as the abuser. In most of these cases, the abuse inflicted was part of an overall pattern typical of teenagers using and abusing drugs and, therefore, can be confronted like any other destructive behavioral pattern.

Whenever possible, it is better to defer treatment of abuse and neglect issues until the recovering teenager has progressed to the committing and transmitting plateaus of recovery. Treatment strategies abound in the literature on this subject. Rencken (1989), for example, provides an excellent text outlining intervention strategies for both the victims of sexual abuse and for the offenders.

Children of Chemically Dependent Parent(s)

An increasing number of adolescents entering treatment for a chemical dependency problem come from homes where one or both of the parents are abusers of alcohol and/or other mind-altering drugs. This home situation creates many challenges for the recovering teenager and his or her therapist(s). Specifically, this case usually requires the recovering teenager to remain accountable to an authority figure such as the therapist for a much longer period of time, for the parents are usually so involved in their own recovery issues that they find it difficult to provide the structure required to help the recovering teenager grow and mature. Most recovering teenagers not only have the handicap of being in recovery, they also must overcome the handicap of simply being teenagers, now that their use of drugs has subsided.

Often, recovering teenagers growing up in homes where one or both of the parents are users, failed to learn how to assimilate standards of right and wrong in determining behavior choices. In such cases, a complete provision of parenting is necessary if the teenager is to have a reasonable chance of recovery.

As with issues of abuse and neglect, care must be taken to ensure that recovering teenagers do not use their parents as an excuse to avoid taking responsibility for their drug problem. The so-called "adult child" issues that emerge when one or both parents are chemically dependent also need to be dealt with at a later stage in treatment, preferably after the recovering teenager has fully committed himself or herself to a program of recovery. Even at this stage, caution must be used to discourage the recovering teenager from hooking on to "adult child" issues to avoid current challenges and responsibilities.

Death, Divorce, and Adoption

Many chemically dependent teenagers come from a family where one or both parents have died, or the teenager was living in a single-family home usually with the father being absent, or both parents had divorced and remarried, or the teenager had been adopted at an early age. Each of these conditions creates unique challenges for recovering teenagers and can provide them opportunities to avoid facing their drug problem. Care must be taken to address the many hurts and pains that often accompany death, divorce, and adoption, but at the same time, these concerns must not be used as an excuse to avoid current challenges and responsibilities.

Physical Disabilities

It is also not uncommon to encounter recovering teenagers with physical disabilities. The key to treating these recovering teenagers is preventing them from using their self-pity to solicit sympathy for their physical impairment and to avoid taking responsibility for their drug problem.

Court-Ordered Teenagers

Court-ordered teenagers usually require additional attention in that several counselors are often involved in their treatment (e.g., parole officer, social worker, lawyer), thereby increasing their opportunities to manipulate and play off against one another the various counselors. Treatment plans must carefully stipulate that the drug treatment agency is responsible for development and implementation of primary treatment and that other interested parties must subordinate their interests and concerns to the chemical dependency counselor. Unfortunately however, legal concerns and medical necessities are often incompatible (see Ross, 1990b).

Court-ordered chemically dependent adolescents must be carefully monitored to determine to what extent an acting-bad or antisocial personality disorder may have developed. Chemically dependent adolescents who demonstrate emerging antisocial personality characteristics usually show, after considerable time in treatment, little if any remorse for their past wrongs and for the hurt and pain they have inflicted on others. Additional group and individual counseling may be indicated to address specific issues presented by these teenagers. Samenow (1984) provides an excellent discussion and outline of treatment strategies helpful in dealing with these types of teenagers.

The Role of God in Recovery

The issue of a creator being, a higher power, or God is extremely important and needs to be addressed at some point in the treatment of a chemically dependent adolescent. Experience has indicated that most recovering teenagers are very confused about this issue and for the most part, have either denounced the idea of a higher power or feel guilty and ashamed to develop a relationship with a higher power.

When confronted with the issue in treatment, their initial response is either to deny the existence of God or to be angry with a God that allowed them to suffer so many unpleasant and negative consequences, such as being confined to a treatment center. Many recovering teenagers will often give lip service to God to impress their counselor and parents of the miraculous changes being made but, when hard pressed, will admit they are still very angry with God, or still do not believe in God.

One method used to help recovering teenagers begin to confront this important issue is to challenge openly their denial of God's existence by asserting that they do, indeed, believe in God. Many will vehemently argue they do not believe in God. After patiently listening to their protests, calmly remind them that they do believe in God—for each of them thought and acted as if they were God; thinking and acting as if they were "invincible, almighty, and omnipotent." Calmly correct their delusion and remind them that they are not God.

As effective therapists, it is important not to sidestep the issue of a higher power when questioned by recovering teenagers. For example, if asked by a teenager in treatment how I have personally resolved the issue of God in my life, I would have no hesitation sharing my convictions. I would be careful, however, not to impose my convictions on the client or in any way suggest that he or she could not get off drugs unless he or she accepted any particular religious views. We need to remember that our goal as therapists is to help the teenager to stop using drugs. Therapists with strong religious convictions will better serve their clients by remembering this important insight.

The use of pastoral counselors who are familiar with chemical dependency treatment can provide meaningful counsel to adolescents grappling with spiritual issues, especially during the later stages of recovery.

Self-Help Support Groups

Many chemical dependency treatment programs for adolescents make use of self-help support groups such as Alcoholics Anonymous (AA) and Narcotics Anonymous (NA). However it is important to recognize their limitations and understand their strengths within the context of the recovery process (Clark, 1987).

It is important to understand that self-help programs provide support, not treatment. Many novice chemical dependency counselors, mental health professionals, and family members are deceived into believing that self-help groups are sufficient for recovery after initial intervening treatment has been provided. Although this may often be the case for the successful treatment of adults—that is, completing a 21- to 30-day treatment program and then attending 90 self-help support group meetings (i.e., AA meetings) in 90 days—this regimen does not prove very successful for adolescents and often is unsuccessful for the adult polydrug and cocaine user.

Adolescents, unlike their adult counterparts, require much more structure and longer treatment to address not only their chemical dependency issues but also maturation issues that have been interrupted and, in some cases, seriously affected by drug use. As one clinical director of an adolescent treatment program explains, "Drug dependence can be seen as one near fatal disease and puberty as another" (Ehrlich, 1987, p. 312)

Self-help support groups are not designed to provide authority and structure. Instead, they are designed to provide support and encouragement. But recovering adolescents need authority and structure as well as support and encouragement if recovery is to be achieved.

Effective chemical dependency treatment programs for adolescents must combine support and encouragement coupled with authority and structure. They must provide ongoing cognitive-behavioral therapy group sessions that carefully blend adolescents new to recovery with teenagers more advanced in treatment. Additional group therapy is also needed for those more advanced in treatment (see Nay & Ross, 1993). Only after the recovering teenager's willingness to change has clearly emerged, should self-help groups such as AA be presented, and only as an auxiliary to, not a substitute for, ongoing treatment.

Self-help groups for the families of chemically dependent adolescents (e.g., Alanon, Families Anonymous) are useful in helping family members, especially parents, overcome co-dependent enabling behavior (Galanter, Gleaton, Marcus, & McMillen, 1984). An effective treatment program will encourage participation by family members in such support groups and also provide group therapy sessions that address issues surrounding co-dependent enabling behavior, communication and family interaction patterns, and in some cases, parental chemical dependency and mental disorders.

Twelve Steps

Many treatment programs for adolescent substance abusers use the twelve steps of Alcoholics Anonymous as a major therapeutic tool in recovering teenagers' ongoing treatment. The first three steps of AA help chemically dependent adolescents become more honest, decide to stop using drugs, and embark on a new course of action. Steps four through nine of AA are action steps designed to help recovering teenagers continue to be more honest, develop and implement a plan of action to change, and rectify past mistakes when possible and desirable. Steps ten through twelve are growth steps designed to encourage recovering teenagers to continue to work a program of recovery as they grow in sobriety[2]

Used appropriately, the twelve steps combined with cognitive-behavioral therapy, family therapy, and other treatment approaches help provide a basis for "understanding recovery as a process of new knowledge construction including the progressive development and integration of behavior, cognition, and affect" (Ehrlich, 1987, p. 313).

For example, twelve-step terms such *powerlessness* and *unmanageability* serve as useful vehicles to explain further the role of dysfunctional and self-defeating self-talk and emerging cognitive structures. One indeed is powerless, and one's life does become unmanageable when certain dysfunctional emotional and behavioral responses to life situations become automatic.

Summary

In this chapter, treatment options and the treatment environment were discussed. Treatment options ranged from outpatient treatment to hospitalization. Three important aspects of a healthy treatment environment were also discussed. They included treatment climate, staffing patterns, and supportive services.

Endnotes

1. Most chemically dependent adolescents do not require hospitalization but do require medical attention and need to be placed in an environment where their behavior can be monitored and access to mind-altering substances and tobacco products is eliminated. The symptoms and medical dangers of physiological addiction usually subside in three to five days. Hospitalization is indicated when alternative means of monitorong physical withdrawal symptoms are unavailable, when other serious medical complications accompany the chemical dependency, or when the acting-out behavior of the adolescent poses a direct physical threat to the life of the teenager or others.
2. A detailed discussion of how the twelve steps of AA are used as therapeutic techniques is presented in Chapters 5 and 6.

5

Treatment Strategies: Admitting and Submitting Plateaus

Past and current articles and books written on treating chemically dependent adolescents mostly report types of treatment available (e.g., inpatient or outpatient), present models for treatment (e.g., family emphasis, multidisciplinary approach), or discuss important issues in treatment (e.g., dual diagnosis, treating minorities).[1] However, the reporting of specific treatment strategies within a framework of a defined treatment rationale that outlines a process of recovery with stated goals and objectives is lacking. Articles and books reporting specific treatment strategies that have been shown to be useful in treating chemically dependent teenagers are also quite sparse.

In this chapter, 15 treatment strategies will be introduced within a framework of a defined treatment rationale that outlines a process of recovery with stated goals and objectives. Specifically, four plateaus of recovery will be explained in relationship to the emerging personality and cognitive structure of the teenage substance abuser. These plateaus include (1) *admitting,* (2) *submitting,* (3) *committing,* and (4) *transmitting.* Treatment objectives for the first two plateaus of recovery will then be listed, followed by treatment strategies that have been shown useful in helping teenage substance abusers reach the admitting and submitting stages of recovery.

Treatment objectives for the committing and transmitting plateaus and strategies proven useful in reaching them are introduced in chapter 6.

Four Plateaus of Recovery

In an excellent oral presentation, Dr. Forest Richeson (1977) outlines four dimensions of recovery that serve as excellent markers for the understanding of a treatment process for adolescents suffering from the disease of chemical dependency. He explains that a recovering individual must overcome four distinct but interrelated plateaus which he labels admitting, submitting, committing, and transmitting. Each plateau represents an important stage of the treatment process and contains a distinct set of distorted thinking patterns.

Figure 5-1 lists the four plateaus of recovery in relationship to the emerging personality and cognitive structure of a chemically dependent adolescent.

Emerging Personality	Cognitive Structure	Plateau
Psychological Addiction	I just can't stop using the drugs. The only way to manage my life is to get high.	Admit
Denial	Magical Thinking Wishful Thinking Denial Rationalization Projection	Admit
Refusal	Indifference Self-sufficiency Self-righteousness Defiance Rejection Belligerence	Submit
Self-destructive Attitudes	Damnation of Others Damnation Of Self Tyranny of Should's Awfulizing I can't stand it "itis"	Commit/ Transmit

FIGURE 5-1 Emerging Personality and Cognitive Structure in Relationship to the Four Plateaus of Recovery

Admitting: The First Plateau

For many drug-abusing teenagers, the first recovery plateau, *admitting*, may take months to reach, and unfortunately, for a percentage of teenage substance abusers, is never achieved. Goals that must be completed in order to reach the first plateau focus on identifying, examining, and confronting the denial mechanisms that maintain dishonesty and keep teenagers from honestly admitting their drug problem. The therapeutic challenge is to break through a well-rehearsed cognitive structure that maintains the two outer layers of the emerging personality of the teenage substance abuser: psychological/physiological addiction and denial of feelings and actions.[2]

These two layers of the personality contain a distinct self-talk that includes an erroneous belief that "getting high on drugs is the only way to be happy and manage one's life." In addition, the self-talk includes a myriad of excuses justifying the drug usage (rationalizations), a constant blaming of others for current and previous unpleasant circumstances (projection), unrealistic expectations about the present and the future (wishful and magical thinking), and a continual self-deception or lying to oneself and others about present and past realities (denial). These deeply entrenched elements of a distorted cognitive structure must first be shattered before the drug-abusing teenager can admit that he or she has a drug problem.

Shattering these two layers of self-destructive thinking requires a well-planned therapeutic approach utilizing cognitive-behavioral, gestalt, and reality therapies. This approach must initially focus on the teenager's feelings and behavior while restricting the teenager's access to any mind-altering drugs. A process can then begin that challenges the erroneous a posteriori belief, the obsession that "I must get high to have fun or manage my life."

Each day that the chemically dependent teenager avoids getting high provides experiential evidence that contradicts the obsession and diminishes the physiological effects of the drugs. Therefore, the first step in providing an effective treatment intervention is to place the drug-abusing teenager in a structured drug-free environment where medical needs can be addressed and the processing of emotional and behavioral experiences begins.

Experience has indicated that treatment approaches depending heavily on antipsychotic and antidepressant medications, especially during this early admitting stage of treatment, usually have proved to be ineffective in the treatment of chemically dependent adolescents. One national authority (King, 1988, p.48) on the treatment of teenage substance abuse also cautions that "parents in pain should be warned away from any type of counseling or therapy that sides with the child and makes the parent feel somehow responsible for the child's chemical abuse." He further explains that one should avoid individual counseling "that expects the adolescent to respond by forming a 'trust' relationship with the therapist." This is to say that "if the adolescent and his therapist appear to be getting along too well in the initial weeks of therapy, then the professional has failed." In that "stripping away the teenager's belief system is part of the goal of therapy," he concludes, "such a fundamental change cannot be accomplished through agreement and conciliatory behavior on the part of the authority figure—in this case, the therapist."

Reaching this first plateau is arduous and time consuming. Complicating matters is the length of time required for the effects of the mind-altering chemicals on the brain to disintegrate. For example, chronic users of marijuana may require four to seven months before the final traces of the marijuana will be eliminated from their bodies and their minds be totally free of the drug's influence.

In the meantime, recovery can be enhanced by engaging the teenage substance abuser in a group process utilizing cognitive-behavioral, gestalt, and reality therapies. The group process must begin to identify current and past feelings and behaviors. It also must repeatedly confront the substance abuser with the reality that much of the pain and misery experienced both in the past and now was and is a direct result of his or her drug habit and faulty belief structure.

Submitting: The Second Plateau

For many teenagers in treatment, eventually *admitting* that they have a drug problem is commonplace. Getting them to *submit* to a process of recovery, however, is a different matter. This is the challenge that must be overcome in order to reach the second plateau.

A major obstacle is refusal. The barriers of refusal are quite impenetrable at times and usually reinforce denial patterns. The "I don't care " (indifference), "I can get off drugs by myself" (self-sufficiency), "I already know how to get off drugs" (self-righteous), "I'm not worth it" (rejection), "You can't make me" (defiant), "It's my life and no one is going to tell me what I can and cannot do" (belligerent) attitudes are powerful forces to combat.

Individual cognitive-behavioral or other kinds of individual therapy usually prove ineffective at this stage of treatment. What is needed, is a well-structured cognitive-behavioral group process that consistently challenges the teenager's irrational beliefs, points out the inconsistency of these beliefs, and graphically reminds the teenager of the realities resulting from adhering to such beliefs. An effective method will use the experience of other teenagers who are more advanced in their recovery and have already successfully worked through the challenges that this plateau presents (Nay & Ross, 1993).

Progress begins when the teenager starts to honestly admit that he or she has a drug problem, does not know how to solve it, and asks the group for help with it. Until admission and submission take place, the teenager's denial and refusal layers are continuing to dictate and control the teenager's future. Submission occurs when the teenager is willing to hold himself or herself accountable to the group and the group therapist(s).

Committing: The Third Plateau

Reaching the third plateau of treatment, *committing,* requires the teenager to begin acting on a new set of beliefs and to struggle with the ambivalence and dissonance that accompany any change. As the teenager begins to develop a new, positive, more rational, functional self-talk and begins to experience the emotional and behavioral responses that result from it, *ambivalence* and *dissonance* begin to emerge. This new self-talk and the previously well-rehearsed old "druggie" thinking patterns compete for the heart and soul of the recovering teenager. Unfortunately, the drug-abusing teenager will not give up old "druggie" thinking patterns without a battle and, often, without a long arduous struggle. In addition, the teenager will feel awkward or ambivalent as he or she attempts to address life's challenges sober.

The experience of ambivalence and dissonance is similar to asking people to tie their shoes starting with their left hand when they had been used to tying their shoes by starting with their right hand. At first, they will feel very awkward and uncomfortable when performing the task and will have a strong inclination to resort back to their old way of tying their shoes. However, with ample time and correct practice, the new way of tying their shoes would become more comfortable and the old inclination would become less favorable.

Critical to reaching the committing plateau is helping the teenager stay focused on the benefits of adhering to and enacting new thinking patterns and continually reminding the teenager of the consequences of choosing to pay attention to their old "druggie" style of thinking. The development of a healthy fear of one's past, positive realistic expectations about one's future, and a willingness to act on one's new found beliefs are tantamount in developing a commitment to reach the third plateau and in making a solid commitment to live a drug-free life style.

Transmitting: The Fourth Plateau

The fourth and final plateau, *transmitting*, requires the recovering teenager to realize that, in order to continue to receive the benefits which accompany a drug-free life style, the new thinking patterns need constant rehearsal and must be implemented on a daily basis. Many recovering individuals have referred to this challenge as the acceptance hurdle, for recovery takes more than just admitting, submitting, and committing.

To reach the transmitting plateau, the recovering teenager must learn how to manage and effectively minimize the impact of strong self-destructive attitudes that resulted from and/or occurred prior to drug usage. Damnation of self and others, the tyranny of shoulds, awfulizing, and I can't stand it-itis thinking patterns are still quite prevalent as are the accompanying emotions of anger, resentment, self-pity, guilt, worry, and apprehension. Transmitting requires the acceptance that continuing to practice new formed habits are essential for sustained recovery.

For most recovering teenage substance abusers, reaching the transmitting plateau takes several years (usually five) to achieve and a lifetime to perfect. Recovering teenagers striving to reach this final plateau benefit immensely from individual cognitive-behavioral counseling and group processes that provide opportunities for teenagers to share accomplishments, continue to challenge distorted thinking patterns, and assist each other in recognizing and eliminating self-defeating thinking. Reaching out and assisting other teenagers new to recovery is also important. Such activity reinforces one's commitment, helps reduce selfishness and self-centeredness, and reminds the teenager that he or she could still be engaged in a self-destructive "druggie" life style.

Treatment Strategies: Admitting and Submitting

As described previously, initial treatment of the teenage substance abuser requires a structured environment that is free of all mind-altering chemicals and includes a group process that will begin to challenge the psychological/physiological addiction, denial, and refusal layers of the chemically dependent personality. Effective treatment also requires the prudent use of several treatment strategies.

A *treatment strategy* is a therapeutic tool or process designed to assist therapists in helping chemically dependent adolescents identify and change self-defeating emotional and behavioral responses. It is a method that directly or indirectly identifies, challenges, or changes the distorted a priori and a posteriori cognitions that make up the self-defeating cognitive structure so prevalent in chemically dependent teenagers.

In addition, effective treatment also requires that treatment strategies be used within a framework of clearly defined treatment objectives. Treatment objectives for the admitting and submitting plateaus include:

1. Identification of how drug usage significantly interfered with work, school, family, friendships, leisure time, society, finances, and self
2. Recognition of impaired ability to manage daily activities and make reasonable life decisions
3. Acknowledgment of a drug problem
4. Recognition of a tendency to blame others or circumstances for drug usage problem
5. Identification of feelings of anger, guilt, resentment, hostility, self-pity, loneliness, apathy, hopelessness, rejection, despair, isolation, embarrassment, and shame
6. Identification of the irrational thinking patterns of denial and refusal that perpetuate emotional and behavioral responses that block the development of willingness and readiness to work a program of recovery
7. Development of the belief that others in the group and group therapist(s) can provide significant help and support if asked
8. Development of the belief that change is possible
9. Recognition of fallibility and correctiveness
10. Increase in tolerance for frustration and stress
11. Demonstration of willingness to follow rules, accept structure, and follow directions of people in authority
12. Beginning the rebuilding of a family relationship
13. Remaining free of all mind-altering chemicals and tobacco products
14. Identifying and addressing any medical and/or psychological complications that might complicate or disrupt treatment

Several treatment strategies have been proved useful in helping recovering teenage drug abusers achieve these treatment objectives, thereby reaching the admitting and submitting plateaus of recovery. These techniques are effective in helping teenage substance abusers overcome the barriers of psychological/physiological addiction, denial, and refusal by enhancing awareness, providing an alternative means to manage feelings, and fostering hope by explaining how change is possible.

Techniques that *enhance awareness* include the awareness wheel, the feeling log, the ABCDEs of emotion and behavior, daily moral inventories, developing a life plan, the rebel without a cause syndrome, steps one, two, three, styles of manipulation and actualization, and the searching and fearless moral inventory.

Techniques that introduce *alternative means to manage feelings* include the three signs, the serenity prayer, and the fallible and correctable human being.

Techniques that explain *how change is possible* include five steps to change, the law of the harvest, and getting straight.

Figure 5-2 lists these 15 treatment strategies for the admitting and submitting plateaus of recovery and describes their purpose.

Enhancing Awareness

An explanation of several treatment strategies for enhancing awareness follows. These strategies have proven useful in helping recovering teenagers become more aware of their feelings, actions, the consequences of their choices, and the impact that their decisions have had on both themselves and others. Awareness is the first step in helping teenage substance abusers develop a healthier cognitive structure.

Awareness Wheel

The awareness wheel (S. Miller, Nunnally, & Wackman, 1991, pp. 15–25) is an excellent therapeutic tool to help recovering teenagers learn how to (1) distinguish their thoughts from their feelings, (2) examine their present and past behaviors, (3) clarify their wants and desires, (4) understand the role of self-talk in the formation of emotional and behavioral responses, and (5) express themselves more openly and honestly, especially in a group setting. The awareness wheel is divided into five distinct but interrelated parts.

Part one of the awareness wheel helps recovering teenagers identify *sensations*—a person's perceptions of an event or situation as experienced through the senses of sight, touch, taste, smell, and sound. Questions like What did you hear? What did you see? What did you taste, smell, or feel? help teenagers identify sensations.

Part two, *thoughts*, helps teenagers identify the beliefs, values, and attitudes they rely on to make sense out of or attach meaning to what they have seen, touched, tasted, smelled, and heard. Teenagers describe their sensations, form and express opinions or make judgments about them, and construct expectations around them. Their resulting descriptions, opinions, and expectations in turn determine the emotional response they will experience in the situation.

Treatment strategy	Purpose
awareness wheel	enhances awareness
feeling log	enhances awareness
ABCDE's of emotion and behavior	enhances awareness
daily moral inventory	enhances awareness
developing a life plan	enhances awareness
rebel without a cause syndrome	enhances awareness
steps one, two, and three	enhances awareness
styles of manipulation and actualization	enhances awareness
searching and fearless moral inventory	enhances awareness
three signs	manage feelings
serenity prayer	manage feelings
fallible and correctable human being	manage feelings
five steps to change	change process
law of the harvest	change process
getting straight	change process

FIGURE 5-2 Admitting and Submitting Treatment Strategies in Relationship to their Purpose

Part three of the awareness wheel helps the recovering teenagers get in touch with *feelings*. Initially, it is very important to provide opportunities for recovering teenagers to openly and honestly express their feelings. The awareness wheel provides a useful tool to help them to focus on their feelings. Feelings can be categorized into six basic emotions: mad, sad, glad, worry, fear, guilt (regret).

Part four of the awareness wheel is designed to help recovering teenagers clearly identify and examine their *intentions*. Teenagers in recovery are usually very confused about their wants, wishes, and desires and have usually thought very little about them. Also, their drug usage has either destroyed or severely damaged many of their dreams and has resulted in the formulation of unrealistic and very unhealthy wishes and desires. This part of the awareness wheel provides an excellent opportunity for the therapist to begin to uncover many of these unhealthy desires as well as to help recovering teenagers focus on their many shattered dreams.

Part five, *actions,* is designed to help recovering teenagers focus on their behaviors, both in the past and present. This part of the awareness wheel provides an excellent vehicle for the therapist to focus on past self-defeating behaviors and to help recovering teenagers become more aware of how they currently act.

Feeling Log

The feeling log is another useful tool to help recovering teenagers become more aware of their feelings. As the name implies, the teenager is requested to keep a daily log of his or her feelings and to write down what event or situation was occurring when experiencing the feeling(s). It is recommended that the teenager monitor his or her feelings three times daily: at noon, at dinner, and just prior to going to bed. The exercise is usually more effective if the therapist provides the teenager with a list of feeling words from which the teenagers can select those feelings that most closely describe his or her state of emotion.

Figure 5-3 depicts the format of a feeling log.

	Feelings	Situation
Noon		
Evening		
Bedtime		

FIGURE 5-3 Format of a Feeling Log

ABCDEs of Emotion and Behavior

The ABCDEs of emotion and behavior (Ross, 1978) is a therapeutic tool similar to the awareness wheel. This tool is especially helpful in teaching recovering teenagers how their self-talk creates and maintains their emotional and behavioral responses. It also helps teach recovering teenagers how they develop both constructive and self-defeating automatic emotional and behavioral responses to events and situations in their lives.

This particular technique helps recovering teenagers learn to distinguish between self-talk that creates and sustains emotional responses and self-talk that creates and sustains behavioral responses. Understanding this distinction is important in recovery. It becomes imperative that recovering teenagers change their self-talk that leads to getting high before they change their self-talk that results in unnecessary emotional turmoil. *Soberness must come before sobriety.*

The first step in introducing the ABCDEs of emotion and behavior is to define what each letter represents:

A = Event or situation
B = Thoughts about A (the event or situation)
C = Feelings or one's emotional response to A
D = Thoughts about C (feelings or emotional response)
E = Behavioral response to A

Our thoughts or beliefs (B) about events or situations (A) are three in nature. We describe an event or situation, we express our opinions about it, and we form expectations. Collectively, our descriptions, opinions, and expectations about an event determine our emotional response to the event. When we think about an event in the same way over and over again, our thoughts (B) become linked or connected with the event (A), whereby we now only have to experience the situation in order to emotionally respond to it. Once our thoughts (B) have become linked with the event (A), an automatic emotional response will occur.

Similarly, we develop thoughts or beliefs about our emotions (C). We attempt to describe our emotions, evaluate whether we like the emotions, and express how we are going to act on, or what we intend to do with, our emotions. How we describe our emotions, evaluate them, and decide what we will do about them (intentions) will determine our behavioral responses (E). When we think about our emotions in the same way over and over again, our emotions (C) and our thoughts (D) become linked, whereby we now only have to experience the emotion in order to behaviorally respond to them. Once our thoughts (D) have become linked with our emotions (C), an automatic behavioral response will occur.

Combined, automatic emotional and behavioral responses to an event or situation is called an attitude. An attitude occurs when we go from (A) to (C) to (E) automatically, without having to consciously think about it. Recovery requires identifying attitudes that result in destructive emotional and behavioral responses and replacing them with attitudes that result in constructive emotional and behavioral responses.[3]

Figure 5-4 provides a schematic presentation of the ABCDEs of emotion and behavior.

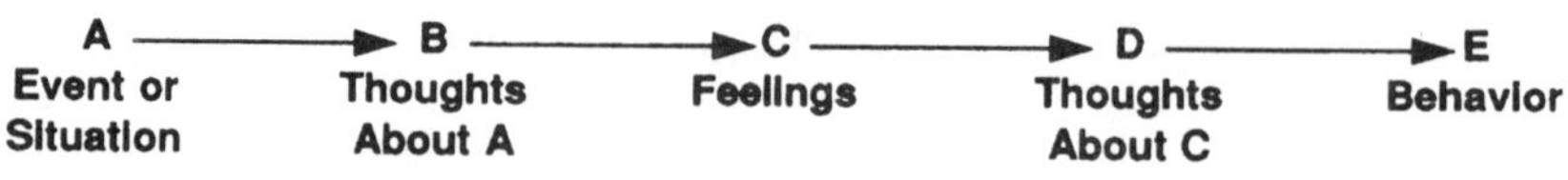

B Thoughts (Beliefs)
- **describe** a situation or event
- express **opinions** about a situation or event
- express **expectations** about a situation or event

B Thoughts → C Feelings (Beliefs)

A becomes associated with B

A → C

automatic emotional response

D Thoughts (Beliefs)
- **describe** how a person feels
- **evaluate** whether a person likes the feelings being experienced
- **expresses** what a person will do (**intentions**) about the feelings

D Thoughts → E Actions (Beliefs)

C becomes associated with D

C → E

automatic behavioral response

A → C → E

automatic emotional and behavioral response (Attitude)

FIGURE 5-4 ABCDEs of Emotion and Behavior

Daily Moral Inventory

The daily moral inventory (Ross, 1983b) is an adaptation of the tenth step of Alcoholics Anonymous as outlined in the AA publication *Twelve Steps and Twelve Traditions* (Anonymous, 1986, pp. 88–95). The inventory serves as a daily log to be written nightly by recovering teenagers.

The log is divided into four sections: challenges, strengths, goals, and blessings.

The first section of the inventory, *challenges*, provides an opportunity for recovering teenagers to write down the difficulties they encountered during the day. In paragraph form, they outline the situation they experienced, identify what they thought, express how they felt, record how they acted, and indicate what they would like to change or do differently if the situation were to reoccur. For example, a teenager will ask himself or herself:

> *During the day, did I experience any of the following: false pride, condemning self, dishonesty, impatience, hate, resentment, overcomplicating, suspicion, envy of others, laziness, procrastination, insincerity, negative thinking, taking self too seriously, selfishness, taking care of everyone else but self? When and under what circumstances did I find myself engaging in these self-defeating feelings and actions? What specifically could I begin doing tomorrow to decrease the frequency of these self-defeating feelings and actions?*

In section two of the inventory, the recovering teenagers are instructed to list their *strengths*. They are asked to review those situations where they experienced rational or more functional feelings and behaviors. They are encouraged to list their strong points and the changes they were able to make for that day.

For example, when and where had they demonstrated gratitude, humility, valuing self, honesty, patience, love, forgiveness, simplicity, trust, appreciation of others, positive activity, promptness, straightforwardness, positive thinking, sense of humor, or taking care of self?

Section three of the inventory is a place to list *goals* for the next day. These goals are to be achievable, believable, concrete, and desirable. They often stem from the challenges listed in section one of the inventory.

Section four is a place to list one's *blessings*. What am I thankful for this day? What kind of successes have I experienced? What kind of experiences have enriched my life today? How and in what ways can I show more appreciation and gratefulness in my life?

Therapeutically, this daily log serves many useful purposes. For one, it provides a written account by which the therapist and recovering teenagers can measure their progress in treatment. Second, the log reveals many of the irrational thinking patterns that need to be challenged in the group therapy sessions. Third, the log can be used to instruct recovering teenagers on how to begin to bring about constructive change in their lives. In addition, careful monitoring of the log can be used to detect those teenagers who are experiencing difficulties in their recovery and who are on the verge of relapse.

Figure 5-5 depicts the format of a daily moral inventory.

Developing a Life Plan

Developing a life plan is yet another strategy that can be used to confront the layers of thinking that keep the teenager from reaching the admitting and submitting plateaus of recovery. Adapted from Bassin (1971), this particular exercise asks teenagers in treatment to respond to four general areas of questioning.

First, the teenagers are asked to think about their life goals. What kind of life do they want ultimately? What do they want to accomplish in the next year, three years, five years?

I. Challenges - **(In paragraph form)**

Situation

Thoughts

Feelings

Change

II. Strength - **(In paragraph form)**

Strong point in your character

III. Goals - **Specific course of actions listed by numbers. These need to relate to challenges in Section I.**

IV. Blessings - **(In paragraph form)**

"What am I thankful for?"

FIGURE 5-5 Format of a Daily Moral Inventory

Next, the teenagers are asked to focus on their situation today. What kind of fears or problems do they have? Before coming into treatment, how would they spend a typical day?

Additionally, the teenagers are asked to think about the question of harmony or balance in life. For example, how much time did they spend alone? What proportion of their day was spent getting high? How much of their time and energy was being spent on their education and other activities that would enable them to make a legitimate living?

Lastly, the teenagers are asked to seriously examine their overall life style. How and in what ways were they investing their time and energy? What results do they have to show for their various efforts?

Collectively, these questions usually result in revealing just how warped their lives had become and how much their lives were centering on a lot of magical and wishful thinking. This exercise usually creates many opportunities for the therapist to directly challenge magical and wishful thinking and the other thought processes that make up the denial layer of the teenager's drug personality.

Rebel Without a Cause Syndrome

The rebel without a cause syndrome is an excellent tool to assist recovering teenagers in overcoming their tendency to blame others for all of their current and past challenges and to address a critical therapeutic issue: force versus choice. This technique is also very useful in dealing with clients who demonstrate strong defiant and belligerent attitudes.

At the core of this syndrome is a set of irrational or dysfunctional thoughts that results in the recovering teenager feeling irrate and acting in a defiant and resisting manner (see Maultsby, 1978, pp. 22, 211–212). The recovering teenager erroneously believes

> *I have been forced into treatment, and I have no choice about being in treatment. Others are trying to control me and if I comply with treatment, that proves that they do control me. If I do what someone else in authority asks me to do, that proves that they are better than me or that I am inferior to them.*

Introducing the rebel without a cause syndrome enables the therapist and other group members to help the angry and defiant teenager (rebel) begin to examine this dysfunctional thinking pattern. Hopefully, the rebellious teenager will realize that, unless someone is physically overpowering him or her, he or she is always choosing to do what he or she does. It is further explained to this teenager that in many instances one's choices might be limited. For example, if the teenager leaves treatment, he or she may be arrested and have to appear before a judge and possibly be sentenced to a juvenile detention center. But nonetheless, the teenager has chosen to be, and is not being forced to be, in treatment.

> *No one else can ever control another person, except physically, because you are always in control of what you think and subsequently how you feel and act, unless of course you have brain damage or are on drugs. Besides, doing what another person wants you to do simply means that you have decided to do it, and in no way proves that others are better than you. Therefore, rebelling for the purpose of proving that someone can't make you do something that you don't want to, when they can't make you do something in the first place, simply does not make sense. Instead of rebelling against something that doesn't exist to begin with, let's begin examining how you can begin to make some rational choices given the alternatives that currently are available to you.*

Introducing *rational alternatives* to the recovering teenager's rebel without a cause thinking begins the process of empowering the teenager to take responsibility for his or her own recovery. This process also sends the important message that if the teenager continues to dwell on and focus on irrational thoughts, he or she will continue to feel miserable, act in ways that will create significant conflict with others, and may result in consequences he or she does not wish to experience.

Steps One, Two, and Three

Steps one, two, and three of Alcoholics Anonymous are most applicable to the admitting and submitting plateaus and serve, in harmony with all of the twelve steps of AA, as excellent therapeutic tools for intervention and treatment of teenage substance abusers.[4] Steps one, two, and three read:

> *We admitted we were powerless over alcohol—that our lives had become unmanageable. Came to believe that a power greater than ourselves could restore us to sanity. Made a decision to turn our lives and will over to the care of God* as we understood Him *(Anonymous, 1986, pp. 21–41).*

These three steps begin by asking the teenager to admit *powerlessness over drugs.* The drug by itself has no power over anything. Powerlessness occurs only when an automatic emotional and behavioral response has formed. A set of well-rehearsed self-talk permeates the teenager's thinking emphasizing, quite erroneously, that the only means to manage life is to take drugs (i.e., psychological addiction).

Careful review of the words contained in each of these three steps and a discussion of their meaning provide an opportunity for the therapist to introduce the relationship between emotion, behavior, and how a person talks to himself. Indeed, a person is powerless over a drug as long as one continues to deny the realities and consequences (the unmanageability) that ensues as a result of taking the drug. Indeed, a person is insane to continue to believe that repeated consumption of the drug will result in no physical, emotional, and spiritual harm, especially in light of concrete evidence to the contrary.

But as step two emphasizes, the drug-abusing teenager must come to *believe* that alternative means are available to manage one's life and that significant others (power greater than oneself) can help one develop a set of thinking patterns that will result in more sane and desirable emotional and behavioral responses. And, as step three emphasizes, the drug-abusing teenager must *decide* to allow significant others to help him or her develop and implement a new pattern of thinking that will result in more sane and desirable outcomes.

Introducing these three steps and discussing their meaning provide another mechanism for the therapist to confront the psychological/physiological addiction, denial, and refusal layers of thinking that keep the teenager from reaching and progressing beyond the admitting and submitting plateaus of recovery. Discussion centering on these three steps helps the therapist assist the teenager in developing a new self-talk that (1) emphasizes the recognition of a severe drug problem, (2) admits ignorance in how to solve the problem, and (3) decides that significant others can help provide a workable solution, if one is only willing to ask for the help and do what others advise. Or as Alcoholics Anonymous would explain: "I can't, God can, if I let Him."

Styles of Manipulation and Actualization

Styles of manipulation and actualization is a treatment strategy developed by Shostrom (1968, pp. 11–30). In introducing the technique, Shostrom identifies personality traits that, depending how the person uses them, result in either manipulation or actualization. These personality traits include (1) strength, (2) sensitivity, (3) control, (4) dependency, (5) aggression, (6) warmth, (7) criticalness, and (8) support. Shostrom also depicts these personality traits as four separate but interrelated continuums: strength versus sensitivity, control versus dependency, aggression versus warmth, and criticalness versus support.

Shostrom views a *manipulator* as "a person who exploits, uses, controls himself or others as 'things' in self-defeating ways." He identifies eight specific styles of manipulation, each characterized by the exaggeration of a particular personality trait. He explains:

> *The dictator exaggerates his strength.... The weakling exaggerates his sensitivity.... The calculator exaggerates his control.... The clinging vine exaggerates his dependency....The bully exaggerates his aggression....The nice guy exaggerates his caring.... The judge exaggerates his criticalness.... The protector exaggerates his support.*

He further explains that opposites on the personality trait continuums usually attract one another in order to act out their manipulations. That is, the dictator seeks out the weakling. The calculator seeks out the clinging vine. The bully seeks out the nice guy. The judge seeks out the protector. Resulting are four polar opposites consisting of eight manipulating types.

Figure 5-6 depicts the eight manipulative types.

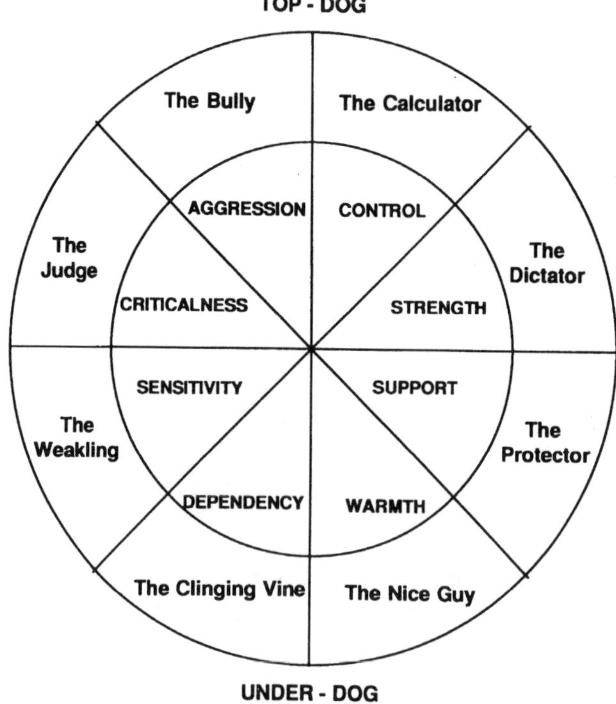

FIGURE 5-6 Manipulative Types

From *Man, The Manipulator,* Everett L. Shostrom Copyright 1967 by Abingdon Press. Used by permission.

Shostrom views the *actualizer* as a person who is "marked by four opposing characteristics: honesty, freedom, awareness, and trust," compared to the manipulator's characteristics of "deception, unawareness, control, and cynicism." He identifies eight actualizing types who have learned how to turn "antagonist opposites" into complementary opposites. He explains:

> *From the dictator develops the leader.... The complementary opposite of the leader is the empathizer.... From the calculator develops the respecter.... The complementary opposite of the respecter is the appreciator.... From the bully develops the asserter.... The complementary opposite of the asserter is the carer.... From the judge develops the expresser.... The complementary opposite of the judge is the guide.*

Shostrom further explains each actualizing type by giving an example from history of a person who exemplified the particular characteristics of the actualizing type.

Figure 5-7 depicts the eight actualizing types and also notes a historical figure representative of that type.

Introducing both the manipulative and actualizing types enables the creative therapist to use these conceptual frameworks to help recovering teenagers become more aware of their past actions and learn how to act differently in the future. This technique can also be used to help them understand their dominant personality type. Just as importantly, the therapist can explore with them the kinds of self-talk that create and sustain each of the manipulative types and the kinds of self-talk that will produce actualizing types.

Searching and Fearless Moral Inventory

A searching and fearless moral inventory[5] (Anonymous, 1980a, pp. 64–71; Anonymous, 1980b, chap. 5; Anonymous, 1986, pp. 42-54) is an extremely useful therapeutic tool to help recovering teenagers identify and confront character defects (self-defeating emotional and behavioral responses) that significantly retard their quest for sobriety and often hamper their efforts to maintain soberness. The fourth of twelve steps in the program of recovery outlined by Alcoholics Anonymous, a searching and fearless moral inventory helps recovering teenagers become more honest with themselves as they embark on a new road designed to initiate and encourage the development of character strengths.

Completing a searching and fearless moral inventory enables the recovering teenager to understand the importance of three instincts, or drives: social instinct, security instinct, and sexual instinct. The teenager

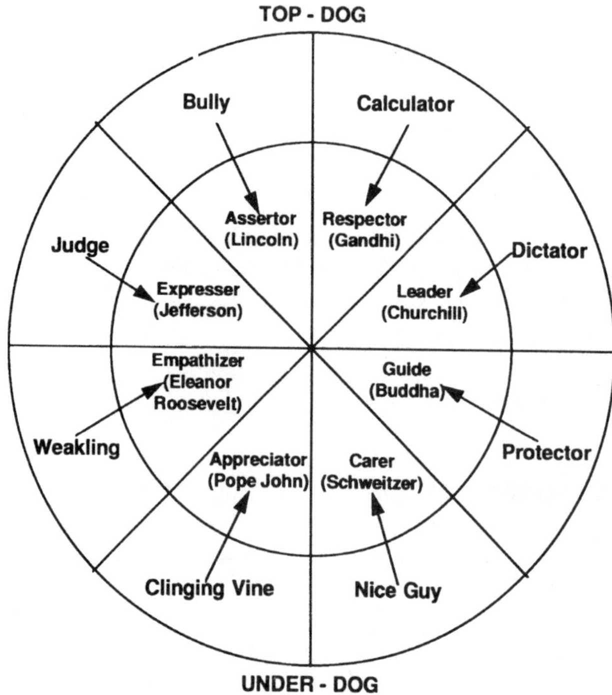

FIGURE 5-7 Actualizing Types

From *Man, The Manipulator,* Everett L. Shostrom copyright 1967 by Abingdon Press. Used by permission.

learns that, left unchecked, these instincts create unnecessary and disabling emotions of resentment, fear and hurt and often result in hurting and harming others.

Note the comments of the cofounder of Alcoholics Anonymous:

> *Yet these instincts, so necessary for our existence, often far exceed their proper function. Powerfully, blindly, many time subtly, they drive us, dominate us, and insist upon ruling our lives. Our desire for sex, for material and emotional security, and for an important place in society often tyrannize us. When thus out of joint, man's natural desires cause him great trouble, practically all the trouble there is. No human being, however good, is exempt from these troubles. Nearly every serious emotional problem can be seen as a case of misdirected instinct. When that happens, our great natural assets, the instincts, have turned into physical and mental liabilities. (Anonymous, 1986, p. 42)*

The searching and fearless moral inventory is a written exercise designed for the purpose of reviewing past and current resentments, fears, and sexual conduct. Starting with resentments, the recovering teenager is asked to list "people, institutions, or principles with whom we were angry." Then the teenager is asked:

> *... why we were angry. In most cases it was found that our self-esteem, our pocketbooks, our ambitions, our personal relationships (including sex) were hurt or threatened.... On our grudge list we set opposite each name our injuries. Was it our self-esteem, our security, our ambitions, our personal, or sex relations, which had been interfered with?.... Referring to our list again. Putting out of our minds the wrongs others had done, we resolutely looked for our own mistakes. Where had we been selfish, dishonest, self-seeking and frightened?.... When we saw our thoughts we listed them.... We admitted our wrongs honestly and were willing to set these matters straight. (Anonymous, 1980a, pp. 64–67)*

In a similar manner, this process is completed for fears and sexual conduct.

Experience has suggested that it is best to introduce this inventory after the teenager begins to show signs of a willingness and readiness to change. The teenager will be more honest in the process of completing the inventory and show a greater motivation to change the character defects uncovered. Encouraging the recovering teenager to complete a moral inventory every six months is strongly suggested.

Managing Feelings

Prior to treatment, the teenager managed feelings by getting high or using denial. Learning alternative means to manage feelings is the second step in helping teenage substance abusers develop a healthier cognitive structure.

Three Signs

The three signs is yet another technique useful in helping recovering teenagers become more honest with themselves and begin to set some realistic priorities for recovery. The three signs are

Think, think, think
First things first
Easy does it

In the early stages of recovery, the drug-abusing teenager experiences a lot of emotional turmoil, and his or her capacity to handle stress is very low. The teenager's frustration level is low due to an instant reinforcement schedule produced by drug usage. The thinking of the teenager at this stage of recovery is also very irrational at times and quite often delusional. His or her capacity for setting priorities has been significantly diminished, with the bulk of attention having been devoted exclusively to one priority, that of getting high or drunk. No longer drugging or drinking, therefore, feels very frustrating, awkward, and strange and is, from the recovering teenager's perspective, extremely abnormal.

Use of the three signs by the therapist(s) is an effective way to address the issues of low frustration tolerance, emotional instability, and emotional discomfort. Focusing on the first of the three signs, think, think, think, provides the opportunity to reinforce the relationship between thinking, emotions, and behavior and also can be used to encourage the teenager to focus on types of thinking that will relieve emotional discomfort.

Introducing the second of the three signs, first things first, helps recovering teenagers begin to establish and prioritize some concrete achievable goals that will specifically address their most important needs at this point in their recovery. For example, a teenager may be focusing all of his energies on restoring his relationship with his parents, but has not even begun to talk about how he treated his parents, or even begun to admit how unmanageable his own life had become. Using this simple phrase, first things first, is a very nonthreatening way to encourage the teenager to focus more on the issues at hand and provides a handle for the teenager to associate the importance of dealing with more important issues first.

The third of the three signs, easy does it, is an excellent phrase to help the recovering teenager begin to develop some patience. Remember, prior to treatment the teenager's thoughts were "I want what I want and I want it now!" Easy does it emphasizes that the recovery process will take time. The message is "Slow down, not so fast, we have lots of time. We only have to get through today, or this afternoon, or the next couple of hours. You can and are learning how to survive without the use of drugs. The discomfort you are experiencing will diminish over time."

Serenity Prayer

The serenity prayer is an excellent therapeutic tool to teach the recovering teenager how to address an obsessive thinking style that demands that the world must conform to our expectations. Commonly referred to as tyranny of shoulds thinking, this style of thinking guarantees that the recovering teenager will experience often the emotional states of frustration and anger.

In contrast, the serenity prayer, when practiced religiously, helps the recovering teenager learn to accept current realities and teaches the teenager how to impact change on the environment without being angry and frustrated. This time-honored prayer reads:

> *God, grant me the serenity to accept the things I cannot change, courage to change the things I can, and the wisdom to know the difference.*

In his book, Alcohol and Spirituality, Whitfield (1985, p. 111) explains that the first part of the prayer, "God grant me," helps a recovering person "admit the existence of a conscience or a higher Power greater than self... that is able to bestow and give to me and others," and that "it is not wrong to ask for... improvements of my character," for "both I and people around me will be happier."

Whitfield further explains that asking for "serenity to accept the things I cannot change" is "asking for calmness, composure and inner peace" as I am "resigning myself to conditions as they are right now." It involves an acknowledgment that "tragedy, death, suffering, illness, and pain, as a part of life, are neither good or bad." It involves an acceptance of one's "humanness and fallibility... accepting my lot in life as it is until I have the courage to change any part of my life... without doing so grudgingly." Furthermore, "I can't prevent these events or conditions from happening to myself or others."

Whitfield explains that the next part of the prayer, "courage to change the things I can," enables a recovering person "to deal with problems and realities of life without reliance on alcohol or drugs... a strength of my spirit to face and handle the negative... fearless in the practice of faith, humility and honesty." He further states:

> *In facing these negatives directly and honestly, I am asking for myself and my life conditions to be different for me. I am taking an active part in this changing. I am asking for help to make the right decisions. Everything is not the way I would like it to be in my life. I must continue to face reality and constantly work toward my continued growth and progress.*

Whitfield concludes that the final part of the prayer, "and wisdom to know the difference," is asking "to rise above my ego and form sound judgements about myself and my life.... I want to see things differently in my life so that I will be more aware of myself and others."

The use of the serenity prayer as a treatment strategy is an excellent means to help recovering teenagers develop the character quality of acceptance. The serenity prayer is also an excellent way to help recovering teenagers begin to identify and address what Maultsby (1986, pp. 125–133) describes as the "Jehovah complex," believing that they can magically change reality as if they were God. But, as Maultsby explains, "there is no known magic in the real world outside human minds."

As one recovering alcoholic (Anonymous, 1980a, p. 449) summarized:

> *And acceptance is the answer to all my problems today. When I am disturbed, it is because I find some person, place, thing or situation—some fact of my life—unacceptable to me, and I can find no serenity until I accept that person, place, thing, or situation as being exactly the way it is supposed to be at this moment. Nothing, absolutely nothing happens in God's world by mistake. Until I could accept my alcoholism, I could not stay sober; unless I accept life completely on life's terms, I cannot be happy. I need to concentrate not so much on what needs to be changed in the world as on what needs to be changed in me and my attitude.*

Fallible and Correctable Human Being

The fallible and correctable human being (Maultsby, 1975; Ross, 1983c) technique is an excellent therapeutic tool to help recovering teenagers learn to distinguish between their performance and their value or inherent worth as a human being. Most drug-abusing teenagers erroneously believe that their value or worth as a human being is dependent on their performance. Therefore, when they start examining the depravity of their "druggie" life style and begin to get more honest about their past behaviors, they often begin to feel quite inadequate and depressed and loathe in their self-pity. They conclude that they are horrible and terrible human beings who do not deserve to live, or at the very least, should be severely punished. They take an otherwise healthy sense of guilt and remorse and translate it into undeserving shame.

The fallible and correctable human being (FHB/CHB) concept helps the recovering teenager learn how to differentiate irrational self-destructive acts and deeds from one's basic value or worth. To facilitate understanding this concept, the sun and rays analogy is used.

As the sun and its rays are two separate entities, so are our behaviors and ourself. When the sun emits rays, it still remains the sun. In a like manner, when people emit behaviors, they still are people. A person can change the behaviors that one emits, but one cannot change the fact that one is still a person.

To illustrate this point, the teenager is asked to list five behaviors that are done well, mediocre, and poorly. Then the teenager is asked to assume that he or she is able to improve on all of the poorly done behaviors but becomes less proficient in behaviors once done well. The question is then asked; Because some of your behaviors improved and some of them did not, are you a different person? The reality is that you are still you, only now you have improved your performance in some areas and need more work in other areas.

Grasping this important concept encourages recovering teenagers to focus on the benefits of improving their behaviors as opposed to focusing on how they can become better people. The FHB/CHB concept helps recovering teenagers learn that they are no more valuable or worthwhile than the teenagers who are still using drugs. The only difference between them and the teenagers still using drugs is that they have had the opportunity to learn and practice more effective ways to manage their lives and are beginning to reap the benefits derived from choosing to live a drug-free life style.

Using the FHB/CHB concept helps eliminate derogatory names used to belittle or put oneself down (e.g., stupid, dumb, idiot, low life) and gets rid of terms such as "good kid" or "good person." As the FHB/CHB concepts implies, the best one can ever hope to be and the worst one ever will be is a fallible and correctable human being. No matter how hard we try, we can never improve on this fact.

Figure 5-8 depicts the sun and rays analogy.

Change Process

Explaining the change process is the third step in helping teenage substance abusers develop a healthier cognitive structure.

Five Steps to Change

Five steps to change is one treatment strategy to help drug-abusing teenagers understand how change is possible. Recovering teenagers are introduced to a five-step process of change: (1) awareness, (2) commitment, (3) identification of irrational thought patterns, (4) substitution of rational thought patterns, and (5) practice–dissonance.

The first step of change is becoming *aware* of the irrational ACEs or automatic self-defeating emotional and behavioral patterns (character defects) that are significantly interfering with the teenager's attainment of soberness and sobriety. Other treatment techniques such as the awareness wheel, daily moral inventory, and steps one, two, three, and four of Alcoholics Anonymous serve as excellent vehicles to enhance self-awareness.

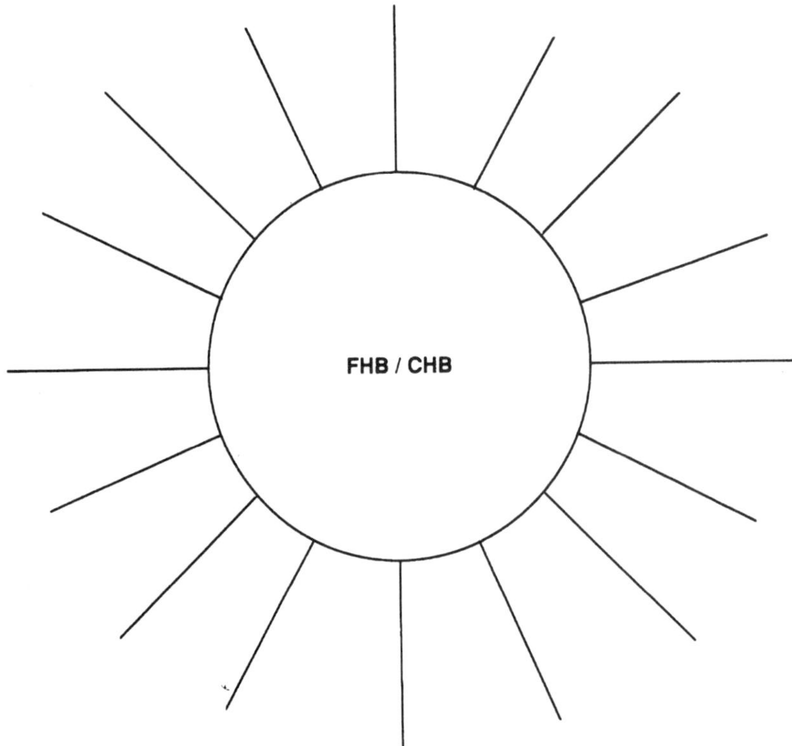

FIGURE 5-8 Sun and Rays Analogy

Once the character defects (irrational ACEs) that the recovering teenager desires to change have been identified, step two of the change process can proceed. This step involves making a no-excuse *commitment* to do whatever is rationally necessary to accomplish the newly desired character traits.

Step three of the change process is to *identify* the irrational beliefs and attitudes that create and sustain the undesirable character defects and to understand clearly why these beliefs and attitudes are irrational or dysfunctional. Armed with this knowledge, the recovering teenager can then develop rational beliefs to substitute for the previously held self-defeating beliefs.

Step four in the change process is to create and sustain rational or functional belief patterns that will *displace* the previously practiced character defects and maintain the newly desired character traits. The seven steps to a happy (F)ACE (to be introduced in Chapter 6) prove quite useful in creating these new rational belief patterns.

The final step in the change process is accomplished by *practicing* the rational or functional belief pattern that creates and sustains the newly desired character trait. It must be practiced a sufficient number of times to overcome the dissonance, or awkwardness, that occurs as the previously learned self-defeating ACE continues to compete with the newly developing rational ACE. Sufficient practice is necessary in order for the newly desired character trait to become more dominant than the previously learned character defect. Recovery scripts coupled with prayer and meditation (to be introduced in Chapter 6) enhance this process immensely.

Understanding the change process provides the recovering teenager and the therapist a frame of reference to evaluate progress. This understanding also helps the recovering teenager avoid an unnecessary relapse, as he or she can now anticipate going through some initial discomfort (dissonance) as he or she develops new character traits. The teenager now realizes that this discomfort is quite normal and expected. The teenager can also better appreciate the adage "no pain no gain" and understand more completely why those further along in recovery emphasize "faking it until you make it." Relapse thinking such as "this is not the real me" or "I am acting like a phony" can be confidently replaced with "this is really me developing and practicing a new way to feel and act."

Law of the Harvest

The law of the harvest (Swindoll, 1987a) is based on the biblical text (Ryrie, 1978) of Galatians 6:6–10.

> *And let the one who is taught the word share all good things with him who teaches. Do not be deceived, God is not mocked; for whatever a man sows, this he will also reap. For the one who sows to his own flesh shall from the flesh reap corruption, but the one who sows to the Spirit shall from the Spirit reap eternal life. And let us not lose heart in doing good, for in due time we shall reap if we do not grow weary. So then, while we have opportunity, let us do good to all men, and especially to those who are of the household of the faith.*

Four important principles for recovery are derived from this biblical text. First, we reap what we plant. Secondly, we reap in a different season than when we plant. Thirdly, we always will reap more than we plant. Finally, we cannot change last year's harvest, but we can do something about next year's harvest. Discussing each of these principles within a group setting provides the therapist an opportunity to encourage the recovering teenager to focus on several key therapeutic issues involving the process of recovery.

The first principle, *reaping what we plant,* focuses on the therapeutic issue of taking responsibility for our past actions and deeds and stresses that we did not get addicted to drugs by chance or by accident. If you plant corn, you will reap corn. If you plant carrots you will reap carrots. If you plant drug usage and destructive attitudes, you will reap addictive and destructive behavior. Introducing this first principle helps to dispel much of the magical and wishful thinking that is so prevalent during the early stages of recovery.

The second principle, *reaping in a different season than we sow,* stresses that recovery is not going to happen immediately and that our diligent efforts may not begin to show results for several months. Just as we did not develop our addictive and destructive behavioral patterns overnight, we will not harvest the fruits of recovery overnight. Understanding this second important principle will help recovering teenagers develop realistic expectations about their recovery and learn the importance of patience.

The third principle, *reaping more than we plant,* is especially useful in helping the recovering teenager examine honestly the many undesirable consequences that have occurred as a result of planting the seeds of drug usage and self-destructive attitudes. The principle is also a source of encouragement. Hope is fostered when it is learned that planting new seeds of a drug-free life style and constructive attitudes will bear more fruit than initially planted.

The fourth principle, *last year's harvest is gone, but we can change future harvests,* is a very encouraging notion that can provide the motivation to begin to plant different kinds of seeds. This fourth principle serves as a cornerstone of hope; it attacks directly the attitudes of indifference and rejection.

In summary, discussing the laws of the harvest, enables therapists to assist recovering teenagers in an honest examination of their past plantings, focusing on the types of harvests they have reaped, and encouraging them to think more seriously about the kinds of harvests they desire in the future. Then the critical question can be addressed: "What kind of seeds do I need to begin planting today if I want to have a different kind of harvest in the future?"

Getting Straight

Getting straight is a treatment strategy developed by Ross (1988) for the purpose of helping chemically dependent adolescents become more motivated to make a commitment to change from a life style of drugs and misery to a life style of soberness and sobriety. In a four-part lecture, recovering teenagers are taught what getting straight is not, what getting straight is, what getting straight requires, and the benefits derived from getting straight.

Getting straight is not (1) a once and for all accomplishment, (2) an emotional high, (3) reserved for the perfect, (4) an independent achievement, or (5) something that happens passively as we sit on the sidelines.

Getting straight does require a commitment derived from consciously applying steps one, two, and three of Alcoholics Anonymous—admitting that I have a problem, that I don't know how to solve it, and submitting to others more informed who can help me, if I only ask.

Getting straight requires action, a willingness to learn and apply on a daily basis steps four through nine of Alcoholics Anonymous.

Getting straight requires aim, an aspiration and unquenching desire to be free of alcohol and drugs. It also requires discipline as one continues to develop habits that replace a "will run riot" with self-control and continues to practice a program of recovery and shares it with others, as encouraged by steps ten, eleven and twelve of Alcoholics Anonymous.

Getting straight requires a spiritual rebirth, that is, a change in attitudes. It requires faith as emphasized in step two, "came to believe." It requires the embracing of truth, that is, developing new attitudes based on winning principles.

Getting straight requires (1) an acceptance of reality, (2) asking for help, (3) giving up control, (4) looking inside ourselves, (5) sharing our pain, (6) wanting something different, (7) a request for release, (8) being accountable to make amends, (9) showing others our change, (10) maintaining a clear conscience, (11) seeking God's will, and (12) giving to others.

Getting straight results in

> *...new freedom and new happiness. We will not regret the past nor wish to shut the door on it. We will comprehend the word serenity and we will know peace. No matter how far down the scale we have gone, we will see how our experience can benefit others. That feeling of uselessness and pity will disappear. We will lose interest in selfish things and gain interest in our fellows. Self-seeking will slip away. Our whole attitude and outlook upon life will change. Fear of people and economic insecurity will leave us. We will intuitively know how to handle things which used to baffle us. We will suddenly realize that God is doing for us what we could not do for ourselves. (Anonymous, 1980a, pp. 83–84)*

Examination of ideas expressed in this lecture provides several opportunities to teach recovering teenage substance abusers what their program of recovery is all about and what can be accomplished if they are willing to put forth the required effort. Combined with other techniques, this procedure can help chemically dependent teenagers focus more clearly on the task at hand, getting sober and experiencing sobriety.

Summary

In this chapter, four plateaus of recovery were introduced: admitting, submitting, committing, and transmitting. Treatment objectives for reaching the admitting and transmitting plateaus of recovery were outlined. In addition, 15 treatment strategies found useful in enhancing awareness, providing alternative means to manage feelings, and explaining how change is possible were introduced.

Endnotes

1. See for example, Gabe (1989), Isralowitz and Singer (1983), G. G. Lawson and A. W. Lawson (1992), Selekmand and Todd (1991), Snyder (1993), Wheeler and Malmquist (1987).
2. Refer to chapter 2 for detailed explanation of the emerging personality and cognitive structure of an adolescent substance abuser.
3. Refer to chapter 2 for a detailed explanation of attitudes.
4. The Twelve Steps in their entirety are listed in Appendix B. The Twelve Steps and other AA excerpts appearing in this publication are reprinted with permission of Alcoholics Anonymous World Services, Inc. Permission to reprint this material does not mean that AA has reviewed or approved the contents of this publication, nor that AA agrees with the views expressed herein. AA is a program of recovery from alcoholism *only*—use of the Twelve Steps and other excerpts in connection with programs and activities which are patterned after AA, but which address other problems, does not imply otherwise.
5. The Twelve Steps in their entirety are listed in Appendix B.

6

Treatment Strategies: Committing and Transmitting Plateaus

In this chapter, 15 additional treatment strategies are introduced. These techniques have been shown useful in helping chemically dependent adolescents identify self-defeating self-talk, change it, and avoid relapse. They have been shown to help chemically dependent youth reach the committing and transmitting plateaus of recovery.

Treatment Strategies: Committing and Transmitting

The committing and transmitting plateaus can best be described by the word "action." Whereas reaching the first two plateaus, admitting and submitting, necessitates a willingness and readiness to change, these last two plateaus require teenage substance abusers to take personal responsibility for their recovery by daily participation in activities that foster change. Treatment objectives for these two plateaus include

1. Identification and development of a plan of action to change self-defeating irrational thinking patterns that maintain and perpetuate (a) drug usage, (b) destructive emotions and behaviors, (c) family discord, (d) poor school and/or work performance, (e) conflict with authority

figures, (f) conflict with peers, (g) attitudes of selfishness and self-centeredness, (h) resentments, fears, anger, pity, and depression, and (i) low frustration tolerance (impatience).

2. The practicing of new rational thinking patterns that will maintain and perpetuate (a) abstinence, (b) constructive emotions and behavior, (c) family harmony, (d) improved school and/or work performance, (e) decreased conflict with authority figures, (f) reduced conflict with peers, (g) attitudes of gratitude and sharing, (h) attitudes of forgiveness and tolerance, and (i) high frustration tolerance (patience).

3. Demonstration of a willingness and readiness to (a) actively pursue educational and vocational pursuits, (b) work a twelve-step program of recovery, (c) make constructive use of leisure time, (d) develop solid drug-free friendships, (e) accept responsibility for one's recovery, (f) develop skills in effective management of financial resources, (g) develop healthy patterns for dating and courtship, and (h) remain free of mind-altering drugs and tobacco products.

Several treatment strategies are useful in helping recovering teenage drug abusers accomplish these objectives, thereby enabling them to reach the committing and transmitting plateaus of recovery. These techniques help teenage substance abusers directly confront the self-destructive attitudes of damnation of self, damnation of others, tyranny of shoulds, awfulizing, and I can't stand it-itis. These techniques are also effective in helping to identify other self-defeating self-talk, changing it, and preventing the return of denial and refusal thinking patterns (i.e., relapse prevention).

Techniques that identify self-defeating self-talk include (1) the five criteria, (2) styles of thinking, (3) self-downing and self-acceptance cycles, (4) language of anger and resentment, and (5) secondary virginity.

Techniques that illustrate how to change self-talk include (1) steps five, six, and seven, (2) seven steps to a happy (F)ACE, (3) recovery scripts, (4) changing dislike behaviors, and (5) the Lord's Prayer.

Relapse prevention techniques include (1) steps eight and nine, (2) steps eleven and twelve, (3) ten most common causes of failure, (4) relapse signs and symptoms, and (5) goal setting.

Figure 6-1 lists 15 treatment strategies for the committing and transmitting plateaus of recovery and describes their purpose.

Identifying Self-Defeating Self-Talk

Recognizing self-defeating self-talk is the fourth step in helping teenage substance abusers develop a healthier cognitive structure.

Treatment strategy	Purpose
five criteria for rational thinking	identify self-defeating self-talk
styles of irrational or dysfunctional thinking	identify self-defeating self-talk
self-downing and self-acceptance cycle	identify self-defeating self-talk
language of anger and resentment	identify self-defeating self-talk
secondary virginity	identify self-defeating self-talk
steps five, six, and seven	changing self-talk
seven steps to a happy (F) A-C-E	changing self-talk
recovery scripts	changing self-talk
changing dislike behaviors	changing self-talk
Lord's prayer	changing self-talk
steps eight and nine	relapse prevention
steps eleven and twelve	relapse prevention
ten most common causes of failure	relapse prevention
relapse signs and symptoms list	relapse prevention
goal setting	relapse prevention

FIGURE 6-1 Committing and Transmitting Treatment Strategies in Relationship to their Purpose

Five Criteria for Rational Thinking

The five criteria for rational thinking (Maultsby, 1986, pp. 5–6) is a systematic and objective means to help recovering teenagers challenge their erroneous a priori and a posteriori cognitions. The five criteria address the important question of How does one decide what to believe? Because our thoughts lead to feelings and actions, and when continually repeated, become habits and eventual life patterns, the five criteria provide a mechanism to challenge our self-talk, clarify our thinking, and ensure that our thinking leads to healthy habits and life patterns. Our thinking is said to be rational, functional, or in our best interest if we can honestly say yes to three of the five following questions:

1. Is my thinking based on fact?
2. Does my thinking help protect my life and health?
3. Does my thinking help me achieve my goals now and in the future?

4. Does my thinking help me prevent unwanted and unnecessary conflict with others?
5. Does my thinking help me feel the way I need to?

If our thinking, or self-talk, cannot pass at least three of these five criteria, than our self-talk most probably will keep us from achieving our goals, result in unwanted trouble with others, impair our health in some way, and lead us to feel tense or unhappy. In the case of a recovering teenager, it will lead back to a life of drug usage.

Introduction of the five criteria provides a convenient neutral reference point for the therapist(s) and other group members to draw on when challenging the irrational or dysfunctional self-talk of group members. Take, for example, some of the self-talk commonly used to justify drug usage:

> *Everyone else does it. It doesn't hurt me. I can think better when I'm high. Helps me with my school work. My friends look up to me when I do drugs. I can handle it. No one loves me. I'll slack off when I get older. The world is coming to an end soon, so I may as well live it up. I have problems that no one else could ever understand...different problems. If a good reason ever came along, I could quit drinking or drugging. I don't have anything else better to do. I know what I am doing. The only kind of parties that are fun are drug parties. I wanted to be known as someone who did drugs. I felt big.*

Applying the five criteria to each of these justifications quickly reveals their irrationality and helps the individual and the group begin to realize just how dysfunctional their thinking had become. Rational or functional alternatives to these justifications can then be proposed, thereby helping the recovering teenager begin to develop a new self-talk that is in his or her best interest.

Styles of Irrational or Dysfunctional Thinking

Several styles of irrational or dysfunctional thinking have been identified as contributors to unnecessary and unpleasant emotional turmoil. Introducing these dysfunctional styles of thinking to the recovering teenager is an effective means to accelerate emotional recovery, especially if the teenager is able to identify specific styles of irrational thinking that he or she most often uses. Ross (1978) identified 15 styles of irrational thinking. They include:

ABSOLUTES: Viewing the world in absolutes. Ex: My parents are *always* criticizing me. I *never* can do anything right.

WHAT-IFING: Negatively anticipating the future. Ex: Preparing a homework assignment and thinking, *what if* I do it incorrectly or fail the assignment.

HAVE TO–GOT TO–MUST: Motivating oneself with fear by making life a series of rules to follow instead of acting on the basis that you will personally benefit from the actions you choose. Ex: I *have to* get straight. I *got to* pass this course. I *must* be more polite to my mother.

SHOULD AND OUGHT: Demanding that the world, others, or yourself be different from the way they are. Ex: I *should* never have taken drugs. My father *ought* to be more considerate of my feelings.

AWFULIZING: Viewing life's experiences as being awful or terrible. Ex: It will be just *awful* if I flunk the course. It will be *terrible* if they don't like the speech.

GOOD PEOPLE–BAD PEOPLE: Viewing others as being either good or bad, right or wrong. Ex: The problem is all those teachers. If they would just leave me alone and mind their own business.

HARD AND EASY: Appraising tasks as being either too hard or too easy and therefore deciding to do nothing. Ex: Getting straight is just *too hard*. Working the twelve steps is a *piece of cake*.

TRYING VERSUS DOING: Saying you tried to accomplish something but never doing the necessary things to accomplish the task. Ex: I really *tried* to stop drinking. I really *tried* to go to the AA meeting.

CAN'T: Saying you cannot do something that you are perfectly capable of doing when you really chose not to do it because you were afraid to or simply did not want to. Ex: There is no way, I *can't* get straight.

YES–BUT: Saying you want to change or do something about a problem and than making excuses not to do the things required to change the problem. Ex: Believe me, I really want to get straight, *but* it is just too hard. I really want to stop drinking, *but* I don't have the time to go to AA meetings.

THE DOUBLE BIND: Thinking that you have to or must do something and at the same time being afraid to do it. Ex: I *have to* get straight, but I *can't*. I *must* get my high school education, but I *can't*.

ROMANTICIZING: Viewing the world through rose-colored glasses; fantasizing about accomplishments, people, or self, but never examining the facts and realities involved. Ex: She is the *most fabulous* person in the world. He could *never do anything wrong*. This is the *most fantastic* opportunity I will ever have.

ABUSE OF GENERALITIES: Viewing the world in abstract, nebulous, undefined terms. Ex: I just want to be *free*. I've got to be *independent*. I got to be *genuine*.

SELECTIVE LISTENING: Listening to what others are saying but only hearing what you are thinking. Ex: Therapist explains to the client that you don't have to get angry if someone says no to you. Client responds; "But I do have feelings." As the client listened to the therapist, he or she heard himself or herself saying; "Only a person who doesn't have any feelings would not get angry," instead of listening to the therapist's message that there are other alternatives other than becoming angry.

THINKING IN VIVID IMAGES: Imagining the worst things possible; picturing catastrophic: results; visualizing what you don't want to happen; seeing yourself failing at a task. Ex: Before starting a new job, picturing yourself making all sorts of mistakes leading to your dismissal.

Maultsby and Hendricks (1974, pp. 83-106)[1] identified 11 commonly held irrational or dysfunctional beliefs that cause people unnecessary and often painful emotional turmoil. These beliefs include:

1. I have to feel the way I feel. And that's it. That's just me. I have no choice in the matter.
2. I can't accept myself without the love and/or approval of those I want it from.
3. If I don't do everything exactly right, or if I'm not first, that proves that I'm a worthless slob.
4. Other people or things outside of me make me feel the emotions I feel.
5. If I don't like a job, or the people or institution that requires me to do the job, they have no right to be mad at me or to punish me if I mess the job up or refuse to do it altogether.
6. My way is the only "right" or "correct," or "just" way to do things.
7. I should use all my abilities fully and achieve as much as I can. If I don't, I should feel guilty.
8. The way I act tells me what type of person I am. (If I act foolishly then I am a fool.)
9. I have to feel bad if the person I love leaves me or dies. My willingness to suffer proves how much I loved that person. If I don't feel bad, that proves I never really loved that person in the first place.
10. I can't accept myself unless I'm married, have friends, or am loved by really worthwhile people or unless I am involved in a cause that's greater or more worthwhile than I am.

11. I just have to be upset if people (especially those close to me) don't behave the way they should.

Samenow (1987) identified 17 errors of thinking often practiced by persons with antisocial personalities. These thinking patterns are also frequently observed in many teenagers recovering from substance abuse. These errors of thinking include:

VICTIM STANCE: Attempts to blame others for current conditions. Refuses to accept responsibility for one's own actions.

I CAN'T: A statement of inability that is really a statement of refusal.

LACK OF CONCEPT OF INJURY TO OTHERS: Does not stop to think how his or her actions harm others (except physically).

LACK OF EFFORT: Unwilling to do anything which he or she finds boring, disagreeable. Engages in self-pity and looks for excuses. Psychosomatic aches and pains to avoid effort. Complains about a lack of energy.

REFUSAL TO ACCEPT OBLIGATION: Says I forgot. Does not see something as an obligation to begin with. Does that which he or she wants and ignores the obligation.

ATTITUDE OF OWNERSHIP: Demands of people as though asserting their rights. Ex: I have a *right* to steal from you.

TRUST (NO CONCEPT OF): Blames you for not trusting him or her; tries to make you feel as though it is your fault. Says that he or she cannot trust you.

UNREALISTIC EXPECTATIONS: Thinking makes it so. Because he or she thinks something will happen, it must. He or she expects others to fall into line and accommodate his or her wishes, whims.

IRRESPONSIBLE DECISION MAKING: Makes assumptions; does not find facts. Does not suspend judgment. Blames others when things go wrong.

PRIDE: Refuses to back down even on little points. Insists on his or her point of view to the exclusion of all others. Even when proved wrong, clings to his or her initial position.

FAILURE TO PLAN AHEAD OR THINK LONG RANGE: Future is not considered, unless to accomplish something illicit or else a fantasy of tremendous success.

A FLAWED DEFINITION OF SUCCESS AND FAILURE: Success equals being number one overnight. Failure equals being anything less than number one and if not, then considering oneself a zero.

FEAR OF BEING PUT DOWN: Does not take criticism without flaring up or blaming others. Considers even minor inconveniences or failing to achieve unrealistic expectations as a putdown.

REFUSAL TO ACKNOWLEDGE FEAR: Denies being afraid. Views fear as a weakness. Fails to realize that fear can be constructive.

ANGER: Anger is used to control people and may take the form of direct threat, intimidation, assault, sarcasm, and annoyance. May not be openly expressed, resulting in indirect aggression, that is, "I don't get mad I get even." May also take anger out on innocent people.

POWER TACTICS: Enjoys fighting for power for its own sake. Gets a "high" from overcoming and dominating people.

Helping recovering teenagers learn how to identify and change these irrational and dysfunctional thinking styles is an essential component of the committing and transmitting stages of recovery. Changing these irrational belief patterns and replacing them with more rational or functional ones result in recovering teenagers experiencing a greater peace of mind and serenity as they begin to enjoy the benefits of a drug-free life style. They also experience less frequently the resentments, fears, anger, pity, frustration, and depression that accompany self-defeating "druggie" thinking.

Self-Downing and Self-Acceptance Cycle

The self-downing and self-acceptance cycle (Maultsby, 1982b) is a treatment strategy that can be used to help recovering teenagers overcome the often-observed self-defeating thinking patterns of *have to, I'll try,* and *I can't.* These thoughts mask an underlying fear of making mistakes, reinforce an irrational belief of equating one's value with performance, and result in half-hearted attempts to achieve desirable goals.

Figure 6-2 depicts the *self-downing cycle:* When faced with a task, thinking irrational thoughts such as I can't, I'll try, and I have to results in an uncompleted task and an erroneous conclusion of worthlessness.

In contrast, the *self-acceptance cycle* illustrates how to eliminate the self-downing cycle by replacing the irrational thinking pattern of I can't, I'll try, and I have to with a rational thinking pattern of I'm capable, I'll do my best, and I'm choosing to because. Figure 6-3 depicts the self-acceptance cycle.

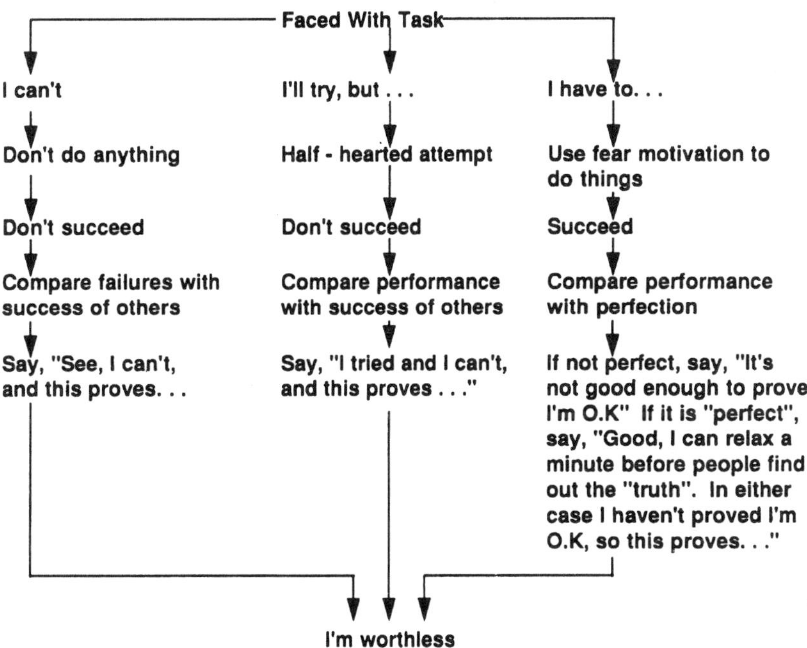

FIGURE 6-2 The Self-Downing Cycle

Replacing the previously held self-downing belief pattern with I'm capable, I'll do my best, and I'm choosing to because thinking results in improved performance and unconditional self-acceptance. If efforts prove unsuccessful, then a person can calmly evaluate what went wrong and procede to correct the error. As Maultsby, (1982b) explained:

> *The worst thing anyone can find out about me is that I'm fallible like everyone else. What other people think cannot change me. Even if they think I'm bad, I am the same fallible human being. I may not like what they think; they are entitled to their opinion. I cannot control what they think, therefore I'll do what is in my best interest. I'll make mistakes, because I'm fallible. I can learn to correct them. I can do some things well, and I will look at my mistakes as an opportunity to learn. Mistakes are made in the process of creating and learning. Therefore I will feel accepting and calm when I make mistakes.*

Language of Anger and Resentment

The language of anger and resentment (Ross, 1990a) is a therapeutic tool to help recovering teenagers more effectively manage and reduce the frequency of anger and resentment. A recovering teenager who is experi-

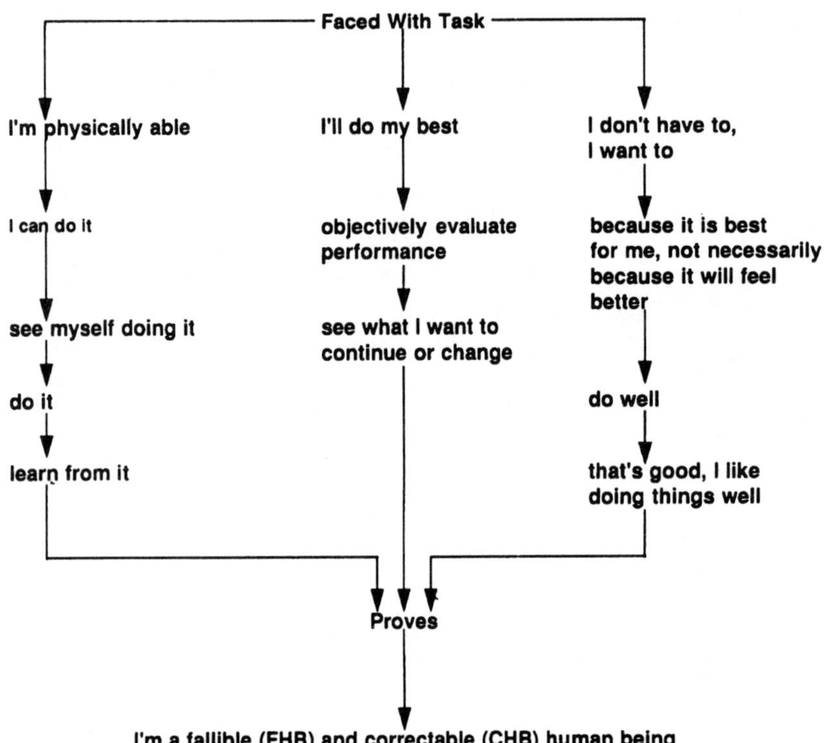

FIGURE 6-3 The Self-Acceptance Cycle

encing anger or resentment usually is rehearsing one or more of seven thinking patterns that create and sustain an angry and/or resentful response. These thinking patterns include:

SHOULDS: Demanding that reality be different than it currently is.

AWFULIZING: Believing that a situation is worse than it actually is.

IT'S NOT FAIR: Concluding that someone has broken or violated a contract with you when someone doesn't give you what you want or desire or respond positively to your request.

NAME CALLING: Labeling others as something other than a fallible and correctable human being.

FORCE VERSUS CHOICE: Believing that someone is forcing you to do something, when they are actually giving you limited options.

DAMNATION OF OTHERS: Blaming others for your mistakes.

DAMNATION OF SELF: Putting self down for making a mistake or not getting what you want or desire.

Identifying and replacing these thinking patterns with more rational or functional thinking patterns will significantly reduce the response of anger and resentment. Shoulds are replaced with "I would have liked or preferred." Awfulizing thoughts are replaced with "It is inconveniencing, but not horrible or terrible." Unfairness is replaced with "Where is the contract?" Name calling is replaced with "They are fallible and correctable human beings. Being forced is replaced with "It's my choice, I control how I feel and act." Damnation of others and self is replaced with "We are both fallible and correctable human beings."

Secondary Virginity

Many teenagers in recovery have experienced multiple sexual encounters prior to treatment, and for some, they may have become sexually addicted. For others, sex and drugs were synonymous. For these teenagers, sexual encounters can easily trigger a desire to get high, especially in the early stages of recovery.

The concept of secondary virginity helps address these challenges. Secondary virginity is another important treatment strategy proven useful in helping recovering teenagers regain their self-respect and learn healthier beliefs about the role and function of sex in their lives.

Developed by Mast (1986, pp. 45–46), "secondary virginity is the decision to stop having sex until after marriage, and the acting out of that decision." Mast goes on to explain:

> *Any person who wants it can have it by deciding to change, detaching oneself from old habits, from people, places, and situations which weaken self-control, and developing new, nonphysical ways to share. So even though you may have lost your physical virginity, you can still return to the qualities of psychological virginity and all its advantages. Don't buy the myth that once you've "lost it" you can no longer control your sexual impulses.*

Introducing the concept of secondary virginity to recovering teenagers releases them from the damaging belief that they must be sexually active because they have no control over their sexual impulses. Discrediting this irrational belief and replacing it with the belief of secondary virginity empower previously sexually active teenagers to direct their sexual energy toward other more-pressing challenges of recovery—staying sober and achieving improved levels of sobriety.

Changing Self-Talk

Changing self-talk is the fifth step in helping teenage substance abusers develop a healthier cognitive structure.

Steps Five, Six, and Seven

Steps five, six, and seven of Alcoholics Anonymous (Anonymous, 1986, pp. 55–76) are specifically designed to enable the recovering teenager to focus directly on character defects and to develop a plan of action to turn them into character strengths.[2] These three steps read:

> *Admitted to God, to ourselves, and to another human being the exact nature of our wrongs. Were entirely ready to have God remove all these defects of character. Humbly asked Him to remove these shortcomings (Anonymous, 1986, pp. 6–7).*[2]

Step five, "admitting our wrongs," helps the recovering teenager face point blank those aspects of character that are in dire need of change and fosters courage, that is, dealing with problems and realities of life without reliance on drugs. The recovering teenager is encouraged to review with another person, often a minister or counselor, their resentments, fears, and sex conduct previously outlined in their searching and fearless moral inventory. The result is a clear conscience and the development of a healthy fear of one's past. Guilt and shame begin to decline as the recovering teenager begins to experience forgiveness, worth, and self-acceptance.

Armed with the clean slate, achieved by completing steps four and five, the recovering teenager is now prepared to take steps six and seven. Taking these two steps expresses a *willingness*, without reservation, to discard old willful thoughts and habits, to be freed of the dysfunctional thinking that maintained drug usage and other self-defeating emotional and behavioral responses. These steps involve making a *commitment* to develop and implement a plan of action that will challenge and eventually replace dysfunctional thinking with rational functional thinking that leads to soberness and sobriety. Steps six and seven clarify the need to ask continually for the help of others to accomplish these and other important goals of recovery.

Seven Steps to a Happy **(F)ACE**

The seven steps to a happy *(F)ACE* is a process adapted from Maultsby (1978, pp. 122–137) and revised by Ross (1983d) to help recovering teenagers develop more functional automatic emotional and behavioral responses to life's situations (i.e., functional *(F)ACEs*).[3] The seven steps is a therapeutic tool that provides a systematic way for recovering teenagers to (1) factually describe events and situations, (2) identify self-talk, (3) identify feelings and behaviors, (4) critique self-talk, (5) create new self-talk, (6) create script that results in new feelings and behaviors, and (7) practice script.

Step one of the process is to record accurately and factually an event or situation *(A)* where undesirable emotions and behaviors were experienced. It is important to record only those thoughts that factually describe what was experienced—simply state the facts as if a camera or recorder was doing the reporting. Avoid recording opinions, expectations, and intentions; these thoughts are recorded in step four.

Step two is to record actual feelings *(C)* and desired feelings *(C-1)* in the situation *(A)*.

Step three is to record actual actions *(E)* and desired actions *(E-1)* in the situation *(A)*.

Step four is to record descriptions, judgments, and expectations *(B)* about the situation *(A)* and the opinions and intentions *(D)* with regards to feelings *(C)* about the situation *(A)*.

Step five is to critique the descriptions, judgments, expectations *(B)*, opinions, and intentions *(D)* recorded in step four. This is accomplished by applying the previously introduced technique of the five criteria for rational, functional, or in your best interest thinking to each of the thoughts recorded.[4]

Step six is to replace all thoughts in step five that would not pass the five criteria test with new rational or functional thoughts that will pass it.

Step seven is to develop a rational or functional script based on the thoughts developed in step six that, when consistently practiced, will result in the desired emotional *(C-1)* and behavioral *(E-1)* responses expressed in step two and step three. The goal, therefore, is to create a functional *ACE (A–C-1–E-1)* to replace the previously established dysfunctional *ACE (A–C–E)*.

For example, John, a 16-year-old in recovery for five months, uses the seven steps to resolve a conflict that he is having with his mother:

A Situation: Mom and I got into an argument about a shirt I wanted to wear to church

C Feelings: Anger, frustration, pity

C-1 Desired Feelings: Calm, relaxed

E Behavior: Close minded, yelled at mom, walked away and slammed the bedroom door

E-1 Desired Behavior: Open minded, listening, accepting of mother's authority, respectful

B/D Self-talk:

1. Why don't you quit playing God!
2. She just wants to make me angry.
3. I'm sick of her treating me like a baby!
4. I can make my own decisions.
5. The only reason she wants me to dress up is so she can look good in front of her friends.
6. The only reason she does this now is because she knows she can.
7. Nobody ever listens to what I want!
8. I hate living here.
9. When I turn 18 I am going to dress and act however I want.
10. I wish I was back in treatment where people care about me.
11. I do everything they tell me to do and I am doing good in school, so I should get something for it.
12. You're (mother) so selfish and inconsiderate.
13. You never think of anyone but yourself.
14. We can't ever settle anything because she won't ever listen!

Critique of Self-Talk

1. It is not a *fact* that Mom is playing God. Believing that she is does not promote my health or well-being, for believing and demanding her to be something she isn't causes me to feel unnecessary anger. Believing this thought does nothing to help me achieve my short- and long-term goals of getting closer to my mother and being more patient and respectful with authority figures. This thought results in considerable conflict with others and does not help me to feel and act the way I desire.

2. It is not a fact that my mother makes me angry. I make myself angry by the way I choose to think about my mother. Believing that she makes me angry does not promote my health or well-being, help me achieve my goals, or avoid conflict with myself (feel and act the way I need) or my mother.

3. It is not a fact that mom is treating me like a baby, and it's also not a fact that I get sick when she says no to my request or asks me to dress in a certain way. Believing this thought does not promote my health or well-being, help me achieve my goals, or reduce conflict with myself or mother.

4. It is not a fact that by making a request of me, she is keeping me from making my own decisions. Also, she does have a right to make requests of me, whether I agree with the requests or not. Believing the contrary does not promote my health or well-being, help me achieve my goals, or reduce conflict with myself or my mother.

5. It is not a fact that the only reason she wants me to dress up is to make her look good in front of her friends. I know for a fact that she wants me to learn how to take pride in my dress and appearance. Believing this idea also violates the other four criteria for rational thinking.

6. Believing this idea does not help me to achieve my goal of learning to be more patient and respectful with authority figures and grow closer to my mother. This thought also violates the other rules for rational thinking.

7. This thought is not based on fact. It also violates the other four criteria for rational thinking.

8. It's not a fact that I hate living here. I really hate making myself so angry when I don't get my own way. This thought also violates the other four criteria for rational thinking.

9. There is nothing magic about turning 18. My mother will still make requests of me, and I will most likely still need her financial support. This thought also violates the other four criteria for rational thinking.

10. This thought implies that my mother does not care about me. This is not factual. Because my mother disagrees with me does not mean that she does not care about me. This thought also violates the other four criteria for rational thinking.

11. It is not a fact that I do everything that my parents tell me to do. Also, getting good grades in school has resulted in a lot of benefits for me. This thought violates the other four criteria for rational thinking.

12. It is not a fact that when my mother says no to me, it does not mean that she is selfish and inconsiderate. Also violates other four rules for rational thinking.

13. It is not a fact that my mother was only thinking about herself when she asked me to change my shirt. Also violates other four rules for rational thinking.

14. It is not a fact that my mother does not listen to me or that we have never been able to resolve any conflicts. Also violates other four rules for rational thinking.

New Self-talk: She's not playing God, she is doing what God wants her to do, being a parent to me and setting some standards and expectations for me. She is not forcing me to become angry. I am the only one who can choose to become angry. My mother cannot make me angry. My mother has a right and responsibility to challenge my decisions. She also has a right to tell me what to do. Because my mother does not agree with me does not mean that she does not love and care about me or that she is selfish and inconsiderate. Because my mother says no to me does not mean that she does not listen to me. The facts are that my mother has been very patient and supportive with me over the past several years, even when I have made some very poor decisions and even when I have been involved in situations where she felt very embarrassed about me.

Script: My mother makes a request of me. I calmly listen to her request and respectfully comply with it. If I disagree with her request or think it unfair, I will calmly state my reasons and ask her to consider my reasons for not wanting to comply with her request. I express my disagreements calmly and respectfully. If my mother still insists that I comply with her, I will calmly do so, keeping an open mind to what she is telling me and respecting her decision.

Mary, a 19-year-old in recovery for 18 months, uses the seven steps to resolve a conflict with her mother:

A Situation: Disagreeing with my mother

C Feelings: Distant, dominant, quiet, angry, evasive, contemptuous, panicky, locked in, belligerent, hard, cold, defiant, tense, defeated, threatened, resentful, hopeless, abused

C-1 Desired Feelings: Close, cooperative, self-assured, open, happy, calm, confident, warm, soft, relaxed, affectionate, grateful, compassionate, empathetic, humble, hopeful, loving, respectful

E Behavior: Tune out, turn away from her, push feelings down, fiddle with something

E-1 Desired Behavior: Pay attention, have open mind, be empathetic, look at her, listen, express my feelings

B/D Self-talk: God, she's a bitch. Quit whining. She's blowing it out of proportion. I didn't do it on purpose. It was a mistake. God, I hate her. I don't want to hear this. Why does she have to personalize these things? I don't want to hear it. Leave me alone. She's trying to make me feel bad because she is getting ready to cry. She's faking it. She has no right to tell me how to act or feel. I wish she would die. I'd be better off if she died. I want out of here. I want to beat the shit out of her. Just tell her to fuck off. I want to move out. She tells me all of her problems. She is trying to embarrass me. My foster sisters think she is crazy. Thank God she is not my real mother. Shut up. Is this going to be worth it? She is so weak. Here we go again.

Critique of Self-talk: It is not a fact that my mother is a bitch, is crazy, or is weak. The fact is that my mother is a fallible and correctable human being who does not always act the way I would prefer her to act. Believing otherwise does not promote my health or well-being, help me achieve my goals of getting straight and improving my relationship with my mother, nor does it significantly reduce conflicts with myself or others. Just because my mother says or does things that I don't like, I have no right to judge her by my expectations of her. The fact is that my mother *should* be doing whatever she is doing, saying whatever she is saying, thinking whatever she is thinking, and feeling however she is feeling at any given moment in time. Thinking otherwise does not promote my health or well-being, help me achieve my goals, or significantly decrease conflicts with myself or others.

My mother is not to blame because I don't like what she says or does. The fact is that I don't hate my mother, but I hate myself when I treat her the way I do. The fact is that my mother can't make me feel bad or embarrassed. The fact is that my mother does have a right to tell me what she expects of me, but that does not mean she is trying to control me. I have shown many times in the past that she has no control over me. I control how I want to feel and act by what I am thinking. I am also responsible for how I feel and act. Believing otherwise does not promote my health or well-being, help me achieve my goals, or significantly decrease conflicts with myself or others.

Unpleasantness exists, and avoiding it won't make it go away. The facts are that I can stand it, and if I want to be less miserable, I can change how I respond to my mother and myself. Believing otherwise does not promote my health or well-being, help me achieve my goals, or reduce significantly conflicts with myself or others.

The fact is that I, not my mother, am blowing this entire situation out of proportion. It is not awful or terrible that my mother and I don't agree on everything or that we still have challenges in relating to one another. Believing otherwise does not promote my health or well-being, help me achieve my goals, or significantly reduce conflicts with myself or others.

New Self-talk: I am a fallible and correctable human being and so is my mother. Everything is always as it should be at any given moment in time. I cause how I feel and act. I can and will learn how to tolerate and accept not getting everything I want. Nothing is really awful or terrible, just inconvenient. There is no law in life that says I will never be inconvenienced.

Script: I picture myself discussing points of disagreement with my mother. I calmly share with her my point of view and how I feel about it. I calmly listen to her viewpoint. I remain polite and respectful to my mother, keeping in mind that she has a right to disagree with me and, as long as I am living in her house, has the right to set down rules and regulations for me to follow. I calmly accept the results of our discussion.

John and Mary both illustrate the importance of learning how to utilize this cognitive-behavioral technique. When confronted with these challenges in their past, they would have used the situation as an excuse to go and get high. Instead, they are not getting high but are learning the skill of problem solving and how to identify and change the irrational self-talk that has kept them so miserable. Specifically, they are learning how to manage and change more effectively the self-destructive attitudes of damnation of self, damnation of others, tyranny of shoulds, awfulizing, and I can't stand it-itis. These attitudes usually emerge in recovering teenagers when they are not getting what they want.

Recovery Scripts

The recovery script is another important treatment strategy useful in the treatment of teenage substance abusers. Scripts are the result of examining a self-defeating response to a situation by carefully exercising the seven steps to a happy (F)ACE. They are effective in promoting both soberness (free of mind-altering drugs) and sobriety (developing peace of mind and serenity). They are designed to be read or listened to frequently throughout the day in order to help the recovering teenager visualize desired emotional and behavioral responses (functional ACEs) that will promote soberness and sobriety. They also serve as excellent sources on which to meditate. For example, examine carefully the following soberness script prepared by a 17-year-old teenage girl in recovery:

> *I am offered drugs by a friend and immediately I think to myself, "I don't want to use drugs because I remember all the consequences I received before I got into recovery." I was arrested six times for shoplifting and running away. I had a really bad reputation with the police department and with druggie friends and my family. I fought constantly with my parents and still feel guilty for hurting them. My relationship with my brothers was almost nonexistent. I rarely had anyone to talk to I felt so lonely and insecure. My druggie friends lied and stole from me, and I did the same thing back. I depended on my outer appearance and guys to feel good about myself. I threw up countless of times and was almost killed in drunk driving accidents. I remember being passed out in ditches. I was grounded almost half of my teenage years. I started failing in school and made very low grades. I was majorly dependent on drugs and getting high—I felt obsessed. I thought I could do it on my own—and I relapsed. I fell hard. I blamed everyone else for my problems. Any good friends that I had, I ended up using and pushing away. I was suicidal and had no respect, and I let myself be used. I cried almost every night by myself in my room—I was so depressed. I was never satisfied with anything. I ended up in jail, and it was miserable. None of my so-called friends stuck around to support me. I hated and resented myself very much.*
>
> *Since I've been in recovery, I have gained so much back. I am learning how to talk and communicate with my family and friends. I am learning how to stand up for myself and be assertive, to show myself respect and not tolerate being used. I have strong friendships now and friends who will stick by me and help me. I have learned how to deal with my challenges constructively. I am learning how to feel good and accept myself for who I am. I'll never give up my sobriety! Therefore, I tell this person that I am doing good things for myself now and I don't need drugs to feel good. Then I proudly walk away.*

This particular script illustrates two important points in writing effective recovery scripts. For the habit of drug usage to cease, the recovering teenager must develop a negative attitude (ACE) toward drug usage and a positive attitude (ACE) toward non-drug usage. Therefore, the recovery script must elicit a healthy fear of a "druggie" past and a realistic hope for the present and future. This teenager's script would not be effective, however, if she had not first experienced the pain of her past choices and the joy and relief that emerged from making the choice to discontinue drug usage and to learn to think and act differently. Her soberness script, therefore, vividly reminds her of the horrible consequences of doing drugs and the magnificent benefits of staying clean.

Her soberness script also reminds her that she still has much work remaining on learning how to be happier and more content with herself. She would benefit immensely from writing and practicing a variety of recovery scripts to help her cope more effectively with her anger, resentment, pity, guilt, procrastination, selfishness, and self-centeredness.[5] For example, she could benefit immensely from practicing daily a sobriety script recommended by Alcoholics Anonymous (1980a, pp. 86–87).

> *...we ask God to direct our thinking, especially asking that it be divorced from self-pity, dishonesty, or self-seeking motives.... In thinking about our day we may face indecision. We may not be able to determine which course to take. Here we ask God for inspiration, an intuitive thought or decision. We relax and take it easy. We don't struggle.... We usually conclude the period of meditation with a prayer that we be shown all through the day what our next step is to be, that we be given whatever we need to take care of such problems. We ask especially for freedom from self-will, and are careful to make no request for ourselves only. We may ask for ourselves, however, if others will be helped. We are careful never to pray for our own selfish ends.... As we go through the day we pause when agitated or doubtful and ask you for the right thought or action. We constantly remind ourselves that we are no longer running the show, humbly saying many times each day, "Thy will be done." We are then in much less danger of excitement, fear, anger, worry, self-pity or foolish decisions. We become much more efficient. We do not tire so easily, for we are not burning up energy foolishly as we did when we were trying to arrange life to suit ourselves.... So we let God discipline us in the simple way we have just outlined.... When we retire at night, we constructively review our day. Were we resentful, selfish, dishonest, or afraid. Do we owe an apology? Have we kept something to ourselves which should be discussed with another person at once? Were we kind and loving toward all? What could we have done better? Were we thinking of ourselves most of the time? Or were we thinking of what we could do for others, of what we could pack into the stream of life? But we must be careful not to drift into worry, remorse or morbid reflection, for that would diminish our usefulness to others. After making our review we ask God's forgiveness and inquire what corrective measures should be taken (Alcoholics Anonymous, 1980, pp. 86-88).*

In writing effective recovery scripts, caution must be taken to ensure that the scripts do not contain many of the previously practiced self-defeating beliefs that led to and reinforced undesirable emotional and behavioral responses. Carpenter (1982) introduced several positive replacements for previously practiced self-talk:

Old Self Talk	*Positive Replacement*
It upsets me.	I control how I feel.
It's too hard.	It'll take conscious attention.
I can't.	I can, and I will.
It shouldn't take this much effort.	It takes as much effort as it takes. My goal is worthwhile to me, so I will do it.
It doesn't feel right.	It is right—that's what counts. I'll do it until it feels right.
What if?	If it happens, I'll do the best I can.
Problem.	Opportunity, challenge.
He/she should...	Where's the law? I think it would be best...I'd like...I'd prefer...
I should have done better.	I should have done as well as I did, given my knowledge, skills, experience, beliefs, and goals at the time.
I'll never get this right.	I'm learning.
I'm stupid.	I am a fallible and correctable human being who made a mistake.
I did awful.	I made a mistake. I will learn from it.
I have to.	I choose to because...
I'll try.	I will.
Yes, but...	Yes, and...
It's not fair.	Where's the law? I think it would be best.

Changing Dislike Behaviors

Changing dislike behaviors is a cognitive-behavioral technique developed by Weinberg and Kosloske (1977). The technique encourages recovering teenagers to make a searching and fearless inventory of their dislike behaviors by first specifying how they act out the dislike behaviors, and then pinpointing how they talk to themselves and others to create and maintain the dislike behaviors.

Weinberg and Kosloske facilitate this initial step by providing the recovering teenagers with a list of dislike behaviors that includes blaming and resentment, intolerance, self-pity, jealousy, fear of rejection, fear of failure, oversensitivity, nonassertiveness, perfectionism, false pride, short-term self-interest, and worry. In addition to introducing and defining each of these dislike behaviors, this technique also illustrates the kinds of self-talk used to generate these types of dislike behaviors.

After recovering teenagers complete the dislike inventory, Weinberg and Kosloske then introduce a pattern of new self-talk that will turn the teenagers' dislike behaviors into desired like behaviors. With subsequent practice of this new pattern of self-talk, blaming and resentment is replaced by acceptance, intolerance is replaced by tolerance, self-pity is replaced by coping with reality, jealousy is replaced by helping others prosper, fear of rejection is replaced by self-approval, fear of failure is replaced by reasonable efforts to succeed, oversensitivity is replaced by self-approval, nonassertiveness is replaced by assertiveness, perfectionism is replaced by the fallible and correctable human being concept, false

Dislike behaviors	Like behaviors
blaming-resentment	acceptance
intolerance	tolerance
self-pity	coping with reality
jealousy	hoping others prosper
fear of rejection	self-approval
fear of failure	reasonable efforts to succeed
over-sensitivity	self-approval
non-assertiveness	assertiveness
perfectionism	fallible & correctable
false pride	playing straight
short term interest	short & long term interest
worry	one day at a time

FIGURE 6-4 Comparison of Dislike with Like Behaviors

pride is replaced by playing straight, short-term interest is replaced by long-term interest, and worry is replaced by one-day-at-a-time thinking.

Figure 6-4 compares dislike behaviors with like behaviors.

My clinical experience has indicated that this exercise is very useful, and for the most part, recovering teenagers indicated that they frequently experienced each one of the dislike behaviors. This exercise is also enhanced by having the teenagers rank, in order of severity, each dislike behavior. The teenager can then focus on their most severe dislike behaviors and apply the techniques of seven steps to a happy (F)ACE and recovery script writing to their particular dislike behaviors. Once a teenager achieves success at reducing the frequency of the highest ranked dislike, he or she would then procede to tackle the next highest ranked dislike on his or her list.

The Lord's Prayer

The Lord's Prayer is an excellent therapeutic tool in helping the recovering teenage drug abuser overcome feelings of inferiority, depression, anxiety, guilt, resentment, and fear.

> The Lord's Prayer
>
> *Our Father who art in heaven,*
> *Hallowed be thy name.*
> *Thy kingdom come, Thy will be done,*
> *On earth as it is in heaven.*
> *Give us this day our daily bread;*
> *And forgive us our debts,*
> *As we also have forgiven our debtors;*
> *And lead us not into temptation,*
> *But deliver us from evil. (Ryrie, 1978, p. 1454)*

Closer examination of this prayer reveals six phrases for meditation that, if recited consistently over time, provide the building blocks to reconstruct a positive and healthy self-esteem. (Schuller, 1982).

The first building block to a better self-esteem, *Our Father who art in heaven, Hallowed be thy name,* helps the recovering teenager surmount feelings of inferiority. By engraving this phrase onto one's memory and meditating daily on its meaning, the recovering teenager will begin to realize that a power greater than him- or herself was responsible for his or her creation. Therefore, by definition of creation, the teenager is of value and worth. Embracing this concept allows one to experience a new type of vulnerability that encompasses love, trust, humility, and honor.

The second building block, *Thy kingdom come, Thy will be done, on earth as it is in heaven,* contains the seeds of enthusiasm. Having excitement in life can be achieved by thinking about, designing, and acting out positive constructive plans that will serve others. The recovering teenager can begin to experience enthusiasm by reaching out to and serving others in the therapeutic group as he or she overcomes the self-pity and depression so typical of teenagers in recovery.

The third building block that helps create a more positive self-esteem is contained within the phrase *Give us this day our daily bread.* Recovering teenagers need a "spiritual" food that will enable them to cope calmly with today's challenges without having to rely on any kind of mind-altering drug, to give them a mind set that will help them view recovery as a unique opportunity to build a more positive and caring character that others will desire to emulate.

The fourth building block, *And forgive us our debts,* helps the recovering teenager gain a new lease on life. A second chance is available for the recovering teenager to start anew. New opportunities are available, if these adolescents are willing to accept the gift of life, let go of their past mistakes, and forgive themselves.

The fifth building block, *As we have forgiven our debtors,* contains the letting go part of reconstruction. Forgiveness of others is an important cornerstone to one's new life as he or she learns how to develop a more positive relationship with others. The recovering teenager can ill afford to continue to hold on to past resentments if he or she is to have any chance of recovering from the disease of chemical dependency.

The sixth and final building block, *And lead us not into temptation, But deliver us from evil,* is essential to overcome fear. Fear, left unchecked, will lead to apathy and inactivity. Recovering teenagers need to develop perserverance, or "stick-to-it-ness," to make the changes necessary to recover from their chemical dependency.

Figure 6-5 depicts the six roadblocks to self-esteem juxtaposed with the building blocks to self-esteem.

Relapse Prevention

Relapse prevention is the final step in helping teenage substance abusers develop a healthier cognitive structure.

Steps Eight and Nine

Steps eight and nine of Alcoholics Anonymous (Anonymous, 1986, pp. 77–87) are additional action steps designed "to put into practice a working course of conduct which will directly rectify the harm or injury our drinking may have imposed upon others and thus start harmoniously relating us to God and to our fellow man" (Anonymous, 1970, p. 91). The steps read:

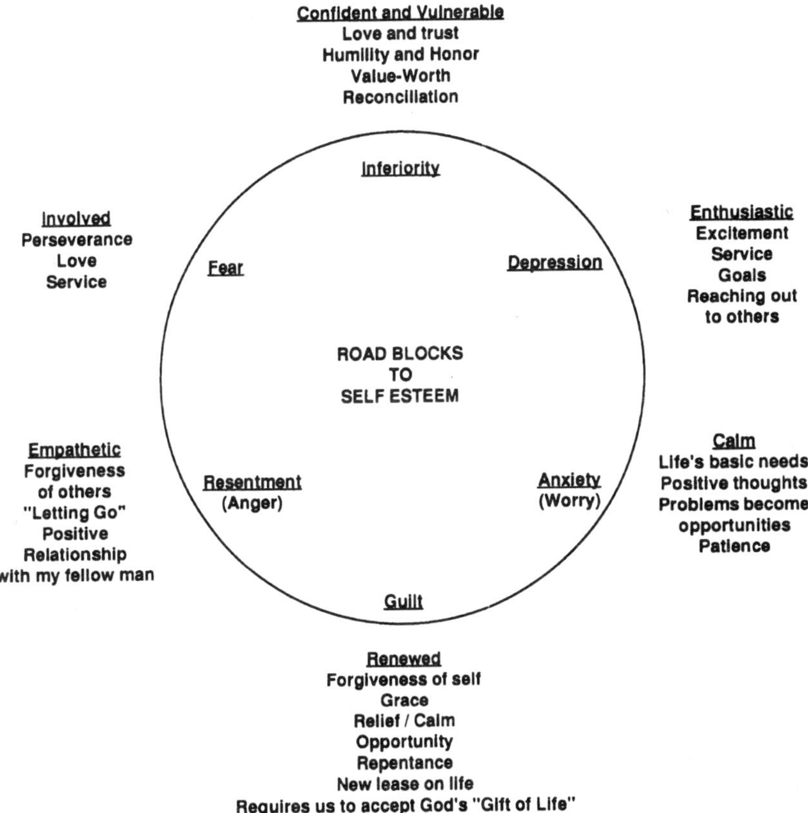

FIGURE 6-5 Six Building Blocks to Self-Esteem

> *Made a list of all persons we had harmed and become willing to make amends to them all. Made direct amends to such people whenever possible, except when to do so would injure them or others (Anonymous, 1986, p. 7).*[6]

The recovering teenager is encouraged to put his or her name at the top of the list and start by first making amends to him- or herself. Others would include drug-free friends, family members, teachers, principals, counselors, and people who were stolen from or vandalized. This process of listing people the teenager has harmed and making direct amends to them fosters attitudes of tolerance and forgiveness and requires the teenager to take full responsibility for past actions. In addition, these two steps help the recovering teenager rebuild self-respect, courage, and confidence.

Steps Eleven and Twelve

Steps eleven and twelve of Alcoholics Anonymous (Anonymous, 1986, pp. 96–125), in combination with the tenth step, can be viewed as the transmitting steps. Steps eleven and twelve read:

> *Sought through prayer and meditation to improve our conscious contact with* <u>God as we understood Him</u>, *praying only for the knowledge of His will for us and the power to carry that out. Having had a spiritual awakening as the result of these steps, we tried to carry this message to alcoholics, and to practice these principles in all of our affairs (Anonymous, 1986, p. 7).*[7]

Changes in one's character occur as a result of discovering new ways of thinking about oneself and others, acting on these insights, and experiencing the benefits derived from thinking and acting differently. Continuing to practice new patterns of thinking and acting reinforces the formation of the desired character trait and, eventually, leads to its habituation. Daily review of one's practice helps the individual evaluate his or her progress and make necessary corrections to keep on the right track. Teaching one's success to others helps reinforce and internalize the value of the character change one is attempting to achieve as he or she learns more effective means of coping with one's self and others.

Steps eleven and twelve are designed to help accelerate the process of character change that has begun to emerge in the recovering teenager and also helps ensure the process's continuation. These two steps also underscore the importance of realizing that yesterday's successes will not ensure tomorrow's victories.

After reaching the transmitting plateau, the recovering teenager begins to experience the benefits derived from thinking about and acting on the knowledge gained from working the first ten steps of Alcoholics Anonymous and applying other treatment strategies. There is a real temptation at this point, however, to believe erroneously that final victory has been achieved and additional and continuing work is unnecessary. Operating under the *illusion of success,* many recovering teenagers will stop implementing the new thought and action patterns that have resulted in their success and, much to their surprise, wake up one day back in the old self-defeating patterns that they labored so vigorously to overcome.

Steps eleven and twelve provide the recovering teenager four accelerating principles that offer a solution to this dilemma and help them hurdle the illusion of success. They include prayer and meditation, power, spiritual awakening, and practice.

Daily prayer and meditation help the recovering teenager stay focused. This involves a spiritual conditioning. One asks God to:

> *make me a channel of thy peace—that where there is hatred, I may bring love—that where there is wrong—I may bring the spirit of forgiveness that where there is discord, I may bring harmony—that where there is error I may bring truth—that where there is doubt, I may bring faith—that where there is despair, I may bring hope—that where there are shadows, I may bring light—that where there is sadness, I may bring joy. Lord, grant that I may seek rather to comfort than to be comforted—to understand, than to be understood—to love, than to be loved. For it is by self-forgetting that one finds. It is by forgiving that one is forgiven. It is by dying that one awakens to Eternal Life (Anonymous, 1986, p. 99).*

This daily process enhances the recovering teenager's understanding of the nature of *power* and its origin and reinforces the principle that power to elicit and sustain desired change is achieved by staying focused on a new set of beliefs. A recovering teenager learns that newly achieved successes came not from one's own will (old ACEs), but from the new insights (new ACEs) gained from seeking out and asking for the help and advice of those already successfully demonstrating desired changes. By acting on these new insights, different and more desirable results were achieved and a new state of consciousness, *a renewal of the mind, a spiritual awakening* occurred.

The recovering teenager now understands that acting on a new more rational functional set of beliefs will result in a more happy, harmonious, peaceful, and drug-free life. The adolescent appreciates that continuing to *practice* these new beliefs in all daily affairs and sharing the good news with others reinforce the newly desired results, making them easier to maintain.

Ten Most Common Causes of Failure

The ten most common causes of failure (Binstock, 1982) is a treatment strategy used to teach recovering teenagers common pitfalls to avoid when attempting to change their lives. Adapted from an article written by Louis Binstock, the causes of failure include (1) blaming others, (2) blaming oneself, (3) having no goals, (4) choosing the wrong goals, (5) taking the short cut, (6) taking the long road, (7) neglecting little things, (8) quitting too soon, (9) burden of the past, and (10) illusion of success.

Adolescents in recovery are encouraged to take an inventory of themselves by seriously asking, "To what degree and extent do each of these stumbling blocks currently interfere with my efforts to remain drug free and redirect my life along more positive drug-free avenues?"

After the soul searching required for this exercise, it is not uncommon for teenagers in each of the four plateaus of recovery to discover that they are still blaming others for current and past mistakes and they have done little work to genuinely forgive themselves for their past wrongdoings. They also discover that they have not truly committed themselves to a new direction in their lives and that they are still being lured by old self-defeating thinking patterns, being convinced that they can return to old friends, old places, and old things and not run any risk of relapse.

These recovering teenagers learn that they vacillate between looking for an easy, painless road to recovery that involves little if any effort and making recovery an arduous, complicated task that is void of any pleasure. Recovery either becomes too easy or too hard, thus resulting in little action or overzealous action. They find it difficult to accept daily routines, and paying attention to little things on a daily basis soon becomes boring and uneventful. They discover that they are not really different than other people and can only achieve their ambitions by developing successful daily routines. But in their past, nonroutine had become their routine.

They learn that giving up or quitting too soon is a common habit of recovering teenagers, especially in the initial stages of treatment but also in the later stages. They begin to appreciate the challenge of increasing their capacity to handle frustration.

Completing this inventory helps recovering teenagers appreciate that the burden of the past, or unresolved guilt, is a major hurdle in recovery. They learn that to be successful, they not only must develop a healthy fear of their past as a primary motivator but also must engage in an extensive effort to forgive themselves for their past mistakes. This forgiveness enables them to redirect their energies toward the development of new habits that will keep them from repeating their past mistakes.

Taking this inventory shows recovering teenagers how vulnerable they are to the illusion of success, especially during the transmitting plateau. Having achieved success from committing themselves to a new way of thinking and acting, and having experienced the benefits derived from following this new life style, many recovering teenagers now erroneously think that they have arrived. Therefore, they conclude, it is no longer necessary to continue to engage in the kind of activities that have produced their success. Recovering teenagers learn to avoid this trap when they fully understand that recovery is not an end in itself, but is a continuing means to grow and mature.

Combined, the ten most common causes of failure are symptomatic of a much deeper challenge for recovering teenagers, the challenge of accepting and taking responsibility for their own recovery. Recovering teenagers must be made aware of these pitfalls, be conscious of their consequences, and learn how to avoid them. But for some recovering teenagers, these ten pitfalls soon become excuses for not continuing to grow and mature in recovery. These pitfalls become a hiding place for them to avoid taking responsibility for their recovery and often serve as excuses to return to a life style of drug use.

Relapse Signs and Symptoms List

The relapse signs and symptoms list (Monahan, 1985, p. 8) is another treatment strategy designed to increase awareness of several potential pitfalls that a teenager may encounter in recovery. Monahan explains that "relapse can be sneaky, hiding behind various signs and symptoms" These signs and symptoms include:

1. Becoming overconfident in recovery
2. Trying to force recovery on others
3. Avoiding talking about challenges encountered in recovery
4. Behaving compulsively (over/underwork; overtalk/withdraw; isolation/socialization)
5. Overreacting to stressful situations
6. Getting depressed, living in past, or engaging in haphazard planning
7. Avoiding having fun
8. Overanalyzing self and becoming preoccupied with one area of life
9. Becoming easily angered and irritated with family and friends
10. Blaming everyone else for your problems
11. Losing daily routine, sleeping irregularly, becoming listless
12. Sporadically attending self-help meetings such as AA or aftercare, or not attending at all
13. Developing an "I don't care" attitude
14. Developing aches and pains
15. Overusing money, sex, or power
16. Feeling powerless, helpless, sorry for oneself, and beginning to lose confidence in oneself
17. Fantasizing about drinking, rationalizing drinking, start visiting old "druggie" places or getting together with old "druggie" friends
18. Increasing usage of nonprescription drugs or attempting controlled usage of mind-altering drugs

Teenagers in the latter stages of recovery benefit immensely from receiving and reviewing this checklist and being reminded that "relapse is a process, just as recovery is a process. Relapse begins when movement toward recovery ceases, because recovering persons have to keep moving ahead just to stay even" (Monahan, 1985, p. 8). Or as Gorski and Miller (1982, p. 56) explain, "Relapse begins in a behavioral dynamic which reactivates patterns of denial, isolation, elevated stress, and impaired judgment."

Goal Setting

Goal setting is another important treatment strategy useful in preventing relapse; especially during the committing and transmitting stages of recovery. The goal-setting exercise encourages the recovering teenager to make a minimum of three 6-month goals in each one of nine life areas: (1) physical self-improvement, (2) emotional self-improvement, (3) spiritual self-improvement, (4) family relationship, (5) education and vocation, (6) leisure time, (7) drug-free friendships, (8) service, and (9) financial. Each of the 6-month goals must be achievable, believable, concrete, and desirable.

Once having completed the listing of the goals, the recovering teenager is asked to develop an implementation plan by applying Zig Ziglar's (1985) seven steps to better goal setting.

1. Identify clearly what you want.
2. Set specific dates when you expect to get what you want (reach your goal).
3. List obstacles that you need to overcome to reach your goal.
4. Identify what you need to know to reach your goal.
5. Identify people, groups, organizations, companies, etc. that you need to work with in order to achieve your goal.
6. Develop a comprehensive plan of action.
7. Specify in detail the benefits of achieving your goal and the consequences if you do not.

When a sound implementation plan is completed, the recovering teenager is taught to develop weekly goals that, when accomplished, will contribute toward the obtainment of the identified 6-month goals. Once a week the recovering teenager is encouraged to complete a weekly planning calendar that lists (1) things that must be done at a specific time, (2) things that must be done but no specific time, (3) things that are desirable but must be done at a specific time, and (4) things that are desirable but can be done anytime. Then, on a daily basis, the recovering teenager is taught to spot check his or her goals by listing the six most important tasks that need to be accomplished for that day.

Overall, this exercise teaches the recovering teenager how to plan for and implement realistic goals and at the same time reinforces the importance of the principles outlined in the previously introduced treatment strategy, the three signs: think think think, first things first, and easy does it.

Summary

In this chapter, treatment objectives for the committing and transmitting plateaus of recovery were outlined. Fifteen treatment strategies were introduced that help recovering teenage substance abusers identify self-defeating self-talk, change it, and avoid relapse.

Endnotes

1. *You and your emotions* is available by mail at $9.50; I'ACT, Inc., 3939 W. Spencer Street (P.O. Box 1011), Appleton, WI 54515-1011.
2. The Twelve Steps in their entirety are listed in Appendix B.
3. Refer to chapter 2 for a detailed explanation of automatic emotional and behavioral responses. See also The ABCDEs of Emotions and Behavior in chapter 5.
4. For a detailed explanation of the five criteria, see The Five Criteria in chapter 6.
5. Maultsby (1986) provides an excellent resource for those seriously committed to reducing irrational thinking that creates and substains irrational self-defeating emotional and behavioral responses such as anger, self-pity, etc.
6. The Twelve Steps in their entirety are listed in Appendix B.
7. The Twelve Steps in their entirety are listed in Appendix B.

7

Treating the Family of the Adolescent Substance Abuser

This chapter outlines several treatment strategies useful in treating parents, siblings, grandparents, and other relatives of adolescents recovering from a problem of substance abuse. Special attention is given to a unique self-defeating self-talk that emerges when relatives live and/or interact with a chemically dependent adolescent.

Treating Co-Dependent Enabling Parents

Whereas a chemically dependent adolescent becomes psychologically and/or physiologically addicted to drugs, the parents become psychologically addicted to their child. The parents begin to believe erroneously that their worth as human beings is dependent solely on the success or failure and the happiness or unhappiness of their child. Just as damaging, the parents begin to believe that they are responsible totally for the welfare of their child and that they have caused their child's current drug problem. Just as chemical dependency can be viewed as a disease of attitudes that results in physiological, emotional, and spiritual difficulties, so can co-dependency.

Wegscheider-Cruse (1988, p. 8) defines *co-dependency* as "a toxic relationship to a substance, a person, or a behavior that results in increased shame, low self worth, relationship problems and medical complications." Parents of chemically dependent adolescents develop a toxic relationship with their drug-abusing teenagers. Maintaining this state of co-dependency is a faulty cognitive structure similar to the cognitive structure of the chemically dependent adolescent.

Figure 7-1 depicts the emerging personality and cognitive structure of the *co-dependent enabling parent.*

The outer layer of the parents' co-dependent enabling personality consist of an obsessive thinking pattern (psychological addiction) perpetuating the belief that parents are ultimately and totally responsible for the

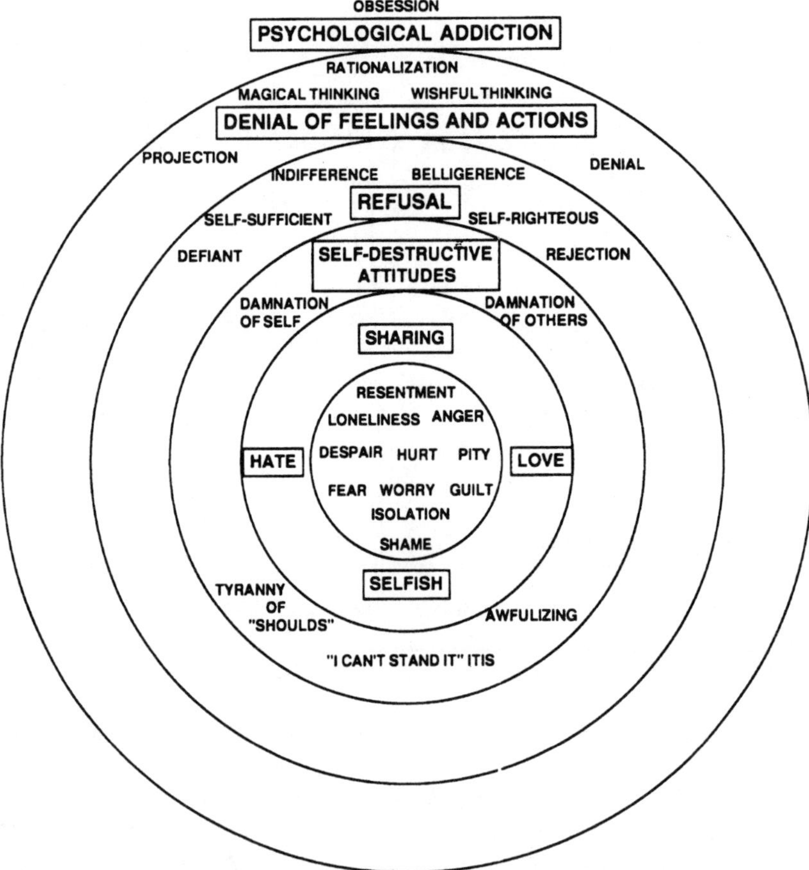

FIGURE 7-1 Emerging Personality and Cognitive Structure of the Co-dependent Enabling Parent

welfare and happiness of their child. Parents have erroneously linked their worth as people with the success or failure of their child. Also, parents have learned how to overcompensate for their child's deficiencies by covering up for and enabling their child's continuing drug usage in order to gain temporary relief from the hurt and disappointment experienced from observing their child's ongoing spiritual, emotional, and physical deterioration. This addictive process is subtle and insidious and is strongly reinforced by attitudes of *denial* and *refusal.*

The denial layer of the co-dependent enabling personality consists of rationalizations, magical thinking, wishful thinking, projection, and denial. *Rationalizations* consist of excuses and justifications that parents contrive to avoid examining and accepting their child's drug usage and accompanying destructive behaviors. *Magical thinking* clings to the false hope that their child will eventually outgrow the problem. *Wishful thinking* falsely believes that if they give their child one more chance, that this time he or she will alter the self-defeating behavior. *Projection* places the blame for the child's condition on their previous failures as parents, on schools or law enforcement agencies, unpleasant childhood experiences, or any other source other than the child. *Denial* is a refusal by parents to examine openly and honestly the facts being presented to them about their child. It is a process of lying to themselves about the reality of their child's condition.

The refusal layer of the co-dependent enabling personality consists of attitudes of belligerence, defiance, self-sufficiency, self righteousness, indifference, and rejection. *Belligerent* parents are prepared to take on and attack anyone who would suggest that their child is anything less than perfect. *Defiant* parents will sabotage the family treatment agenda by refusing to comply with rules, regulations, and guidelines established for the successful treatment of the family. Defiant parents will also consistently challenge and argue about the efficacy of treatment procedures without any sound rationale supporting the challenge. *Self-sufficient* parents will find it difficult to admit the need for, let alone ask for, help, believing that it is a parents' role to solve their own problems independent of outside help. *Self-righteous* parents already know how to solve the child's drug problem and therefore will attempt continuously to impress the therapist and other parents in treatment with their knowledge and expertise and are quick to instruct others in the changes they should be making. *Indifferent* parents will participate reluctantly in treatment, believing for the most part that any effort extended will be futile. These parents' "I don't care attitude" mask a tremendous amount of hurt and disappointment experienced from their child's continuing failure to meet their expectations. Parents exhibiting the attitude of *rejection* will quickly and consistently avoid confronting their child, believing that they are the sole cause for all of the child's shortcomings and drug usage. The child's behavior reinforces the parents' belief of "how much of a failure we are."

The innermost layer of the co-dependent enabling personality consists of five self-destructive attitudes: (1) damnation of self, (2) damnation of others, (3) tyranny of shoulds, (4) awfulizing, and (5) I can't stand-it-itis. The first two sets of attitudes, *damnation of self and others,* has the parents erroneously concluding that it is either their fault or someone else's fault that their child continues to use drugs. The *tyranny of shoulds* results in the parents demanding in their minds that the child's present and past condition be different, that is, "he should not be on drugs and he should have never used drugs." *Awfulizing* results in the parents overexaggerating the consequences and implications of the child being involved in drug usage. The attitude of *I can't stand-it-itis* results in feelings of helplessness, hopelessness, and frustration and is underscored by an erroneous belief that there is no constructive way to manage the emotional pain that accompanies having a child on drugs.

Read carefully the following desperate self-talk of a mother whose daughter is about to walk out of treatment.

> *She's not so bad. She only did it once or twice. She doesn't know what she is doing. She is going to ruin her life. She will end up dead or in prison. Why is this happening to me? This is going to ruin her life. Why can't she change? I am a complete failure. She is going to hate me for the rest of my life. I can't take it anymore. I'll do anything if you just stay in treatment. Our family is totally ruined. She'll grow out of it. It is just a stage she is going through. I should have gotten her help sooner. I should have gotten a court order. Why didn't the schools have a better drug education course. Why can't the police do something about all of these drugs in our community. I'll let her come back home again and give her one more chance.*

Notice the rationalizations or excuses this mother uses ("She's only done it twice. She doesn't know what she is doing."). The magical ("She'll grow out of it.") and wishful ("I'll let her come back home again and give her one more chance.") thinking, the projection ("Why didn't the schools have a better..."), and the denial ("She's not so bad.") that dominates this parent's thinking. Notice also, the self destructive attitudes of blaming self and others ("I'm a complete failure...why can't the police..."), the should or demanding thinking ("I should have gotten a court order."), the awfulizing ("Our family is totally ruined."), and the I can't stand-it-itis thinking ("I can't take it anymore.") evident in the parent's self-talk.

In this example, clear indicators of the obsessive thinking patterns of psychological addiction, denial, refusal, and self-destructive attitudes are present. Each distinct layer of this parent's cognitive structure carefully guards a caldron of emotional pain consisting of worry, fear, guilt, anger, resentment, pity, shame, hopelessness, and despair.

Rehearsed for too long, this parent will soon slip back into a refusal pattern of indifference and rejection, scared to care any longer, for fear of feeling shameful, helpless, and worthless. Left unchallenged, this parent will return to a self-defeating pattern of enabling behavior so typical of the addiction of co-dependency. Left untreated, this parent's continued exposure to her drug-abusing child will result in her life becoming more unmanageable as her powerlessness over her daughter intensifies. This parent must address each of these irrational layers of her emerging personality and cognitive structure that create and sustain her co-dependent enabling behaviors. Only then can her treatment be successful.

Treatment Objectives and Strategies

Objectives

Treatment objectives for co-dependent enabling parents should include

1. Reducing the level of anxiety, depression, and anger
2. Identifying self-defeating irrational thinking patterns that maintain the co-dependent enabling personality
3. Replacing self-defeating irrational thinking patterns with new self-enhancing rational patterns of thinking
4. Practicing new self-enhancing rational thinking patterns
5. Admitting powerlessness over their child's condition and accepting the possibility that their child may not recover from the disease
6. Fostering a willingness and readiness to ask for and accept the help of others in overcoming their co-dependent enabling personality
7. Healing damaged relationships with other family members including the chemically dependent child, spouse, and other children
8. Addressing other psychological and/or chemical dependency issues that diminish the parents' effectiveness to parent their child and act more effectively in other areas of their lives
9. Educating parents about the disease of chemical dependency and co-dependency
10. Developing more effective communication and parenting skills

Overall, the treatment objectives should foster an atmosphere where the parents can openly and honestly accept the condition of their child.

Treatment objectives should help parents honestly confront their child with their feelings of hurt and disappointment as they admit their powerlessness to change their child. Most importantly, treatment objectives should help the parents learn how to live with their hurt and disappointment in more positive and constructive ways. They no longer have to dwell in feelings of anger, resentment, self-pity, guilt, shame, and fear. They no longer have to continue to cover up for and enable their child to avoid the consequences of his or her drug usage.

The following letter to her therapist describes the thoughts of one parent as she reports, her attempts to grapple with her relapsed son and apply her newly learned coping skills. She and her son have been in treatment for nearly two years.

As you remember, my son knows my two Achilles' heels: his artistic talent and college education. He let me have it with both barrels. An institute of art has a location in Florida, and he needs my help to get the financial aid paperwork going. Also, his druggie friend has invited my son to go down there with him for Spring break and he's sure dad will forgive the car payment for one month so he can go. It's of course a minor detail that my son hasn't found a job yet.

The good news is I kept my cool and basically repeated the fact that I love him very much. I'm afraid for him and disappointed that he chose to (1) resume his drug use and (2) betray my trust in him. I will not help him financially or in any other way until he is ready to (1) face his relapse, (2) take steps to get help, (3) and live a life without drugs and druggie friends. I said that I'm here for him. I'm ready to stand by him when he takes those steps. I also said it was not something to be embarrassed about. Once he has the courage to deal with the relapse, he will have even , more to offer others with the disease.

The bad news is I said it too many times and allowed him to deliver any number of verbal left-hooks in between. I probably stayed on the phone 20 minutes. It would have been more effective to state my position and get off the phone once the conning and rationalization began. Round and round we went. If you had been here, you would have kicked me under the table! He denied the drug use and said I was trying to run his life just like I try to run every one else's. That's why I'm broke. That's why I haven't finished my screenplay. I want him to be a geek. I enforce all these rules with him but I still sent his sister to college and she drank. I never paid for any vacations for him and I sent his sister to Europe. He's going to go through life as a college drop-out because I won't help him go to college unless I can run his life. I'm guilty of assuming thinking. I just assume he uses because I found a few seeds in his room. His friend drinks and drugs and his parents don't care. My son went on to say that he was out of control before, but he was only 15 then. Do I realize the trauma I put him through? Having him arrested...sending him away...if I could see all of his druggie friends now. They changed on their own. And they weren't brainwashed.

I'm listing all of this to show myself and you just how CRAZY I was to listen to that. At least (a tiny plus) I did not challenge any of his absurd statements. I just calmly repeated what I have noted above. I did end the conversation by saying there would be no more discussions like this and to call me only when he is ready to get help. In the meantime, I love him and will be praying for him.

Effective treatment objectives encourage co-dependent enabling parents to get honest with themselves and squarely face the reality that they cannot control how their child is going to respond to life emotionally and behaviorally. Effective treatment objectives teach the parents that they have choices as to how they want to respond emotionally and behaviorally to life's circumstances. Effective treatment objectives teach parents that they can live with hurt and pain and still have joy, meaning, and purpose in their life. This parent was well on her way to accomplishing the objectives that were set for her in treatment.

Strategies

Several treatment strategies exist to help co-dependent enabling parents recover by learning how to confront their child's disease of chemical dependency more openly and honestly. They include general, introductory, intermediate, and advanced strategies.

General treatment strategies include (1) the awareness wheel, (2) ABCDEs of emotion and behavior, (3) overcoming denial and refusal, (4) moral inventories, (5) fallible and correctable human being (FHB/CHB), (6) five steps to change, (7) four key words to recovery, (8) serenity prayer, (9) the three signs, (10) five criteria for rational thinking, (11) the Lord's Prayer, and (12) parent weekend.

Introductory treatment strategies include (1) co-dependency and the primary enabler, (2) sympathy kills: learning how to effectively express your feelings to your child, (3) consistency and commitment, (4) emotional ignorance and the importance of self-talk, (5) powerlessness over our kids the challenge of accepting step one, and (6) reaching out to others.

Intermediate treatment strategies include (1) overcoming enabling behavior, (2) seven steps to a happy (F)ACE, (3) self-defeating styles of thinking, (4) script writing, (5) assertiveness training, (6) rule setting, negotiating, and the effective use of motivators, and (7) stress reduction techniques.

Advanced treatment strategies include (1) couples communication, (2) signs of relapse, (3) family relationships, (4) relationships with the opposite sex, and (5) overcoming fears and insecurities.

Each of these four types of treatment strategies should be introduced over a 9- to 14-month period of time, preferably in group counseling sessions. This will give parents an ample opportunity to digest, practice, and fully incorporate newly learned patterns of thinking into their daily lives. Remember, to be successful with the parents, it is necessary to " change their cognitive structure.

Parents identified with severe emotional problems and/or chemical dependency problems will require individual counseling in addition to the group counseling and, in some cases, may require temporary hospitalization. Appropriate screening procedures should be used to determine the mental state of the parents as to whether they are slightly dysfunctional, marginally dysfunctional, dysfunctional due to mental illness, or dysfunctional due to chemical dependence (see Mental State: Parents in chapter 3).

General Treatment Strategies

The first 11 of the 12 general treatment strategies are best introduced over an 11-week period of time, introducing one strategy per week and then assigning homework to reinforce the insights learned. Each of the first 11 general treatment strategies can be introduced in a 45-minute group setting allowing an additional 15 minutes for questions and an opportunity to clarify misunderstandings. The first 11 general treatment strategies form a core of knowledge essential for the parents' recovery and, therefore, should be repeated as many times as possible (preferably three or more times) to continue to reinforce newly emerging thinking patterns. These first 11 general treatment strategies can parallel the presentation of the introductory, intermediate, and advanced treatment strategies and often add to and reinforce their understanding.

The twelfth general treatment strategy, parent weekend, involves a two-day commitment by parents and is introduced after parents have completed the first 11 general treatment strategies. It is also recommended that parents attend this weekend three or four times during the course of their treatment.

Awareness Wheel

This general treatment strategy (S. Miller, Nunnally, & Wackman, 1991, pp. 15–25) has been previously explained in detail in chapter 5. This strategy is particularly useful in helping parents begin to distinguish between their thoughts, feelings, intentions, and actions. Homework assigned after introducing this strategy includes completing two awareness wheels during the week and also maintaining a feeling log (refer to chapter 5). Combined, these two homework assignments help the parents identify their current and past feelings and help them to talk about them more openly and honestly.

ABCDEs of Emotion and Behavior

This strategy (Ross, 1983d) is a therapeutic tool similar to the awareness wheel. It is especially helpful in teaching parents how their self-talk creates and maintains their co-dependent personality. This treatment strategy has been previously explained explained in detail in chapter 5.

Overcoming Denial and Refusal

This strategy helps parents confront the denial and refusal layers of their co-dependent enabling personality as they grapple with concepts outlined in steps one, two, and three of Alcoholics Anonymous. Terms such as *powerless, unmanageable, power greater than ourselves, sanity, decision,* and *will* are discussed, and their implications for recovery explored. (Refer also to Steps One, Two, and Three in chapter 5.)

Introducing these concepts enables the therapist to ask the parents pertinent therapeutic questions such as How were you powerless over your child? How was your life becoming unmanageable and insane? In what ways did you deny your child's drug problem? In what ways did you cover up for and enable your child to continue drug usage? In what ways do you avoid seeking and asking for help for the current emotional pain and turmoil in your life?

Teaching parents how to apply the first three steps of Alcoholics Anonymous helps them admit that their current coping style of dealing with their chemically dependent child is and has been ineffective and that they are in need of learning a more effective coping style. Parents will need to submit to the learning process and to commit themselves to applying a new set of thinking patterns.

Moral Inventories

This strategy is another therapeutic tool to help parents become more honest with themselves and to identify self-defeating behavioral patterns. Two types of moral inventories are introduced a *daily personal inventory* modeled after step ten of Alcoholics Anonymous (refer to chapter 5, Daily Moral Inventory) and a *searching and fearless moral inventory* modeled after step four of Alcoholics Anonymous (refer to chapter 5, Searching and Fearless Moral Inventory). Together, these two tools help parents engage in a fact-finding and fact-facing process where they begin to make an honest examination of their self-defeating irrational emotional and behavioral responses. Parents explore past resentments, fears, hurts, and harms and relate them to current challenges. Parents learn the important spiritual axiom that "every time we are disturbed, no matter what the cause, there is something wrong with us" (Anonymous, 1986, p. 90).

Fallible and Correctable Human Being (FHB/CHB)

This strategy is an excellent cognitive-behavioral therapeutic tool to help parents distinguish between their performance and their inherent worth as human beings (see chapter 5, Fallible and Correctable Human Being). Specifically, parents learn that the best they ever can be and the worst they ever will be is a fallible and correctable human being. Combined with steps five, eight, and nine of Alcoholics Anonymous, parents learn that their performance does not equate to their value as a person. Parents learn a process of how to accept and take responsibility for past wrongs and mistakes, how to apply forgiveness to self and others, and when possible and desirable, how to rectify past shortcomings.

Five Steps to Change

This strategy is an excellent treatment strategy that facilitates parents' understanding of the process they must complete in order to eliminate or significantly diminish self-defeating emotional and behavioral responses and provides them a mechanism to evaluate their progress accurately (refer to chapter 5, Five Steps to Change). Combined with steps six, seven, eleven, and twelve of Alcoholics Anonymous, parents learn that change requires (1) a well-thought-out plan of action, (2) an expressed willingness and readiness to change, (3) the need to ask others to help them and keep them accountable, (4) use of prayer and meditation, (5) a change in their cognitive structure, and (6) correct practice.

Four Key Words to Recovery

This strategy (refer to chapter 5, Four Plateaus of Recovery) helps parents to conceptualize their recovery from co-dependency in distinct stages: (1) admitting, (2) submitting, (3) committing, and (4) transmitting. Parents learn that each stage, or plateau, has unique thought patterns that need to be addressed and changed if complete recovery is to be achieved. Understanding each of these four plateaus helps parents define specific goals that must be reached at each plateau and helps them conceptualize how the twelve steps of Alcoholics Anonymous and other treatment aids can assist them in their efforts.

The Serenity Prayer

This strategy (Refer to chapter 5, Serenity Prayer) is an excellent therapeutic tool to introduce parents to the important concept of acceptance, and it also helps parents combat the tyranny of should thinking. Parents learn that

> *When I am disturbed, it's because I find some person, place, or thing, or situation—some facet of my life—unacceptable to me; and I can find no serenity until I accept that person, place, thing, or situation as being exactly the way it is supposed to be at this moment. (Anonymous, 1980a, p. 449)*

Maultsby (1982a) provides the explanation that

> *Because there is no magic in the real world outside human minds, everything is exactly as it now should be. That fact does not mean that people have to like what is happening or what has happened; nor do they have to think it is best. The rational use of the word should means only that everything necessary to make every current reality happen was done first. Consequently, every current reality had to happen the way it happened and therefore should have happened that way.*

Parents learn that they do not necessarily have to like a situation, but they can choose how they want to respond emotionally and behaviorally to the situation.

Three Signs

Think think think, First things first, and Easy does it (refer to chapter 5, Three Signs) serve as important cognitive reminders for parents that they must choose to restructure their thinking, realign their priorities, and learn patience if they are going to confront and successfully overcome their pattern of co-dependent enabling behavior. These three signs also serve as excellent anchors to teach parents more effective time management techniques as they learn to set goals and prioritize their time in areas of self-improvement physically, emotionally, and spiritually; family relationship; education/vocation; leisure time; meaningful friendships; community service; and financial.

The three signs reinforce the concepts outlined in steps six and seven of Alcoholics Anonymous as parents set achievable, believable, concrete, and desirable 6-month recovery goals in each of the listed areas. They develop a plan of action to accomplish their goals and then proceed to implement their plan. In the process they learn how to establish and maintain a more balanced life style and to set priorities in their lives.

Five Criteria for Rational Thinking

This strategy (Maultsby, 1986, pp. 5–6) is a systematic and objective means to help co-dependent enabling parents learn to challenge their erroneous thinking patterns that maintain their self-defeating emotional and behavioral responses (refer also to chapter 6, Five Criteria for Rational Thinking). This cognitive-behavioral technique helps parents address the important question How do you know if what you are thinking is worth thinking? Parents learn that their thinking, especially as it related to their chemically dependent child, was quite logical, but their underlying assumptions were quite irrational. Their assumptions about their child and themselves were not in their best interest and, in fact, were quite dysfunctional.

The Lord's Prayer

This treatment strategy serves as an excellent aid to help parents begin to address their feelings of inferiority, depression, anxiety, guilt, resentment, and fear (refer also to chapter 6, The Lord's Prayer). Studying the meaning of each phrase of this beautiful prayer and learning how to meditate on it help parents replace self-esteem–strangulating, negative emotions with positive, health-generating emotions. Coupled with the concepts taught in step eleven of Alcoholics Anonymous, parents take steps to become more confident yet vulnerable, more enthusiastic, and less fearful of failure. They learn how to be calmer in the midst of adversity. They learn how to be renewed in spirit, more forgiving and empathetic of others, no longer afraid to embrace life, but willing to stay involved and demonstrate authentic perserving love.

Parent Weekend

The parent weekend is a 2-day therapeutic experience designed to assist parents in becoming more aware of their particular treatment issues and to provide them an opportunity to grow closer to their chemically dependent child. In addition, the weekend also serves as an opportunity for parents to grow closer to other parents in treatment and discover how they can help each other overcome their co-dependent enabling tendencies.

During the first day of the weekend, the parents are involved in several group discussions. The morning sessions review the program basics that were introduced in the first 11 general treatment strategies.

Particular attention is centered on how to write an effective searching and fearless moral inventory. Emphasis is placed on having parents write down ten experiences in their lives when they experienced the most anger/resentment. They then are encouraged to share these experiences with other group members. Usually, a significant percentage of these experiences involve childhood experiences centering around parent-child relationships.

The afternoon sessions consist of two group experiences with an exercise period in between. The first group session involves healing the past. An audio tape is played to the group featuring a young man sharing the anger and resentment that he had held toward his father. Eventually, after many years, he is able to go to his father and reconcile their differences. The tape is quite emotional in parts and stresses the importance of parents verbally expressing their love to their children. Following the tape, parents are encouraged to share with each other any thoughts and emotions they experienced while listening to the tape. Usually, many parents will share strong feelings of anger, resentment, and guilt that they have held toward their parents.

After the exercise period, parents are introduced to family sculpturing. Using other group members and other available props (e.g., chairs), parents are encouraged to make a sculpture of their childhood family. They are then encouraged to explain the meaning of the sculpture to the other parents. Other parents are also encouraged to ask questions and to share observations about the experience. Usually, parents gain many insights about their childhood and how it has helped shape their current emotions and behaviors.

The evening of the first day closes with a general review of the day's happenings. Parents are encouraged to share with each other particular insights that they may have learned about themselves. Parents are also encouraged to share with other parents insights that they learned about each other.

The second day of the parent weekend involves an afternoon of family time activities where parents are encouraged to participate in a series of games with their teenager in treatment. The games usually consist of four square, volleyball, and basketball. After the completion of the family time activity, a dinner is served. After the dinner, a combined evening group therapy session involving the parents and their teenager is conducted. Parents and their teenager are encouraged to share the thoughts and feelings they were experiencing during the afternoon family activities session. For many parents and their drug using child, this may have been the first time in years that they had participated in a meaningful family experience.

Introductory Treatment Strategies

The introductory treatment strategies are best presented over a 6-week period, teaching one strategy each week and assigning homework assignments in between sessions. They are most effectively introduced in a group but can be taught in a one-on-one setting. Each strategy requires 45 minutes to an hour to present and discuss.

Co-Dependency and the Primary Enabler

This treatment strategy builds on the concepts introduced in Sharon Wegscheider-Cruse's books, *The Co-Dependency Trap* (1988) and *The Family Trap* (1983). The role of the primary or chief enabler is introduced to each of the parents.

> *The chief enabler is often the spouse or the parent of a chemically dependent person. It is the person who is closest and most depended on by the dependent. As the illness grows, so does the involvement of the enabler. With the growth of the illness comes the increased repression of feelings and the development of a set of survival defenses for the enabler. The role of the chief enabler in the system is to provide responsibility. As the dependent increasingly loses control, the chief enabler makes more choices to compensate for the dependent's lack of power. (Wegscheider-Cruse, 1983, pp. 10–11)*

The co-dependent enabling parents use the denial and refusal layer of their emerging personalities to cover up the hurt, anger, guilt, fear, and overall emotional pain being experienced. Parents act out these feelings by being super-responsible and manipulating, becoming overly serious, self-blaming and emotionally fragile, and by dwelling in thoughts of powerlessness and feelings of self-pity. Over time, the co-dependent enabling parent "compulsively covers up the true feelings and the enabler lives in the trap of self-delusion" (Wegscheider-Cruse, 1983, p. 11).

Once introduced to the concept of the *co-dependent enabler*, parents are then asked to think about how they were an enabler to their son or daughter. How did they act out the emotional pain they were experiencing? One parent in treatment explained:

> *My son had a school assignment to prepare a report on a subject of his choice and give a talk on this subject to the class. He was also to prepare a poster or some other visual aid to go along with the talk. As the time neared for this assignment to be completed, I attempted to assist him by taking him to my office at work where he would be away from the many distractions available at home.*

When we arrived, I suggested he work in the office adjoining mine and while he began the writing process, I would assist him by making copies of pictures from the library books we had brought with us. (I had gone to the library and found and checked out the books needed for the report.) As the evening passed, he wrote the report with considerable encouragement, suggestion, and editorial work from me. I typed the text as he wrote it and used the word processor to rearrange and smooth out his writing. We then did the layout and the paste-up of the poster.

Some weeks later, I attended the teacher conference day where parents were given an opportunity to talk with their child's teachers. (This was not a favorite experience in those days.) When I talked to the teacher who had given the assignment of the report, I was told that my son might not have failed the grading period had he given the report that had been assigned. Despite my assurances that I had personal knowledge of the report having been prepared, the teacher steadfastly maintained that my son had said he was not prepared and did not give the report.

Much later, my son advised me that he was high during the class and was in no condition to give a report. After we took him out of school and put him in treatment, we found the poster in his locker.

Other parents in the group session could immediately relate to this type of insane behavior. The parents in the group were beginning to get in touch with and experience their pain and how ineffectively they were coping with it.

After completing of this treatment strategy, parents are asked to read *The Co-Dependency Trap* and *The Family Trap* in their entirety and, as a homework assignment, determine what role they played in their family when they were growing up: the family hero, the family scapegoat, the lost child, or the family mascot. Also, they are asked to examine what roles they and their children are currently playing in their family.

Sympathy Kills

This strategy is an effective therapeutic tool to teach parents how to express their feelings more openly and honestly to their chemically dependent child while avoiding the good parent trap. Most parents in the initial stage of treatment reek with sympathy for their child, feeling sorry for both their child and themselves. Effective treatment must quickly dispel such useless emotion, for as long as the parents dwell in their self-pity and feel sorry for their child, they will greatly diminish any negotiating power they have left. For the child will quickly surmise that his or her parents will continue to rescue him or her from the natural consequences of poor choices and most likely will withdraw him or her from treatment, if he or she acts miserable enough. *Parents must be taught immediately from "the get go" that sympathy kills!* Or as one counselor bluntly explains, "In the dictionary you find sympathy between suicide and syphilis."

At the core of the parents' sympathy is an underlying belief that their value as people is dependent on how happy or unhappy their child feels. Their mistaken belief starts with the assumption that a happy child equals a good parent and an unhappy child equates into a bad parent. Subsequently, if I am a bad parent, that must mean I am a bad person. If I am a bad person, therefore I must feel miserable. Therefore, to avoid feeling miserable, I must do everything I can to keep my child happy. Carpenter (1979, p. 1) explains:

> *Parents in the "good parent trap" are victims of their intense fear of being "bad parents." They make their worth as a person dependent upon how happy their children feel and how well they behave....They are afraid for their children to feel unhappy because, in their minds, that would prove they are "bad parents."*
>
> *Thus, when their children act upset and unhappy, these parents feel panic stricken about the possibility of having done the wrong thing. And that panic quickly leads to an intense feeling of guilt. Their intense guilt leads them to reverse themselves to say "yes" if they have said "no" and to cancel practiced discipline.*
>
> *Their children get what they want, so they're satisfied. But what about their parents? They get the very behavior they don't want from their child, and they feel miserable about it. In reality, they feel miserably guilty about not doing what they know is in their children's best interests to do.*
>
> *No matter what they do, therefore, parents end up angry with themselves and their children and they feel guilty about that.*

Parents are quickly taught that people don't have to get undesirably upset just because they don't get what they want. They can learn how to calmly accept unavoidable disappointments. Secondly, they learn that there is no such things as good or bad parents, just fallible human beings who can act effectively or ineffectively in raising their children. Effective parenting establishes boundaries and allows children to experience the natural consequences of their poor choices. Thirdly, the parents begin to understand that they don't cause how their children feel and act, and if their child chooses to feel miserable, they don't have to feel the same way. Parents begin to learn that they have more power to negotiate with their children than they thought previously, if they will just get rid of the erroneous assumptions that have kept them in the good parent trap.

Once rid of their sympathy and the good parent trap, parents are able to focus on their intense feelings of hurt and disappointment and are encouraged to express these feelings to their chemically dependent child.

Consistency and Commitment

Consistency and commitment are important cognitive-behavioral concepts for the parents to learn. This particular therapeutic strategy is designed to impress on the parents how important it is for them to work their own program of recovery, independent of their child's efforts. It is explained to parents early in treatment that, unfortunately, many chemically dependent teenagers do not choose to recover from their disease. But this fact does not have to distract the parents from overcoming their co-dependent enabling role. Parents learn, ironically, that as they diminish their co-dependent enabling role with their child, in most cases, their child's chances for recovery increase. Parents learn that their guilt, anger, fear, and self-pity are four major emotional stumbling blocks that significantly interfere with their goal of consistently , maintaining a commitment to overcome their self-defeating feelings and behaviors. The self-talk that maintains these emotional stumbling blocks is then explored.

Emotional Ignorance and Self-talk

This therapeutic strategy reviews with the parents (1) the ABCDEs of emotions and behavior, (2) the five criteria for rational thinking, (3) the underlying attitudes of denial and refusal, and (4) the self-talk of the co-dependent enabling parent. Armed with these new therapeutic tools, parents can now begin to learn how to respond differently, no longer being ignorant of their emotional responses and understanding the important role their self-talk plays in creating them.

Powerlessness Over Our Kids

Understanding and admitting step one of Alcoholics Anonymous is perhaps one of the more difficult hurdles that co-dependent enabling parents must overcome during the course of their treatment. This treatment strategy begins to impress on the parents that as their child became addicted to drugs, they became addicted to their child. Beginning to discuss that they were indeed "powerless over our child and that our lives had become unmanageable" leads to open discussion of the anger, fear, guilt, self-pity, and shame that currently are disabling the parents and encourages an examination of the self-talk contributing to their powerlessness. Parents are asked to reflect on this question, as homework: How have you avoided taking step one in your program of recovery?

Reaching Out to Others

Reaching out to others is a simple treatment strategy that encourages parents to openly share their thoughts and feelings with other group members and to encourage other group members to do the same. A willingness to participate in the group therapy sessions helps all who participate become more honest with themselves and fosters a system of accountability and mutual support.

Parents learn the importance of *carefronting,* helping another person focus on their thoughts, feelings, and behavior, especially those who are self-destructive, being careful to differentiate between their actions and their value as people. Parents learn that a most effective way to carefront another is to share with that person how you can relate to what they are experiencing, because you have already experienced something similar.

Intermediate Treatment Strategies

Intermediate treatment strategies consist of seven treatment interventions that are best introduced over a 12-week span. It is preferable to conduct the strategies in a group, but they also can be taught in a one-on-one setting. Each session requires 45-minutes to an hour to introduce and discuss. Additional sessions are required to review homework assignments and provide feedback on experiences encountered while implementing newly learned skills. Completion of both the general and introductory treatment strategies is a prerequisite for participation in these sessions.

Overcoming Co-Dependent Enabling Behavior

This is an intermediate treatment strategy that stresses the importance of identifying self-defeating self-talk that creates and maintains co-dependent enabling behavior and replacing it with constructive rational self-talk that will severely limit and begin to alter the well-entrenched cycle of co-dependency. During this treatment session, parents review the ABC-DEs of emotions and behavior, the five criteria for rational thinking, and the five steps to change that were introduced in the general treatment strategies. Parents are asked to pay particular attention to their specific self-defeating ACEs that characterize their co-dependent enabling tendency.

Seven Steps to a Happy (F)ACE

This strategy is a process adapted from Maultsby (1978, pp. 122–137) and developed by Ross (1983d) to help parents develop more functional automatic emotional and behavioral responses to life's situations (i.e., functional (ACEs). The seven steps provide a systematic means for parents to (1) factually describe events and situations, (2) identify self-talk, (3) identify feelings and behavior, (4) critique self-talk, (5) create new self-talk, (6) create new feelings and behaviors, and (7) practice new feelings and behaviors (refer also to Chapter 6, Seven Steps to a Happy (F)ACE).

Once introduced, parents are asked to write about challenges they are currently experiencing using the seven steps format. For example, one mother uses the seven steps to resolve a conflict she is having with her son and his treatment program.

> *A Situation*: My son asked staff to get him some notebook (paper and he didn't get any.
>
> *C Feelings*: Angry, anxious, sympathetic, resentful, blaming
>
> *C-1 Desired Feelings*: Calm, accepting, tolerant
>
> *E Behavior*: Asked my son why he did not get the paper, blamed staff for not giving him the paper, and confronted staff about how irresponsible they were.
>
> *E-1 Desired Behavior*: Recognize that it was my son's challenge and encourage him to resolve his challenge with staff.
>
> *B/D Self-Talk*: I need to work out all the details so that things go as smoothly as possible when I am not here. My son has enough challenges without problems with school supplies. What if he needs something right away and gets a bad grade because he doesn't have what he needs? What if he needs to go to the public library and there is no one who can or will take him? My son might get discouraged with the treatment program if he makes bad grades because of this situation. Sometimes it seems like staff deliberately gives him a challenge. If the program gave him a permanent foster family when I'm gone, it would be a lot easier on him. I would get tired of having to stay in a different house every night. The program isn't operating the way it said it would for out-of-town parents.
>
> *Critique of Self-talk*: It's not a fact that I have to work out all of the details for my son's life to go smoothly. It is also not a fact that I'm a bad mother or a bad person if my son experiences some challenges, disappointments, and does not get everything he wants when I am not here. Believing that I must be responsible for my son's happiness does not promote my health or well being, help me to achieve my goal of overcoming my co-depen-

dent enabling tendencies, nor help me to reduce significant conflict with myself or others.

The facts are that he will have as many challenges as he has. In fact when he was drugging, he could not have cared less about any of his challenges and at that time they were far more severe in their consequences than any of the challenges with which he is currently having to deal. It is obvious that I am overexaggerating his challenges and believing that it is awful or terrible that he has to deal with them. Again, it is not a fact that just because he has challenges, I am a bad parent or a bad mother or a bad person. Overexaggerating his challenges and believing they are my responsibility does not promote my health or well-being, help me achieve my goals, or reduce significant conflict with myself or others.

So what if he doesn't get what he needs right away, makes poor grades, or does not get to the library? So what if he gets discouraged or makes bad grades? Besides, in his past, if something was important to him, i.e, getting drugs or tickets to a rock concert, he always found a way to get them. In his past he never even bothered to go to school, let alone do his homework. The worst thing that can happen is that he will decide to get high again, and that is his choice not mine. The facts are that he has been given a set of tools to cope with challenges and discouragements effectively. The fact is also that I have no control over whether he chooses to use these tools. Continuing to believe that I have this control and that I am responsible for his shortcomings does not promote my health and well-being, help me achieve my goal of overcoming my co-dependent enabling tendency, nor reduces significant conflict with myself or others.

The fact is that the staff should be doing whatever they are doing at any given moment in time that is giving him challenges, not giving him a permanent foster home, fostering him out at different homes nightly, and working with out-of-town clients in the manner that they are. Demanding in my head that reality be different than it really is at this moment does not promote my health or well-being, help me achieve my goals, nor significantly reduce conflict with myself or others.

New Self-talk: I am not responsible for my son's happiness nor am I responsible for the choices he makes in his life. Whether he chooses to be happy and makes good choices do not determine whether I am a good parent, a good mother, or a good person. The fact is the best I ever can be or the worst I ever will be is a fallible human being. I cannot control what my son does, but I can control how I choose to respond emotionally and behaviorally to what he does. At best, I can only attempt to influence my son and learn better ways to negotiate with him more effectively. My son and staff should be doing whatever they are doing at any given moment in time. I may not agree with what they are doing, and certainly have the choice as to whether I want to attempt to influence their behavior, but I choose to accept the present reality calmly, and if it is not in their best interest nor mine, allow myself to experience disappointment if I choose to feel that way.

Script: My son expresses to me some challenges he is having. I calmly determine whether his challenges are his issues or our issues. If they are his issues, I encourage him to explore options to solve his challenge and to seek additional help if required. If they are our issues, I will calmly sit down with him and discuss them and resolve them in a manner that is in both his best interest and mine. In negotiating with my son, I remember (insert new self-talk here).

Another mother resolves her ongoing conflicts with her daughter:

A Situation: My daughter not complying with my wishes and desires.

C Feelings: Distant, angry, disappointed, cold, sad, choked up, depressed, uptight, tense, lonely, threatened, weepy, resentful, edgy, and abused

C-1 Desired Feelings: Close, happy, disappointed but calm, warm, affectionate, comforted, hopeful, accepting, tolerant

E Actions: Tense, nervous, shaky, uptight, edgy, argue, accuse, give in to her demands

E-1 Desired Actions: Act calm, negotiate more effectively, define my boundaries

B/D Self-talk: My daughter doesn't love me any more! She never did love me. Drugs have robbed her capability of love for me. I could just shake her! Can't she see I love her? I'm her mother, why can't she show me some respect? Her sister has turned her against me. Her sister has taught her not to love or respect me. Joe has talked to her against me and it's their fault. Can't you see I've proven my love to you by caring to get you off drugs? All I'm asking is that you apply the things you have been taught about respect.

Critique of self-talk: Awfulizing—my daughter does not love me anymore, never did love me, and no longer has the capability to love me. These beliefs however, are not based on fact. I do not need the love or approval of anyone in order to feel good about myself, accept myself, love myself, or to be happy. Yes, it is desirable to receive love from others, but it is not necessary. Continuing to believe the contrary, however, does not promote my health and well-being, help me to achieve my goals of negotiating more effectively with my daughter and overcoming my codependent enabling tendencies, nor significantly reduces conflict with myself or others.

Tyranny of shoulds—She should (1) listen to me, (2) see that I love her, (3) show me respect, (4) not have listened to her sister or to Joe, and (5) apply what she has been taught. The fact is, however, that she should be doing whatever she is doing at this moment in time. I may not like it, it may not be in her or my best interest, but that is what she should be doing. Demanding in my head that reality be different than it is does not promote my health or well-being, help me achieve my goals, nor help me avoid significant conflict with myself or others.

New Self-talk: I do not have to have the love or approval of my daughter in order to be happy. I cannot control what my daughter does, but I can control how I choose to respond to her actions. She should be doing whatever she is doing.

Script: My daughter disobeys one of the house rules. I calmly accept this reality and proceed to implement the consequences previously agreed on if she breaks this rule. My daughter may choose to be unhappy about my decision and respond by withdrawing her love and affection. I calmly remind myself that my emotional well-being is not dependent on her love or approval. I choose to feel good about myself for having defined and reinforced my boundaries with my daughter and remaining calm when she expressed her disapproval.

Both of these cases illustrate the importance of helping parents discover underlying irrational assumptions deeply embedded in their cognitive structure that, if left unchallenged and unchanged, will keep them entrapped in their co-dependent enabling behaviors. Specifically, these two cases illustrate how the irrational, dysfunctional beliefs of (1) other people or events control how I feel, (2) equating one's value or worth with performance, (3) requiring the love or approval of others to love self, and (4) tyranny of shoulds significantly undercut parents' effectiveness to negotiate with their child and diminish their emotional well-being.

Self-Defeating Styles of Thinking

This is an intermediate treatment strategy designed to introduce parents to irrational or dysfunctional patterns of thinking that create and sustain unnecessary emotional turmoil and misery. Parents are introduced to 15 styles of irrational thinking as identified by Ross (1978, pp. 80–82) and 11 commonly held irrational or dysfunctional beliefs as identified by Maultsby and Hendricks (1974, pp. 83–106). (See chapter 6, Styles of Irrational or Dysfunctional Thinking, for a listing of the styles of thinking and irrational beliefs.) Parents are asked to prioritize which styles of thinking and which irrational beliefs they use most frequently and to determine how these thoughts and beliefs contribute to certain types of emotional responses. For example, should and ought thinking create elevated levels of anger and frustration.

Script Writing

Script writing, or recovery scripts, is another important cognitive-behavioral tool useful for parents in their efforts to overcome their co-dependent enabling behaviors (refer also to Chapter 6, Script Writing). Specifically, script writing helps parents to focus on and practice new rational styles of thinking that counter co-dependent enabling styles. Script writing accelerates the parents' development of rational ACEs to cope with their chemically dependent children. One parent wrote a script entitled "For Parents Who Love Their Kids Too Much":

> *I realize that I am a fallible and correctable human being. I realize that I do not need my child's approval, nor does my child have to like me, in order for me to feel good about myself as a person or a parent.*
>
> *I am not God. I do not know all things. I do not have all the answers to my child's problems. But I can be at peace with myself regardless of my child's struggles with life and with me.*
>
> *I realize that problems and pain are sometimes the consequences of wrong choices. They are also a normal part of life. God loves his children enough to allow problems and pain into their lives, so that they may learn and mature in body, mind, and spirit. I must do the same for my own children and resist the urge to protect them from the (consequences of their own actions.*

Though I would often rather my child take advantage of my experiences, do things my way, dress the way I want, and behave the way I want, I realize that I am not responsible for my child's choices. People of different ages see things differently. That does not mean that I am wrong or that my child is wrong...we are just different. I do not have to like it, but I can stand it. God does not require me to be the dictator of my family. He only requires me to be the best influence I can be.

In my effort to influence my child to make good decisions, my child may choose *to make himself or herself angry or reject what I say or do. I realize that my child is making the choice, and I do not have to respond in kind. I choose my own response. My child is entitled to his own opinions...but my opinions are equally worthy and valuable. I realize I can stand it if my child doesn't respect me, as long as I respect myself.*

I resolve to be aware of how I feel and what I want and to share these things honestly with my child. If I am honest in my sharing, I will not have to waste needless mental energy in criticizing myself afterwards. I will say NO when I mean NO and YES when I mean YES. I am only responsible to care for my child's needs *and not necessarily his* wants. *My child's life will not "fall apart" without my efforts and attention.*

I resolve to hold fast to my own personal values, and I will resist the temptation to lower my standards and expectations concerning my child. I realize there are no "good parents" or "bad parents". There are only parents. My own future belongs to me. My child's future belongs to my child. Just as I do not deserve the credit if my child succeeds, neither do I deserve the blame if my child fails.

In the following script, one father prepares himself for the possibility of his son deciding to return to drug usage:

It is unfortunate that at this time my son has chosen to practice old druggie attitudes and behaviors. Although I am disappointed and saddened about this, and concerned for his well-being, I cannot control his behavior or make his choices for him. I will be firm with him, confronting him on his behavior and sharing my concern in a loving way. I am clear that he is capable of change, and that the principles he has learned will work as long as he applies them. I will encourage him to make use of what he has learned, to take one day at a time, and to go forward from here. I understand that the choices my son is making at this time do not tarnish his basic goodness and worth as a human being. Although I will feel sad if he continues to make these choices, and I will not support a druggie lifestyle in any way. I can and will continue to love him and remain available to him if and when he chooses to work a 12-step program. I will not unnecessarily upset myself about his choices, as I have no control over what he thinks, feels, and does. It is in my best interests to let go of worry about my son, but I will continue to do what I can to influence the situation. I will move forward with productive loving interactions with the rest of the world. I know that life is good, and I will appreciate that goodness every day regardless of what my son or others do, because my sense of well-being and connection with sacredness does not depend on any external conditions.

Both scripts, if conscientiously rehearsed over a reasonable length of time (practiced three to four times daily for 60 days), will significantly reduce a parent's co-dependent enabling tendencies and significantly assist a parent in improving his or her overall emotional well-being. In addition, correct use of these scripts will aid parents in their efforts to cope more effectively with the hurt and disappointment that occur when those they love and care about make poor choices for themselves.

Assertiveness Training

Assertiveness training is a key intermediate treatment strategy in helping parents overcome their co-dependent enabling behavior. Whereas the seven steps to a happy (F)ACE and script writing help parents change their cognitive structure, assertiveness training assists parents in translating their new-found beliefs into practical observable actions.

In this strategy, parents are introduced to the concepts of assertive, nonassertive, and aggressive behavior as defined by Lange and Jakubowski (1977, pp. 7–10). Verbal and nonverbal characteristics of each type of behavior are examined, and the feelings experienced by the sender and receiver of each of these different types of message are explored. Payoffs or outcomes for using assertive, nonassertive, and aggressive behavior are also discussed. Parents are then encouraged to insert assertive messages in their overcoming co-dependent enabling behavior scripts and to picture themselves acting in an assertive manner with their children. For example, one father wrote:

I picture my son asking me to leave treatment, explaining he no longer needs the staff's or the group's help and he now can handle the problem of drug abuse on his own. I calmly but firmly explain to him in a relaxed, well-modulated voice tone, with my eyes making direct contact with his, that this is certainly an option he has, but he needs to understand that if he makes this decision, that he will not be able to return home, nor will he receive any financial support from his mother or me. I continue to explain to him, in a relaxed manner with my feet firmly planted and with my hands making warm, smooth motions, that I would be extremely disappointed if he chose to leave treatment and that I do not think that it was in his best interest, but if he persisted, he would have to encounter the consequences of his choice without the financial or emotional support of his parents. I feel confident and self-respecting as I honestly express to him in a direct nonthreatening way how I think and feel about his decision and what I plan to do if he exercises his option to discontinue treatment. I explain to him that I love him very much, but that I cannot in good conscience support his decision to leave treatment.

This father was learning how to express his thoughts, feelings, and intentions in a direct and honest manner that did not violate the rights of his son and at the same time clearly stated his position.

Rule Setting, Negotiating, and the Effective Use of Motivators

This is another key intermediate treatment strategy that enables parents to practice newly learned rational beliefs. In these sessions, parents learn the art of effective negotiation as they are asked to develop and implement a plan of rules and regulations for their children.

First, it is explained to the parents that the implementation of any rule should in some manner help their child develop a value deemed important by the parents. Rules and regulations are a means to help parents equip their children with a set of values that will help them cope effectively as adults. Values may include physical, emotional, and spiritual development; family; education; work; sharing; friendships; fiscal responsibility; leisure time; justice; respect for authority; and patriotism, to mention only a few.

Secondly, it is explained to parents that a rule or regulation is a clearly defined course of action being requested of their child with clearly delineated rewards and consequences for compliance or noncompliance. Parents are then encouraged to read Maultsby's (1980) handout entitled *"Rational Rules for Making Rules."* In the handout, Maultsby outlines 11 insights for making effective rules. These insights are:

1. Effective rules are easy to monitor and they efficiently help your children develop a specified behavioral habit.
2. Two conflicting rules equal no rule.
3. There is no magic that will make children like a new rule instantly and follow it perfectly from the first day.
4. When making rules, utilize the five criteria for rational thinking.
5. There are few rational rules that will apply equally well to children of different ages and sexes.

6. Effective rules carry effective penalties for their infraction. Any other so-called rule is merely an arbitrary personal choice.
7. Inconsistency in enforcing rules will convert the exception into the rule.
8. Inconsistency in enforcing rules leads to the perception of unfairness and eventually to a secondary hostile passive resistance to obedience.
9. Children desire and need frequent evidence of parental love and approval to ensure optimal emotional health.
10. A wish that never becomes a reality is merely a nonmotivating fantasy.
11. Children are people, too. And like all people, children initially may forget a new rule more often than they remember it.

Armed with these insights, parents learn to concentrate on making effective rules, agree in advance on the rules they set, and agree to enforce the rules. They give rules a chance to work before changing them, take into consideration the person they are making the rules for, and clearly explain to their child the consequences for violating rules. They have their child write down the rules and their consequences for noncompliance. They patiently and consistently enforce the rules, being careful to note any temporary exceptions. They praise and compliment their child when he or she obeys the rules and reward the child for complying with the rules.

Parents are then encouraged to make a list of activities, experiences, and materials about which their children get excited. It is then explained that human beings are usually motivated by three emotions: hope, fear, and anger. We are motivated by *hope* when we perceive that we will get something we want (reward) or experience some type of pleasure if we engage in a specific behavior. We are motivated by *fear* if we perceive that we will lose a previously gained want (reward) or believe that engaging in a certain activity will result in pain. Seeking pleasure and avoiding pain are strong reasons to engage in activity. *Anger* usually becomes the primary motivator when rewards and consequences generating either/or hope and fear are not being administered justly or fairly.

In most instances, people engage in an activity because they are motivated by both hope and fear. The same activity, experience, or material can be both a positive (hope) or a negative (fear) motivator depending on how it is introduced and how it is perceived. For example, if I tell my daughter she can use the phone an extra 15 minutes on each night that she completes her homework, I would be motivating my daughter out of hope. In contrast, if I told my daughter she would not be able to use the phone at night if she did not complete her homework, I would be motivating her out of fear. If my daughter did not want her friends to be calling her at home, she would perceive the loss of the phone as a reward. If she did not care whether she used the phone or not, then the phone would have no value as a motivator.

In using motivators, it is more effective not to use the same activity, experience, or material as both a reward and a punishment for performance of a desired behavior. Additionally, people usually acquire new desired behaviors more readily if motivators are used that elicit both hope and fear. Rewards as well as consequences for engaging in a desired behavior should be frequent and consistent at first, and the rewards given less frequently over time.

For example, if my goal is to get my 14-year-old daughter to do her homework each night, I might explain to her that I would give her a coupon worth 50 cents each night that she completed her work and, at the end of 30 days, she could cash in the coupons for a given list of activities or materials. For each night she failed to complete her homework, she would lose the privilege for that night to talk on the telephone. Over time, I would diminish the money bonus for compliance.

It is important for parents to understand that in dealing with their children, they are engaging in an act of negotiation. Four cardinal principles of negotiating are introduced to the parents: (1) never negotiate when you are tired, angry, frustrated, feeling guilty, or depressed; (2) always give a little and demand a lot; (3) never be afraid to say no to a deal that is not in your best interest; and (4) only trust your children to do something when they have consistently demonstrated the appropriate competencies to do the task or engage in the activity.

Parents of adolescents in recovery quickly realize that, in most cases, their children had become amotivational, that is, they were neither motivated by hope nor fear, unless the fear centered on not having access to their drugs of choice or being prohibited from engaging in other types of drug-related activities (e.g., going to a rock concert). Other activities, experiences, and materials became of little value to the drug-using teenager. Parents also realized that, in most cases, they had developed the habit of negotiating with their teenagers in a highly charged emotional state. They usually gave a lot and asked for little in return, were extremely afraid to say no to the most absurd propositions presented to them by their chemically dependent child, and unfortunately, consistently fell for their child's famous retort, "You don't trust me!"

Now that their ability to influence their child effectively is gradually being restored, it becomes quite obvious to most of the parents that if they are going to have an effective influence on their child, they are going to have to make a conscientious effort to change how they negotiate with their child. To do otherwise, would be to continue their pattern of co-dependent enabling behavior.

Stress Reduction Techniques

Stress reduction techniques are the last intermediate treatment strategy introduced to the parents. Parents are requested to complete an individualized stress management assessment (Burnett, Kulhavy, & Krug, 1983) which compares 16 personality factors with identified stress in career, family, and personal-social areas. Individual treatment plans are then introduced, and exercises are prescribed to help the parent reduce job, family, and personal stress. Exercises include (1) planning to make your time work for you, (2) learning to compete for important things, (3) enjoying the challenge of work, (4) smoothing out your working days, (5) reviewing and adjusting important life areas, (6) thinking straight about long-term plans, (7) seeing yourself in a better light, (8) easing closer relationships, (9) getting through to other people, (10) standing up for your personal rights, (11) dealing with the little things that bother you, and (12) getting your thoughts together.

Advanced Treatment Strategies

The advanced treatment strategies consist of eight hours of instruction in couples communication (S. Miller et al., 1979) and four 2-hour combined parent-child sessions. Parents must have completed the general, introductory, and intermediate treatment strategies and their teenagers must be in the commitment stage of recovery before these strategies are introduced. These strategies are more effectively conducted in group sessions, but can be introduced in a single family setting. The four combined parent-child sessions should be repeated a least once a month for six months.

Couples Communication

This treatment strategy teaches parents four important components of effective communication: (1) awareness of self, (2) awareness of the other person, (3) styles of communication, and (4) counting yourself and the other person. Couples learn nine skills, four processes, and three frameworks and are then given ample opportunity to practice the skills, processes, and frameworks.

The nine skills include (1) speaking for self, (2) making sense statements, (3) making interpretive statements, (3) making feeling statements, (4) making intention statements, (5) making action statements, (6) attentive listening and observing, (7) encouraging/inviting disclosure, and (9) checking out. The four processes consist of (1) documenting interpretations, (2) shared meaning process, (3) setting procedures, and (4) flexibility in using styles. The three frameworks are (1) awareness wheel, (2) focus of conversation, and (3) styles framework.

Signs and Symptoms of Relapse

Signs of relapse is an advanced treatment strategy that reviews, in a combined group setting with both the parents and their recovering teenagers, the major elements of relapse (refer also to Signs and Symptoms of Relapse and Ten Most Common Causes of Failure in chapter 6). In particular, the parents and the recovering teenagers are reminded about what Louis Binstock (1982, pp. 46–47) coined "the illusion of success."

> *Success is a fickle goddess; when we think we have her, but she knows better.... Many of us are deceived by an event or an accomplishment; it has all the marks of success, and others act as though it were a success, but it fails to satisfy us. We shrug off our doubts; we agree that we have arrived; we don a mask and accept the high popular opinion of ourselves. ...Further accomplishment seems unnecessary. We have abjured the right to go on to true success.*
>
> *Napoleon knew this (little good it did him!); he said once, "the most dangerous moment comes with the victory." The achievement of success is most precarious when it appears to be permanent. Overconfidence sets in; and when a new problem arises we are puzzled and bitter: how can I have trouble now, when I have already succeeded? The answer is that success, being fickle, must be continuously wooed; she can never be won forever and ever. Victory loses its value unless we use it as a means to even greater ends. Of itself it is only temporary, an essentially useless triumph. Talleyrand once commented, "A man can do everything with a sword but sit on it." The same is true with success.*

The parents and their recovering teenagers are cautioned not to rest on their laurels or sit on their success. They are reminded of the twelve step of Alcoholics Anonymous: "Having had a spiritual awakening as the result of these steps...*practice* these principles in all our affairs."

Family Relationships

Family relationships is a treatment strategy designed to help parents and their recovering teenagers resolve family conflicts and to provide an opportunity for the therapist(s) to assess progress and introduce or reinforce more effective conflict resolution strategies. The parents are encouraged to introduce and discuss with their recovering teenagers their expectations for them and to share openly and honestly with their children any concerns they might have and acknowledge any improvements they have observed. Asking the simple question, how are things going with your family? usually serves as an initiator sufficient to generate useful dialogue and instruction.

Dating and Relationships

Dating and relationships is an advanced treatment strategy designed to assist parents in setting meaningful opposite sex guidelines for their recovering teenagers. In sessions with their recovering teenagers, parents are advised that teenagers should not date in the first two years of recovering. These adolescents should be focusing their efforts on their recovery and concentrating on themselves. Relationships with the opposite sex should be limited to group outings. Concepts such as secondary virginity, unhealthy co-dependent relationships, and love versus infatuation are introduced. Parents and their recovering teenagers are advised that when dating does begin, the recovering teenager should be working a solid program of recovery, should group date at first, and should keep the relationship at a friendship level as opposed to an amorous level. The teenager should be cautioned if you do not want to slip (relapse), do not go where it is slippery. Be choosy about where you go to have fun.

Overcoming Fears and Insecurities

This is an advanced treatment strategy designed to help the recovering teenagers and their parents discuss in an open and frank manner recovering issues such as dating, leaving home, AA involvement, leaving the security of treatment, and developing friendships. This time is usefully spent exploring positive constructive solutions to these challenges and sharing them with one another.

Treating Other Family Members

Treatment of other family members including siblings, grandparents, and other relatives uses the same treatment strategies outlined for the parents, with adaptations made to adjust for the age level of the person being treated. It is only necessary to involve grandparents or other relatives directly if they are providing a parental role for the recovering teenager or they have developed a co-dependent enabling relationship with the drug-abusing adolescent.

Especially helpful for siblings of the chemically dependent adolescent is to read, review, and discuss Sharon Wegscheider-Cruse's booklet, *The Family Trap*, and to identify what role they were playing in the family the family hero, scapegoat, lost child, or family mascot. It is also important to interview siblings to determine whether they have had any involvement in drug usage and to what extent. It is not uncommon for other siblings to be involved seriously in drug usage. It is also important to provide avenues for the siblings to express openly and honestly the feelings they experienced while living with their chemically dependent brother or sister. Often, siblings have been physically, emotionally, and/or sexually abused by their older drug-abusing teenage brother or sister.

Summary

This chapter introduced strategies for treating the family members of adolescent substance abusers. General, introductory, intermediate, and advanced strategies for treating co-dependent enabling parents were outlined and discussed. The importance of treating other families members including siblings and grandparents was emphasized.

8

The Chemical Dependency Counselor: Attributes and Skills

Effective counseling with chemically dependent adolescents and their families requires special attributes and skills. This chapter will examine these attributes and skills.

Attributes

Character Strengths

To effectively impact adolescents suffering from the disease of chemical dependency requires counselors who can openly admit their shortcomings and vigorously work at turning them into positive strengths. Progress, not perfection, is asked, but exemplifying a working example of ongoing recovery is essential. Given that modeling or vicarious reinforcement is a dominant mode of learning, combined with the fact that adolescents can spot a fake a mile away, it is imperative that chemical dependency counselors work on improving their cognitive structure as they strive to perfect their character strengths. Recovering teenagers simply will not respond to counselors who do not demonstrate this attribute. Abstinence from cigarettes, alcohol, and other mind-altering drugs is also a prerequisite.

Confidentiality

A counselor who cannot keep his mouth shut will never be effective with any counselee, let alone recovering teenagers. Chemically dependent teenagers must share sensitive, embarrassing, and potentially harmful thoughts and feelings during the process of recovery. An atmosphere of trust and mutual respect must be established for this to occur. Counselors who do not possess this attribute create much havoc for their clients, destroy their bridge of trust, and sometimes can cause them irreversible harm and immeasurable injury. In addition, they leave themselves and the agencies they work for liable for legal action.

Timing and Tact

For some counselors, timing and tact come easily, but for most of us, it emerges from experience. Knowing when to listen, when to advise, when to be directive or nondirective, when to confront or remain silent can increase the effectiveness of our therapeutic efforts.

Especially important for the chemical dependency counselor is having a detailed understanding of the four plateaus of recovery and accurately recognizing on which plateau the client is. For example, a more directive approach is required for clients in the admitting and submitting stages of recovery in contrast to a more nondirective approach for clients in the transmitting stage.

Listenership

The art of listening is an attribute necessary for the chemical dependency counselor to be effective. The counselor must especially learn to listen for thoughts and intentions as well as feelings. He or she must clearly understand how the clients see the world, the words and images the clients use to describe and evaluate their world, and the expectations they have formed about it. Active listening helps the therapist gain this understanding.

Objectivity and Discernment

Recovering teenagers are highly adept at avoiding responsibility for their actions and are extremely facile at getting others to take responsibility for them. They are also skilled at diverting attention from themselves and/or maintaining conversation at very surface levels. Penetrating the denial and refusal layers of the adolescent teenage drug abuser requires, therefore, a very discerning counselor who is not afraid to ask thought-producing, provocative, and sometimes inflammatory questions. It requires flexibility, spontaneity, a sense of immediacy, and concreteness. To penetrate these layers, a counselor must remain objective, exercise good clinical judgment, and not get caught in the web of co-dependency constantly being spun by the teenager in recovery. Similar pitfalls are also present when working with the parents of the chemically dependent teenager, although they often occur more subtly.

Empathy and Understanding

Empathy and understanding is demonstrated by a willingness to become actively involved in another person's life. This attribute requires a willingness to accept people in their current condition, openly and honestly, being careful to separate the person's self-defeating behaviors from the person. It requires a willingness to experience the hurt and suffering of another person while being careful not to feel sorry for the person or yourself. Empathy and understanding requires a willingness to forgo a "holier than thou" attitude, humbly recognizing that you too could become inflicted with the same challenges and difficulties. It involves a capacity for appropriate self-disclosure. Empathy and understanding is saying, "I care enough to help you develop new skills to cope more effectively with your hurts and disappointments."

Honesty

Chemical dependency counselors with a keen sense of honesty are able, when circumstances warrant, to confront, rebuke, and exhort the recovering teenager openly and directly in a loving and caring manner. They have mastered the art of assertive communication and are not afraid to express openly thoughts, feelings, and intentions. They understand the importance of using open and frank communication to penetrate the hardened shells of denial and refusal. These counselors understand how such honesty will produce positive long-term results, even though the initial communication may seem brutal to the client and result in significant painful conflict.

Genuine Interest and Love

To cultivate and develop this attribute requires the chemical dependency counselor to ask the important question: Why do I want to help this person? A person's motives have an important influence on how genuine his or her interest and love will be. Do I have positive regard for others? Do I believe in the worth of people? Do I prejudge people? Do I have similar problems which may hinder my ability to be objective with this client? What are my honest attitudes toward people who have used drugs? Remember, teenage drug abusers have participated in an array of hideous, disgusting, and often illegal activities for which, initially, they show little if any remorse. However, it is essential for the counselor to demonstrate a sincere and genuine interest in the well-being of the teenager he or she is attempting to help, especially if the counselor hopes to be successful in his or her therapeutic efforts.

Patience and Perserverance

Assisting chemically dependent teenagers over the four plateaus of recovery is a slow and arduous process requiring a remarkable degree of patience and perseverance on the part of the therapist. To begin with, it usually takes between 9 and 14 months before the client has cultivated a genuine willingness and readiness to change. Experience has shown that a minimum of 20% of the teenagers will withdraw from treatment before ever developing any motivation to change. It is a fair bet that a least one third of the clients will develop a temporary motivation to change, but will engulf their parents in old co-dependent enabling habits resulting in the parents prematurely withdrawing their children from treatment. This usually occurs when it becomes evident to the teenager that work is required to produce permanent change. Of those remaining, at least half of them will fall prey to the illusion of success, stop doing the things that helped them succeed, and then relapse.

In general, teenage substance abusers perceive treatment as being forced on them, respond in predictable but highly volatile ways, and initially perceive the therapist as the enemy. Therefore, to be effective with this population requires the therapist to demonstrate a strong stick-to-it-ness, an ability to detach when necessary, and a commitment to stay continually focused on desired outcomes. Setting realistic expectations is also essential.

Summary of Attributes

Character strength, confidentiality, timing and tact, listenership, objectivity and discernment, empathy and understanding, honesty, genuine interest and love, and patience and perserverance, these are the attributes required to be an effective chemical dependency counselor. William Glasser (1972) explained:

The helper must be (1) a responsible person, (2) an interested person, (3) a human person, (4) a sensitive person, (5) an objective person, (6) a flexible person, (7) able to fulfill his/her own needs without doing so at the expense of others, (8) neither aloof, superior, nor sacrosanct, (9) able to discuss his own relationships and troubles, (10) able to demonstrate that his/her actions, values and standards are important, (11) strong enough to become involved, (12) strong enough to have his/her values tested by the helpee, (13) able to withstand intense criticism and anger by the very person he/she is trying to help, (14) willing to admit that he/she is far from perfect, (15) able to demonstrate to helpee that he/she can act responsibly—even though it takes great effort, (16) strong instead of expedient, (17) able to withstand the helpee's request for sympathy no matter how the helpee pleads or threatens, (18) able to reject irresponsible action on the helpee's part, (19) willing to watch the patient suffer anxiety if the suffering helps the patient toward accepting responsibility, (20) knowledgeable and understanding about his/her helpee, (21) able to accept his/her helpee as he is at first, (22) free from fear of the helpees behavior no matter how aberrant he/she is, (23) able to remain stable and steady in the face of unusual behavior, (24) able most importantly of all to become emotionally involved with the helpee. To a great extent the helper must be willing to become involved with his/her helpee to the point of being affected by his/her problems or to even suffer with him/her.

Skills

Basic Counseling Skills

For chemical dependency counselors to be effective, they must be facile in using helping skills for "understanding, comfort and crisis utilization, and positive action" (Brammer, 1979, p. 19). Understanding helping skills include listening, leading, reflecting, summarizing, confronting, interpreting, and informing. Comfort and crisis utilization helping skills include supporting, crisis, intervention, centering, and referring. Positive action helping skills include problem solving and decision making and behavior changing.

Figure 8-1 summarizes these helping skills in chart form.

Cognitive-Behavioral Therapy Skills

Effective chemical dependency counselors should have a sound understanding of the principles of cognitive-behavioral therapy (Beck, 1976; Ellis, 1962; Kelly, 1955; Lazarus, 1966; Maultsby, 1984, 1986; Meichen-

For understanding	For comfort and crisis	For political action
1. Listening 1.1 Attending 1.2 Paraphrasing 1.3 Clarifying 1.4 Perception checking 2. Leading 2.1 Indirect leading 2.2 Direct leading 2.3 Focusing 2.4 Questioning 3. Reflecting 3.1 Feeling 3.2 Content 3.3 Experience 4. Summarizing 4.1 Feeling 4.2 Content 4.3 Process 5. Confronting 5.1 Describe feelings 5.2 Expressing feelings 5.3 Feeding back 5.4 Meditating 5.5 Repeating 5.6 Associating 6. Interpreting 6.1 Explaining 6.2 Questioning 6.3 Fantasizing 7. Informing 7.1 Giving information 7.2 Giving advice 7.3 Suggesting	1. Supporting 1.1 Contacting 1.2 Reassuring 1.3 Relaxing 2. Crisis intervening 2.1 Building hope 2.2 Consoling 2.3 Controlling 3. Centering 3.1 Identifying strengths 3.2 Reviewing growth experiences 3.3 Recalling peak experiences 4. Referring	1. Problem Solving and decision making 1.1 Identifying problems 1.2 Changing problems to goals 1.3 Analyzing problems 1.4 Exploring alternatives and implications 1.5 Planning a course of action 1.6 Generalizing to new problems 2. Behavior modifying 2.1 Modeling 2.2 Rewarding 2.3 Extinguishing 2.4 Desensitizing

Figure 8-1 Summary of Helping Skills

From Lawrence M. Brammer, *The Helping Relationship: Process and Skills,* Fourth Edition. Copyright 1988 by Allyn & Bacon. Reprinted with permission.

baum, 1977, 1985; Mischel, 1973; Mowrer, 1960; Peters, 1970; Poppen, 1988; Rokeach, 1970; Siminov, 1970; Spielberger, 1970) and have had ample supervised opportunities to apply these principles in a therapeutic setting. These counselors require training and skill development in the use of cognitive-behavioral techniques and strategies such as those outlined in chapters 5, 6, and 7 of this book. In addition, the effective chemical dependency counselor must have a sound understanding of the emerging personality and cognitive-structure of an adolescent substance abuser and how they relate to the process of addiction (refer to chapter 2).

Chemical Dependency Counseling Skills

The effective chemical dependency counselor must also have a sound and thorough understanding of the principles of chemical dependency counseling (Gabe, 1989; Kentucky Chemical Dependency Counselors' Professional Certification Board, 1987; G. W. Lawson, Ellis, Rivers, 1984; Schuckit, 1984) and have had ample supervised opportunities to apply these principles in a therapeutic setting.

The Kentucky Chemical Dependency Counselors' Professional Certification Board (1987, pp. 9–10) and the National Certification Reciprocity Consortium (NCRC/AODA) requires each certified counselor to have a working knowledge in the following areas: (1) human growth and development; (2) intervention techniques; (3) assessment, interviewing, and diagnostic procedures; (4) the signs symptoms, and phases of chemical dependency and related medical, psychological, social, and spiritual problems; (5) dynamics of denial; (6) treatment planning methodology; (7) counseling modalities and their appropriateness in meeting individual needs; (8) the philosophy, practice, steps, and traditions of AA, Alafam, Alanon, Alateen, Women for Sobriety, NA, and other self-help groups; (9) referral sources and procedures for making client referrals—setting up and maintaining referral and support systems; (10) confidentiality laws and the practices necessary for releasing client information; (11) individual differences in people due to sexual roles, cultural identification, and age; (12) the recovery process through individual and group involvement—patterns of progression in recovery and rehabilitation; and (13) procedures for development of an aftercare plan, including prevention and intervention.

In addition, they require certified counselors to show competency in the following core functions: screening, intake, orientation, assessment, treatment planning, counseling, case management, crisis intervention, client education, referral, reports and record keeping, and consultation with other professionals.

Knowledge of Developmental Theories

Effective chemical dependency counselors also need to have a working knowledge of the major developmental theories of personality development, social development, and intellectual-cognitive development in children and adolescents. Working knowledge of the developmental theories of Piaget, Erikson, Werner, Kohlberg, Freud, and Bandura (Knudtson, 1980), for example, are extremely useful in working with chemically dependent adolescents.

Understanding and assessing the teenager's current stage of personality and social and intellectual development becomes imperative in planning and implementing treatment strategies. Adolescents suffering from the disease of chemical dependency often regress to previous developmental stages, as a result of drug usage, and seldom progress to higher developmental stages while using drugs. Maturational development is "generally regarded to be impeded or halted when adolescents become chemically dependent" (Cavaiola & Kane-Cavaiola, 1989, p. 18). It is not unusual to find a 19-year-old adolescent exhibiting the developmental responses of a 5-year-old when he first enters treatment, and of a 13-year-old adolescent when the effects of the drug usage have initially subsided.

Unfortunately, many chemically dependent adolescents, especially those who have used drugs for a prolonged period of time, find themselves with severe developmental deficiencies once drug usage has ceased. Helping older adolescents and young adults accept this reality is often very difficult, especially when the deficiencies require the late adolescent or young adult to submit to a structured treatment environment viewed as more suitable for younger teenagers.

Knowledge of Family Systems Theories

A working knowledge of family systems theories is also desirable for the effective chemical dependency counselor. Working knowledge of the conceptual framework of communication theories such as those of Don Jackson, Virginia Satir, and Jay Haley and the structural theories of Murray Bowen, David Kantor, and Salvador Minuchin (Okun & Rappaport, 1980) are very useful in counseling chemically dependent teenagers and their families.

For example, introducing parents to Virginia Satir's (1964) five patterns of communication—placating, blaming, super reasonable, irrelevant, and congruent, and the rewards and consequences for using each style—helps recovering teenagers and their parents to recognize quickly their dominant style and encourages them to explore alternatives to communicating with each other more effectively.

A working knowledge of family systems theories also helps the therapist prepare clients for the inevitable fact that, if one person in the family system changes, the change will influence the responses of other family members. It is important to remember that not only is the chemically dependent adolescent dysfunctional at the time of intake but he or she has also profoundly influenced the functioning of the rest of the family members. In most cases, the chemically dependent adolescent has worsened established communication and structural patterns or has introduced new communication and structural patterns that are detrimental to the well-being of the entire family.

Knowledge of Other Counseling Theories

Knowledge of other counseling theories is also a desirable skill of the effective chemical dependency counselor. A working knowledge of gestalt therapy (Korb, Gorrell, & Van De Riet, 1989), reality therapy (Glasser, 1965, 1984), and actualizing therapy (Shostrom, 1977) can be very useful.

Gestalt Therapy

Korb et al. (1989, p. 20) provide an excellent explanation of gestalt therapy.

> *The essence of gestalt therapy is an understanding of organismic gestalt formation and completion within each person's experience. Events are experienced in figure and ground terms, a natural process of emerging figures that have meaning in terms of the context or background against which they are experienced. This process is an integral part of spontaneous self-regulation. Needs of the individual emerge spontaneously through homeostatic process and are resolved as other needs emerge. Gestalt therapy assumes that (1) every organism is creatively adjusting to the self and the environment at all times, and (2) such creative adjustment is possible because each person who enters therapy has the energy and resources necessary for self-regulation. Neurosis results when natural self-regulating mechanisms are disrupted.*
>
> *Principles of therapy—contact, change process, affirmation, clarity, appropriateness, respect, and experimentation—derive from the basic gestalt principles.*

Korb and his colleagues (1989, pp. 16–18) further explain that *contact* "has been identified as spontaneous concentration... the sense of the unitary interfunctioning of you and your environment." The *change process* "happens through present-centered, spontaneous concentration on any figural aspect of the client's experience." *Affirmation* "is an ingredient of the contact experience... recognition and affirmation of personal truth in present experiences brings a cessation of conflict or confusion because completion of an important gestalt occurs at that time." *Clarity,* "the goal is to bring clarity out of the confusion and conflict the client has been experiencing." *Appropriateness* "describes the kinds of interventions or responses the therapist makes in the therapeutic context." Respect implies that the therapist "becomes a participant-observer in the therapeutic encounter, paradoxically being present and contactful but simultaneously reserving personal judgement in favor of neutral observations." *Experimentation* encourages the client "in the safe emergency of the therapeutic relationship... to experiment with experiences that may generate awareness or remove blockages to self-regulation."

Although the therapist may disagree with many of the philosophical assumptions of gestalt therapy, the ability to use the "I and thou, here and now" gestalt therapy techniques proves especially useful during the admitting and committing stages of recovery. In these initial stages of recovery, the chemically dependent teenager experiences three major conflicts. First, how do I get in touch with thoughts, feelings, and behaviors and make sense out of my world, now that I am no longer under the influence of mind altering drugs and a drug culture? Second, how do I recognize and make sense out of my past mistakes, now that I am beginning to look at my past more honestly? Third, how do I recognize and begin to trust a self-regulatory system that has been severely distorted and damaged by my drug usage and exposure to the drug culture? These become critical immediate issues for the recovering teenager. Experimentation within the supporting boundaries of a well-defined therapeutic community enables recovering teenagers to grapple with these conflicts as they embrace and act on new gestalts on which to frame their continuing existence.

Reality Therapy

At the core of reality therapy is the choice one makes on how to cope with reality. One chooses to deal with reality by becoming withdrawn, deliquent, and irresponsible or chooses loving worthwhile and responsible ways to cope. Glasser (1965, p. 41) explains:

> *In summary, then, our basic job as therapists is to become involved with the patient and then get him to face reality. When confronted with reality by the therapist with whom he is involved, he is forced again and again to decide whether or not he wishes to take the responsible path. Reality may be painful, it may be harsh, it may be dangerous, but it changes slowly. All any man can hope to do is struggle with it in a*

responsible way by doing right and enjoying the pleasure or suffering the pain that may follow.

Six underlying assumptions govern the treatment course prescribed by reality therapists (Glasser, 1965, pp. 44-45).

1. Therapist "do not accept the concept of mental illness...a mentally ill person who has no responsibility for his behavior."
2. "Working in the present and toward the future, we do not get involved with the patient's history because we can neither change what happened to him nor accept the fact that he is limited by his past."
3. "We relate to our patients as ourselves, not as transference figures."
4. "We do not look for unconscious conflicts or the reasons for them. A patient cannot become involved with us by excusing his behavior on the basis of unconscious motivations."
5. "We emphasize the morality of behavior...the issue of right and wrong."
6. "We teach patients better ways to fulfill their needs."

Reality therapy concentrates on the here and now and on the appropriateness of behavior. The reality therapist helps clients to evaluate current behavior and then contracts with them to help them develop plans designed to change undesirable behavior. Encouraging them in the process, the reality therapist accepts no excuses from clients for not changing, but praises and approves the clients' accomplishment of agreed on changes.

Reality therapy techniques are useful in the admitting and committing stages of recovery; however, they are especially helpful during the commitment stage of recovery. Reality therapy techniques that encourage the recovering youth to examine "here and now" behaviors and honestly evaluate their appropriateness foster and help develop a motivation to change. Once motivated, genuine commitment can then be empirically tested by monitoring the extent of behavior changes, the extent the client achieves contracted goals, and the degree to which the client offers excuses for unfulfilled commitments.

Actualizing Therapy

Actualizing therapy "emerges from ten parameters of psychotherapy that have their roots in the works of many established leaders in the field... showing how Rogers, Pearls, and Ellis use them in their work...

actualizing therapy attempts to integrate the central dimensions of each of these approaches" (Shostrom, 1977, pp. 27-28) Whereas Rogers focuses on feelings and the client therapist relationship, and Pearls on awareness and the "here and now," and Ellis on rationality and problem solving, Shostrom's actualizing therapy attempts to synthesize creatively these three approaches to psychotherapy. Shostrom (1977, p. 2) explains:

> *A fundamental thesis of actualizing therapy is that the problem of change is not one change from mental illness to mental health, but rather of change from deficiency to fulfillment and from deadness to aliveness. Actualizing therapy is a fundamental process of educating the potential within...to actually believe that out of one's self-defeating manipulations will come increased actualizing.... Actualizing therapy, therefore, is a positively oriented system of therapy with innovative features particularly designed to motivate clients to move toward actualizing.*

Actualizing therapy is a therapy of hope that assumes individual uniqueness, here and now emphasis, freedom, responsibility, learning, and social interaction.

Although useful in the admitting, submitting and committing stages of recovery, the techniques of actualizing therapy are especially useful during the transmitting stages of recovery. Actualizing therapy is beneficial in helping the recovering teenager to confront the sharing-selfish and love-hate polarities that are at the core of the personality of the adolescent substance abuser and that had become negatively skewed as a result of involvement with drugs and the drug culture. During the transmitting stages of recovery, the teenager not only is committing himself or herself to continue to remain drug free one day at a time, but he or she is also insisting on following a program of action that will help transform weaknesses into strengths, manipulations into actualizing potentials, as he or she strives to develop character qualities that exemplify and typify the elements of sharing and love.

Cognitive-Behavioral One-on-One Counseling

In his book, Rational Behavior Therapy, Maultsby (1984) provides an excellent resource for the novice chemical dependency counselor to begin to learn and understand how to conduct effective cognitive-behavioral one-on-one counseling. Particularly helpful is part 3 and part 4 of the book.

In applying the skills of one-on-one cognitive-behavioral counseling with recovering chemically dependent adolescents, the therapist would be well advised to remember the following: (1) initially, the client has a strong motive to be evasive, resistant, and dishonest; (2) the therapist is always vulnerable to becoming a co-dependent enabler; (3) initially, the self-talk of denial and refusal must be the focus of attention; (4) the goal is to help the teenager develop a self-talk that will create a willingness and readiness to change and that will sustain desired change and to help the teenager through the dissonance that will emerge when attempting change; (5) behavioral changes will preceed attitude changes (i.e., a posteriori cognitions will change before a priori cognitions); (6) setting realistic expectations is essential for the rational well-being of both the therapist and the counselee; and (7) group counseling usually is more effective and efficient and provides the recovering teenager with greater accountability.

Cognitive-Behavioral Group Counseling

Conducting effective cognitive-behavioral group counseling with chemically dependent adolescents requires the careful orchestration of several cognitive-behavioral skills coupled with basic skills of group management. Several factors need to be taken into consideration before, during, and after each group session. These factors include (1) group characteristics such as age, sex, types of drugs used, socio-economic background, psycho-social history, and stage of recovery; (2) group size; (3) therapeutic goals; (4) length of each session; (5) group rules; (6) selection of therapeutic aids and techniques; and (7) type of group, i.e., educational and/or therapeutic.

My personal experience conducting hundreds of cognitive-behavioral group counseling sessions with recovering adolescents has suggested that the more heterogeneous the group, the more effective the learning experience. Group size can vary from a minimum of five to eight teenagers to as many as one hundred, depending on the goals for the group and the type of group activity. It is especially helpful to have a balance of males and females in the group, except in situations where sexually sensitive material needs to be discussed; then, segregating groups by sex and/or individual sessions prove more helpful.

It is extremely important to overload the group with teenagers who are further along in their recovery. Doing so helps establish a positive group norm and provides a stronger basis of support to reach out to and confront teenagers in the early stages of recovery. Remember, the denial and refusal and self-destructive attitude layers of the cognitive structure are well entrenched, especially in newly recovering teenagers.

It is recommended that therapeutic groups be conducted by two therapists, preferably one of each sex. Having more than one therapists helps with group management, is safer, and allows more combinations of therapeutic interactions to occur. Group rules may vary depending on the needs of the group, but three rules seem to apply in general: confidentiality, honesty, and mutual respect for other group members. Time length may vary from 45 minutes to 2 hours depending on the type of group being conducted.

Types of cognitive-behavioral groups with chemically dependent adolescents include (1) educational sessions; (2) carefronting the client's past, present, and future; (3) focusing on family relationships (past, present, and future); (4) focusing on sexually sensitive material (i.e., rape, incest, sexual abuse, homosexuality, abortion, sexual promiscuity); and (5) maintaining committing and transmitting attitudes.

Educational Group Sessions

Educational group sessions provide excellent opportunities to teach the "basics" to recovering teenagers. The basics include a working knowledge of (1) the Twelve Steps of Alcoholics Anonymous, (2) the ABCDEs of emotion and behavior, (3) the three signs, (4) the serenity prayer and the Lord's Prayer, (5) the five criteria, (6) the seven steps to a happy (F)ACE, (7) the five stages to change, and (8) the fallible and correctable human being. Additional helpful information that can be taught in group sessions include the awareness wheel, the feeling log, the daily moral inventory, developing a life plan, the rebel without a cause syndrome, searching and fearless moral inventory of the past, law of the harvest, self-downing and self-acceptance cycle, styles of irrational or dysfunctional thinking, recovery scripts, goal setting, relapse symptoms list, the language of anger and resentment, and secondary virginity. (Refer to chapters 5 and 6 for a detailed description of each of these topics.)

Carefronting, Family, and Sexual Group Sessions

Group cognitive-behavioral sessions that carefront the teenager's past, present, or future, involve a discussion of family issues, or deal with sensitive sexual material are used most frequently during the admitting and submitting stages of recovery. These group sessions are designed to help the recovering teenager get in touch with and identify self-defeating patterns of emotions and behavior and begin to identify the self-talk that creates and maintains these self-defeating responses to life's situations.

These group sessions are greatly enhanced by beginning each group session with a predetermined group topic to which each member of the group can relate, and particularly, by introducing a subject that can begin to jar the memories of the newly recovering teenagers, thereby activating their past experiences and their accompanying emotions.

For example, a group session begins with the discussion of the topic "showing our feelings." The two group facilitators start by relating to the topic and sharing how difficult it used to be for them to share feelings. Then, the group facilitators call on several group members who have already worked through their insecurities of sharing feelings to relate their experiences. The more experienced group members are encouraged to share some of the more difficult situations they encountered, the consequences they experienced from involvement with drug usage, and the feelings that accompanied these experiences. Slowly and ever so gradually the group facilitators eventually center in on newer members of the group and invite them to share some of their experiences and feelings. While this discussion is progressing, the group facilitators listen carefully for self-defeating ideas and beliefs expressed by members of the group and, when appropriate, directly challenge the usefulness of holding on to such beliefs.

Group topics are introduced to generate discussion that will help the facilitators focus on group members' faulty beliefs and self-destructive emotional and behavioral responses. Past experiences are only examined to illuminate present self-destructive patterns of thinking and to examine the consequences of continuing to act on them or to help the teenager vent past hurts and disappointments and begin to examine more effective means to manage them. The future is introduced to emphasize the conse-

Educational	Carefronting	Family Sexual	Committing
powerlessness	honesty	pre-marital sex	unity
unmanagability	images	abuse/neglect	appreciation
five criteria	humility	secrets	commitment
FHB/CHB	ego	relationships	love
moral inventory	insecurity	parents	accomplishment
serenity prayer	priorities	fears	forgiveness
three signs	trust	rejection	faith
steps 1, 2, 3	friendships	dignity	serenity
steps 4-9	rebellion	vulnerability	blessings
steps 10-12	loneliness	compromising	direction

Figure 8–2 Examples of group discussion topics

quences of not changing and the benefits that can be obtained by committing to a new course of action. The present is used to help the recovering teenagers fully understand just how powerless and unmanageable their lives have become by choosing to accept and live by their current set of self-defeating beliefs and the ensuing "druggie" life style that results.

Figure 8-2 lists several examples of group discussion topics that are useful in helping recovering teenagers begin to talk about themselves and discover self-defeating emotional and behavioral responses.

Committing and Transmitting Group Sessions

Teenagers in the committing and transmitting stages of recovery can benefit from cognitive-behavioral group sessions as developed by Maultsby (1981) and adapted by Ross (1985b). Group leaders in these sessions (1) instruct the group in the principles and technologies of cognitive-behavioral therapy, (2) monitor group members as to how well they apply these principles and technologies to their current challenges, and (3) facilitate constructive and supportive group interaction.

Initially, group members review the principles and technologies of these emotional self-help aides: (1) the awareness wheel, (2) feeling log, (3) five criteria for rational thinking, (4) ABCDE's of emotion and behavior, (5) seven steps to a happy (F)ACE, (6) the change process, and (7) script writing. In addition, the recovering teenager is introduced to time management and goal-setting skills.

After they complete their review of the principles and technologies, group members are encouraged to complete and share seven steps to a happy (F)ACE with other group members, thereby deriving the benefit of group feedback to their specific issues. Group members are also encouraged to write and share with the group self-acceptance scripts, say no to drugs scripts, and scripts centering on character defects such as intolerance and resentment, self-pity and depression, anxiety, jealousy, fear of failure, fear of success, false pride, short-term self-interest, and self-centeredness and selfishness (see Weinberg and Kosloske, 1977).

Singing as a Group Facilitator

Singing is an important and often overlooked group facilitator that can be utilized to introduce and reinforce important cognitive-behavioral concepts and other ideas important for recovery. Introducing specific songs at the beginning of a group session often helps to establish a mood conducive to the unraveling of painful experiences, and careful selection of tunes to end a group session not only reinforces any insights gained but creates an atmosphere of hope and renewal, both essential for a recovering teenager coping with the emotional pain of chemical dependency.

Critiquing Group Sessions

Critiquing group sessions (Ross, 1985a) is an excellent vehicle to help both novice and experienced cognitive-behavioral group therapists improve their skills. Questions that can be used in critiquing group sessions include the following:

1. Did the therapists at the beginning introduce songs that help set an appropriate mood and end the group with a song that would reinforce insights learned and/or inspire hope and renewal?
2. Did the therapists determine in advance who they wanted to work with in the group?
3. Did the therapists select a group topic that everyone could relate to?
4. Did the therapists pick a group topic that was relevant to the needs of the group members?
5. Did the therapists relate themselves to the group topic?
6. Did the therapists first call on more advanced teenagers in recovery to encourage the participation of newer teenagers in recovery?
7. Did the therapists allow many people to relate in the session, not spending too much time on only a few group members?
8. Did the therapists call on and encourage the participation of new group members?
9. Did the therapists utilize other group members in providing feedback?
10. Did therapists stay actively involved with the group?
11. Did the therapists change or modify the group discussion when appropriate and take advantage of emerging opportunities to teach new insights?
12. Did the therapists introduce appropriate cognitive-behavioral principles or technologies?
13. Did the therapists have the group or individual group members set any therapeutic goals or assign any homework that would reinforce principles or technologies introduced?
14. Did the therapists summarize or have the group summarize what was learned in the group?
15. Did the therapists help group members identify and examine self-defeating emotions and behaviors or help group members cope more effectively with their feelings of hurt, disappointment, anger, pity, guilt, shame, worry, and fear?
16. Did the therapists effectively use understanding helping skills?
17. Did the therapists effectively use comfort and crisis utilization helping skills?
18. Did the therapists effectively use positive action helping skills?

19. Did the therapists present themselves respectfully (i.e., good posture; appropriate dress; avoiding hands in pocket or mouth; avoiding use of foul language, druggie slang, name calling, labeling, and the use of generalities)?

Summary of Skills

The complete chemical dependency counselor will have developed competencies in basic and chemical dependency counseling skills including a working knowledge of the steps and principles of Alcoholics Anonymous. In addition, the complete counselor will demonstrate competency in one-on-one and group cognitive-behavioral counseling and will have developed a working knowledge of the principles of cognitive-behavioral therapy; related therapies, especially gestalt, reality, and actualizing therapies; developmental theories; family system theories; and (5) theories of chemical dependency counseling. In short, the complete chemical dependency counselor will be competent in counseling theory, practice, and technique.

Summary

In this chapter, the attributes and skills of a chemical dependency counselor were outlined and discussed. Attributes included (1) character strengths, (2) confidentiality, (3) timing and tact, (4) listernership, (5) objectivity and discernment, (6) empathy and understanding, (7) honesty, (8) genuine interest and love, and (9) patience and perseverance.

Skills included (1) basic counseling skills; (2) cognitive-behavioral therapy skills; (3) chemical dependency counseling skills including a working knowledge of the steps and principles of Alcoholics Anonymous; (4) knowledge of developmental theories; (5) knowledge of family systems theories; (6) knowledge of other counseling theories, especially gestalt, reality, and actualizing therapies; (7) cognitive-behavioral one-on-one counseling; and (8) cognitive-behavioral group counseling.

9

Efficacy and Efficiency of Treatment

In this chapter the critical questions of efficacy and efficiency of treatment will be examined. *Efficacy* raises the issue as to whether the prescribed program of treatment has the power to produce a desirable effect or outcome. *Efficiency* raises the issue of cost—what amounts of energy, time, and money are required to produce the desired effect or outcome. If a prescribed treatment program is not efficacious, then it does not matter what it costs. If a prescribed treatment program is not efficient, than those who can benefit from it will be significantly limited.

Current State of the Art

Friedman and Glichman (1986, p. 669) reported that "very little is known about the actual 'state of the art' of the treatment that is being provided for adolescent substance abusers." They elaborated:

> *There is, therefore, a clearly demonstrated need for careful and thorough systematic study, evaluation, and analysis of youth drug treatment programs to determine what types of program orientation, treatment philosophies, counseling and psychotherapy modalities, types of alternative activity programs, and characteristics of the treater are effective. To study the relationship of the treatment process and the context of treatment to treatment outcome is even more difficult.*

Friedman and Glichman's conclusions could not have been more dramatically illustrated than what was presented in a CBS News "Insight Investigation" in May 1985 that charged that many troubled youngsters "are being put away for treatment they don't need." The editorial staff of the U.S. Journal of Drug and Alcohol Dependence (1985) further explained:

> *Questions are being asked about the adequacy of treatment programs for adolescent alcoholics and drug abusers and about the appropriateness of screening and admissions criteria to such programs. So they should be.*
>
> *Hardly a week goes by that we don't hear about yet another adolescent program being opened, about a new treatment method or "style" being tried, about a new crisis thundering around our shoulders that supposedly threatens a whole generation of young people.*
>
> *...This is a very new field of therapy, and you don't build a treatment technology for an illness as complex as alcoholism or drug addiction overnight.... Without some form of program and patient evaluation we can only guess at the value—or the harm—being provided by some programs selling their products in the health care marketplace. (pp. 1–2)*

In the same journal issue, one expert in the field of chemical dependency, Gerald Shulman, emphasized:

> *It's a humbling experience to try to come up with the state-of-the-art in adolescent treatment. For one thing, there has been very little research of CD among youth, and there's been even less scientific investigation of treatment and evaluation. (p. 15)*

Further compounding the problem is the state of the art of the methodology available to evaluate treatment outcome. M. B. Sobell, Serge, Sobell, Roy, and Stevens (1987, p. 113) explained:

> *Although considerable methodological improvements have occurred over time, major methodological deficiencies continue to characterize much of the literature, with inadequate reporting of subjects' pretreatment characteristics (e.g., severity of dependency) being the most striking problem. Pervasive differences across studies regarding the types of data gathered and the ways in which findings are reported seriously impede attempts to compare studies and weaken the types of conclusions that can be drawn about treatment efficacy in general.*

Goldstein, Surber, and Wilner (1984, p. 479) indicated that "outcome evaluation studies in the areas of alcohol and drug abuse have suffered design problems. The lack of control groups, prospective designs, adequate outcome measures, and sufficient follow-up has presented the major difficulties."

Hoffmann, Sonis, and Halikas (1987, pp. 457–458) identified six issues that need to be considered before adequate assessment of relative efficacy of treatment programs can be attempted: (1) differential referral sources, (2) differential characteristics of the patient population, (3) differential characteristics of treatment programs, (4) presence or absence of differential treatment strategies responsive to the particular needs of individual adolescents, (5) differential response of the youngster to the treatment process, and (6) identifying appropriate outcome variables. They concluded, "Evaluation of the efficacy of treatment programming for adolescents with substance abuse issues is therefore a complex and as yet poorly developed field of inquiry."

In summary, the overall state of the art of treatment in the field of adolescent chemical dependency and accompanying methodology for evaluating treatment outcome is, at best, emerging.[1]

Four Types of Evaluation

Practitioners concerned about the efficacy and efficiency of treatment would be well advised to become familiar with the now classic presentation in the field of educational evaluation, *Educational Evaluation and Decision Making,* by Stufflebeam et al. (1971). In this book, evaluation is defined as "the process of delineating, obtaining, and providing useful information for judging decision alternatives" (p. 40). Four types of evaluation that can provide useful information for judging decision alternatives are discussed. They include context, input, process, and product evaluation.

> *Context evaluation is defined as a systematic and macroanalytic process for the purpose of providing a rationale for determination of objectives for the system. It defines the environment, describes the desired and actual conditions pertaining to the environment, identifies unmet needs and unused opportunities, and diagnoses the problems that prevent needs from being met and opportunities from being used. (Stufflebeam et al., 1991, p. 353)*

Context evaluation would address questions such as

1. What specific needs are you attempting to address with your prescribed treatment approach?
2. What is chemical dependency?
3. To what degree and extent are adolescents encountering problems with chemical dependency?
4. What kinds of adolescents are encountering problems with chemical dependency?
5. How is it determined that an adolescent is experiencing a chemical dependency problem?
6. What kinds of treatment programs are currently available and have been available in the past to address adolescent chemical dependency problems?
7. What kinds of treatment strategies have been shown effective in alleviating adolescent chemical dependency problems?

> *Input evaluation is essentially ad hoc and microanalytic, and its purpose is to provide information for determining how to utilize resources to meet program goals. It identifies and assesses relevant capabilities of responsible agencies, strategies for achieving program goals, and designs for implementing a selective strategy. (Stufflebeam et al., 1991, p. 354)*

Input evaluation would address efficiency questions such as

1. What will it cost to address these needs in terms of energy, time, and money?
2. What kinds of professional staffing are required to treat chemically dependent adolescents?
3. What kinds of treatment strategies should be used to treat the problem?
4. Should the prescribed treatment be implemented in an inpatient, outpatient, or other kind of setting?
5. How long in duration should the prescribed treatment be?
6. Should family members be included as part of the prescribed treatment?
7. What should be the goals and objectives of the prescribed treatment?

> *Process evaluation provides periodic feedback to persons responsible for implementing plans and procedures. It has three objectives: (1) to detect or predict defects in procedural designs or its implementation during the implementation stages, (2) to provide information for program deci-*

> *sions, and (3) to maintain a record of procedure as it occurs. (Stufflebeam et al., 1971, p. 354)*

Process evaluation would address quality assurance questions such as

1. Is the treatment being delivered in a timely manner by appropriately trained professionals?
2. What evidence is available that the treatment was actually received by the adolescent?
3. Are prerequisite treatments being successfully implemented prior to the introduction of additional treatments?
4. Is adequate time being allowed for the adolescent to benefit from the prescribed treatment?
5. Does the staff have an adequate working knowledge of the treatment strategies being used?
6. Are the roles and functions of the various staff adequately defined?
7. Is adequate documentation being made of any disruption of the prescribed treatment?

> *Product evaluation measures and interprets attainment at the end of the cycle of the project and as often as necessary during the project term. It assesses the extent to which ends are being attained with respect to change efforts within the system. (Stufflebeam et al., 1971, p. 354)*

Product evaluation would address outcome questions such as

1. What were the intermediate and long-term results of the prescribed treatment?
2. What were the secondary and tertiary outcomes of the prescribed treatment?
3. What were the potential dangers of the prescribed treatment?
4. Did 15-year-olds benefit from the prescribed treatment more than 18-year-olds?
5. Which treatment strategies were shown effective in producing the desired treatment outcomes?
6. Were female counselors more effective with the adolescents than their male counterparts?
7. How effective were the treatment strategies in keeping the adolescent in treatment?

Applying the concepts of context, input, process, and product evaluation focuses attention on global evaluation issues important to determining the efficacy and efficiency of adolescent substance abuse treatment programs. These concepts address the importance of (1) clearly identifying the need being addressed (context), (2) specifically defining the resources and the prescribed treatment required to address the need (input), (3) carefully determining whether the prescribed treatment was adequately administered and actually received (process), and (4) accurately assessing whether the prescribed treatment produced the desired results necessary to alleviate the need (product).

Measuring Program Outcomes

Despite the apparent challenges to conducting effective evaluations of program outcomes, chemical dependency treatment programs for adolescent substance abusers do provide measurable outcomes for determining the effectiveness of treatment. For example, Ross (1983a) adapted from the work of Yochelson and Samenow (1976) the following set of criteria to address the question of program outcome of an adolescent substance abuse program. The criteria include determining the degree to which

1. The teenager is free of all mind-altering substances, tobacco products, and excessive use of sugar products and caffeine
2. The teenager experiences significant reduction in levels of anger, anxiety, and depression and begins to show significant increases in levels of serenity, calmness, and cheer
3. The teenager demonstrates openness and honesty when relating to others in the group
4. The teenager is receptive to new ideas, new ways of thinking, new insights about self, and to other people's point of view
5. The teenager constructively accepts criticism from peers, staff, parents, and significant others
6. The teenager no longer accepts excuses for destructive ways of thinking, feeling, and acting
7. The teenager no longer blames others for his or her mistakes
8. The teenager has replaced an "I can't" attitude with a "I can" attitude
9. The teenager is not afraid to accept new challenges
10. The teenager uses mistakes from the past to plan responsible future behavior
11. The teenager demonstrates patience in achieving goals
12. The teenager demonstrates responsible long-range planning in the achievement of goals

13. The teenager demonstrates sustained effort in the achievement of responsible goals
14. The teenager considers others when making decisions (demonstrates empathy)
15. The teenager demonstrates a sustained concern for others (e.g., peers, family members)
16. The teenager successfully completes responsible obligations to others and self
17. The teenager does not use or step on other people to achieve objectives
18. The teenager has an appreciation for self
19. The teenager demonstrates self-generated responsible initiatives (i.e., does not always rely on others, willingness to fact find, no desire for guarantees or perfectionism)
20. The teenager demonstrates a genuine fear of returning to a "druggie life" style
21. The teenager demonstrates ability to immerse his- or herself in a responsible interest, sticks with it, and allows the interest to develop
22. The teenager has demonstrated the ability to accept faults in other people
23. The teenager has demonstrated to others trustworthiness
24. The teenager no longer views obstacles to achieving something as an injustice or put-down
25. The teenager has realistic expectations for self
26. The teenager recognizes that setbacks are not put-downs, but are important events in life from which one grows
27. The teenager is able to adapt to Murphy's law—"If anything can go wrong, it will"
28. The teenager demonstrates the ability to bounce many balls at once—maintain a family relationship, do well in school, and continue to work a daily program of recovery
29. The teenager no longer insists that his or her way is the only way to do things
30. The teenager no longer believes that self-worth is dependent on achieving a particular goal
31. The teenager has learned to deal effectively with periods of discouragement, boredom, and anger without the use of mind-altering drugs
32. The teenager no longer views power for its own sake, but views power and control as means to help serve others
33. The teenager understands and practices humility
34. The teenager demonstrates the ability to work hard and to do one's best without being excessively tense over factors beyond one's control

35. The teenager does not expect praise or credit for performing routine duties that responsible people carry out automatically
36. The teenager has eliminated old friends, old places, and old things (old "druggie" ties) from his or her life
37. The teenager has eliminated super-optimistic thinking—believing that he or she is in control of everything, has all the necessary information, and no longer needs to work a program of recovery
38. The teenager demonstrates thrift and responsible money management
39. The teenager demonstrates efficient and effective performance at home, school, work, and in working a program of recovery
40. The teenager has grasped and practiced a life style that excludes premartial sex
41. The teenager practices daily a twelve-step program of recovery
42. The teenager feels genuinely proud and happy about no longer living a "druggie" life style

In addition, outcome measures assessing parental change might include the degree to which (1) parental co-dependent enabling behaviors decreased; (2) parental anxiety, anger, and depression decreased; and (3) parental ability to influence their teenager effectively increased.

Additional outcome measures of overall family improvement might include, but are not limited to, (1) strength or weakness of parental coalition; (2) equality of parental power; (3) negotiability of parental roles; (4) clearness, spontaneousness, and responsiveness of family communication; (5) intimacy, autonomy and inter-connectedness of family members; (6) feeling tone of family (fun and energetic versus hostile and cynical); (7) clearness of family values/goals; (8) effectiveness and adaptability of family decision making; (9) clearness and flexibility of family rules; (10) extent of family traditions; (11) frequency of family leisure time; (12) family members' enjoyment of work/school; (13) degree of . spiritual awareness; (14) degree of optimistic orientation to life by family members; (15) degree of involvement in relationship to the outside world; and (16) degree of family spirit (pride).

Summary

In this chapter, issues of efficacy and efficiency of treatment were examined. The current state of the art of adolescent treatment programs and the adequacy of methodologies available to assess their effectiveness were reviewed. In addition, four types of evaluation were introduced: context, input, process, and product. Measurable outcome variables for adolescent treatment programs were also discussed.

Endnote

1. Given the current "state of the art" of chemical dependency treatment and the challenge of measuring its effectiveness, parents and clinicians seeking help for adolescents with a drug problem may encounter difficulties finding appropriate treatment for a chemically dependent teenager and would be well advised, therefore, to exercise the business principle "caveat emptor"—let the buyer beware—when considering and choosing any treatment program.

10

A Model Program for Treating Adolescent Substance Abuse

In this chapter a model program for treating adolescent substance abusers will be introduced.[1]

Rationale

Model Treatment Program, Inc. is a drug prevention and treatment program established to provide cost-effective state-of-the-art treatment for chemically dependent youth and their families. It is an organization dedicated to helping youth involved in alcohol and drug usage redirect their lives along more positive drug-free pathways.

> *Children are our best and most important resource. The quality of tomorrow's world will be determined by the development of our children today. Those who survive the current century may live in a world unrecognizable to us, but we have the responsibility to prepare them to cope, to develop personal goals, to live with themselves and others. Ours is the responsibility to help them make their tomorrow better than our today. (Sunday Patriot News, October 21, 1979)*

Model Treatment Program, Inc. utilizes a comprehensive treatment approach designed to address medical complications resulting from or exacerbated by drug usage, to teach adolescents how to stop using drugs and not return to their use, and to teach adolescents how to achieve maximum mental, emotional, and spiritual health without the use of drugs while maintaining a relationship with self, family, and others and pursuing school, vocational, leisure time, financial, and community goals. This treatment approach is also family-based, as it teaches parents how to more effectively motivate their children and develop better lines of communication and interaction patterns with them.

Chemical dependency is a disease of attitudes leading to the use and abuse of mind-altering substances (e.g., alcohol, marijuana, cocaine) culminating in physical deterioration of the body, emotional instability, and spiritual bankruptcy. It is a progressive disease with four distinct stages: (1) initial usage, (2) problem usage, (3) psychological addiction, and (4) physiological addiction. It also involves the formation of a distinct self-defeating self-talk that left unchallenged will form the foundation of a distinct personality and cognitive structure that will ultimately lead to the untimely death of the youth.

Model Treatment Program, Inc. uses various treatment strategies derived from cognitive-behavioral, reality, gestalt, actualizing, and family systems therapies; developmental theories; the twelve steps of Alcoholics Anonymous, and Judeo-Christian principles. These treatment strategies are designed to help chemically dependent adolescents identify and change self-defeating emotional and behavioral responses and overcome the challenges presented by four distinct but interrelated plateaus of recovery: admitting, submitting, committing, and transmitting.

Each plateau represents an important stage of the treatment process and contains a distinct set of distorted thinking patterns that hinder the physical, emotional, and spiritual recovery of the adolescent. Methods are employed that directly or indirectly identify, challenge, or change the distorted self-talk that makes up the self-defeating cognitive structure of chemically dependent teenagers.

Treatment strategies are only effective if they are presented within a framework of clearly defined treatment objectives. Treatment objectives include:

1. Identification of how drug usage significantly interfered with work, school, family, friendships, leisure time, society, finances, and self
2. Recognition of impaired ability to manage daily activities and make reasonable life decisions
3. Acknowledgment of a drug problem
4. Recognition of a tendency to blame others or circumstances for drug usage problem

5. Identification of feelings of anger, guilt, resentment, hostility, self-pity, loneliness, apathy, hopelessness, rejection, despair, isolation, embarrassment, and shame
6. Identification of the irrational thinking patterns of denial and refusal that perpetuate emotional and behavioral responses that block the development of willingness and readiness to work a program of recovery
7. Development of the belief that others in the group and group therapist(s) can provide significant help and support if asked
8. Development of the belief that change is possible
9. Recognition of fallibility and correctiveness
10. Increase in tolerance for frustration and stress
11. Demonstration of willingness to follow rules, accept structure, and follow directions of people in authority
12. Beginning the rebuilding of a family relationship
13. Remaining free of all mind-altering chemicals and tobacco products
14. Identifying and addressing any medical and/or psychological complications that might complicate or disrupt treatment
15. Identify and develop a plan of action to change self-defeating irrational thinking patterns that maintain and perpetuate
    a. drug usage
    b. destructive emotions and behaviors
    c. family discord
    d. poor school and/or work performance
    e. conflict with authority figures
    f. conflict with peers
    g. attitudes of selfishness and self-centeredness
    h. resentments, fears, anger, pity, and depression
    i. low frustration tolerance (impatience)
16. Practicing new rational thinking patterns that will maintain and perpetuate
    a. abstinence
    b. constructive emotions and behavior
    c. family harmony
    d. improved school and/or work performance
    e. decreased conflict with authority figures
    f. reduced conflict with peers
    g. attitudes of gratitude and sharing
    h. attitudes of forgiveness and tolerance
    i. high frustration tolerance (patience)
17. Demonstration of a willingness and readiness to
    a. actively pursue educational and vocational pursuits

b. work a twelve step program of recovery
c. make constructive use of leisure time
d. develop solid drug-free friendships
e. accept responsibility for one's recovery
f. develop skills in effective management of financial resources
g. develop healthy patterns for dating and courtship
h. remain free of mind-altering drugs and tobacco products

This model approach to treatment understands that treating chemically dependent youth differs significantly from the treatment of chemically dependent adults. Teenagers require a lot more structure than adults. They also require a lot more time to develop a willingness and readiness to change and to take personal responsibility for their recovery. They must consistently participate for an extended period of time in daily activities that foster change. In addition, the treatment of teenagers requires active parental involvement, if maximum chances for success are to be realized.

The treatment approach is designed to foster an atmosphere where the parents can openly and honestly accept the condition of their child instead of denying it. It helps parents honestly confront their child with their feelings of hurt and disappointment as they admit their powerlessness to change their child. Most importantly, it helps parents learn how to live with their hurt and disappointment in more positive and constructive ways. They no longer have to dwell in feelings of anger, resentment, self-pity, guilt, shame, and fear. They no longer have to continue to cover up for and enable their child to avoid the consequences of his or her drug usage. Treatment objectives for parents include:

1. Reducing their level of anxiety, depression, and anger
2. Identifying self-defeating irrational thinking patterns that maintain a co-dependent enabling personality pattern
3. Replacing self-defeating irrational thinking patterns with new self-enhancing rational patterns of thinking
4. Practicing new self-enhancing rational thinking patterns
5. Admitting powerlessness over their child's condition and accepting the possibility that their child may not recover from the disease
6. Fostering a willingness and readiness to ask for and accept the help of others in overcoming their co-dependent enabling personality
7. Healing damaged relationships with other family members including the chemically dependent child, spouse, and other children
8. Addressing other psychological and/or chemical dependency issues that diminish the parents' effectiveness to parent their child and act

more effectively in other areas of their lives

9. Educating parents about the disease of chemical dependency and co-dependency
10. Developing more effective communication and parenting skills

The treatment provided by Model Treatment Program is designed to effect change physically, emotionally, and spiritually for chemically dependent adolescents and their families. Although this program does not advocate or promote any particular religious view, its underlying philosophy does stress a concept of spirituality. New possibilities do occur as teenagers are freed from the shackles of drug usage—their physical and emotional health drastically improve, they become reunited with their families, and they experience a renewing of their mind, a spiritual awakening.

Assessment

Prior to admission of any youth into Model Treatment Program, a comprehensive and extensive clinical assessment is conducted. This assessment involves a thorough physical examination and drug screening, a psychological and psychiatric evaluation, a psychosocial assessment, and extensive interviews with the adolescent and his or her parents and other relevant family members. A determination is made as to the degree of chemical dependency exhibited by the youth, his or her mental state, and the mental state of the parents. A plan for intervention and treatment is then carefully outlined and presented.

Continuum of Care

After the adolescent's clinical picture has been carefully reviewed, the youth and his or her family are assigned to one of several treatment options including:

1. Weekly outpatient individual and family treatment
2. Bi-weekly outpatient individual and family treatment
3. Intensive outpatient individual and family treatment
4. Temporary hospitalization for further observation and testing, detoxification, or other required medical treatment.
5. Intensive day treatment program with temporary assignment to a host home

Weekly or Bi-Weekly Individual and Family Counseling

These first two options, weekly or bi-weekly individual and family counseling, are designed for adolescents showing no or minimal (stage one) drug usage, a mental state indicating acting-up or acting-out patterns of behavior, and whose parents' mental state is slightly to very dysfunctional.

Goals for therapy include helping the adolescents learn how to (1) discontinue any drug usage while carefully monitoring their behavior to ensure that usage has stopped, (2) effectively manage emotions and behaviors in healthy ways, and (3) cope more effectively with their parents, peers, family members, and significant others in their life. In addition, the therapy addresses any self-defeating behavioral patterns in which the adolescent may be engaging. Time is also spent with the parents, helping them to address personal issues that interfere with their effectiveness as a parent and teaching them skills on how to be more effective parents. Many of the treatment strategies outlined in chapters 5, 6, and 7 are used to accomplish these goals.

Intensive Outpatient Individual, Family, and Group Treatment

This option is designed for teenager's who have signs and symptoms of stage two chemical dependency (problem usage) and who also demonstrate a strong desire to stop drug usage. Their mental state is one of acting up or acting out. Their parents' mental state can vary from slightly to very dysfunctional.

Goals for this option are the same as those listed for the first two outpatient options. Treatment involves bi-weekly individual and family therapy with the addition of daily after-school group therapy. The group therapy integrates these new adolescents with adolescents who have been free of alcohol or drug usage for several months. Parents also are required to participate in weekly group sessions with other parents experiencing similar problems with their children. Many of the treatment strategies outlined in chapters 5, 6, and 7 are used in treating these adolescents and their parents.

Temporary Hospitalization

Most chemically dependent adolescents do not require hospitalization, but do require medical attention and need to be placed in an environment where their behavior can be monitored and access to mind-altering substances and tobacco products is eliminated. The symptoms and medical dangers of physiological addiction usually subside in three to five days.

The program's policy is to hospitalize adolescents when alternative means of monitoring physical withdrawal symptoms are unavailable, when other serious medical complications accompany the chemical dependency, or when the acting-out behavior of the adolescent poses a direct physical threat to the life of the teenager or others.

For such adolescents, every effort is made to minimize their hospital stay (most cases require 3 to 10 days) by referring them, as soon as possible, to the program's intensive day treatment program with a host home or other outpatient options.

Intensive Day Treatment Program with Host Home

The intensive day treatment program with a temporary assignment to a host home is recommended for teenagers diagnosed at the problem usage and psychologically/physiologically addictive stage of chemical dependency, who have outward signs of chemical dependency and psychopathology that do not require hospitalization, and who have slightly to very dysfunctional parents.

The duration of the intensive day treatment program ranges from 21 to 90 days, depending on the teenager's treatment needs. Goals for the chemically dependent teenager include stabilization of physical health, stopping the usage of mind-altering substances, honesty with self, admitting to a drug problem, submission to a plan of action to treat drug problem, and treatment for anger, depression, and anxiety.[2] Daily therapeutic activities include three group therapy sessions, one educational session, one exercise session, and individual therapy sessions as needed. Family therapy sessions are provided weekly and as needed.

During this time period, the adolescent's education is temporarily halted with the understanding that initially confronting life-threatening issues must take a higher priority than reading, writing, and arithmetic. In addition, temporary restrictions are placed on the use of the radio, television, records, tapes, and CDs and reading materials. Contact with friends and relatives are also temporarily restricted as well as the use of the telephone and correspondence by mail.

In the evenings and on Sunday, the chemically dependent adolescent lives in a host home, a temporary foster home, with the family of another recovering teenager who is further advanced in treatment. Parents agreeing to be host home sponsors receive appropriate and necessary training and are provided ongoing staff support. They also agree to maintain in their homes (1) fire safety including no locks on bedroom doors, (2) sanitary conditions, (3) adequate provisions of nutritious food and water, (4) adequate sleeping accommodations, (5) a home free of alcohol, illegal drugs, tobacco products, and firearms, and (6) a secure and emotionally warm home environment supervised by the host home parents.

On completion of the intensive day treatment program, these chemically dependent adolescents are advised to continue treatment in the intensive intermediate program. This program follows the same guidelines of intensive day treatment, with the exception that the recovering teenager now lives in his or her own home or a permanent foster home or halfway house instead of continuing to reside in a temporary host home. In addition, the recovering teenager is allowed to enter school and/or begin a part-time job. Duration of the intensive intermediate treatment is four to six weeks.

The intensive after-care component is advised for those recovering teenagers who have completed the intensive day and the intensive intermediate treatment programs. The recovering teenagers attend school or work during the day and attend one group session daily. In addition, they participate each week in at least one family therapy session and educational session and receive individual counseling as needed. Goals for the intensive follow-up treatment include a continuation of previous treatment goals with the added goals of learning how to use free time constructively and learning how to share and give back to others. Duration of treatment is a minimum of six months.

The program provides follow-up therapy for those recovering teenagers who have successfully completed the intensive day, the intensive intermediate, and intensive after-care treatment programs. While participating in this phase of treatment, the recovering teenager weekly attends five group therapy sessions, two educational sessions, and one or more individual therapy sessions. Two or more family therapy sessions are provided each month. In addition, the recovering teenager is required to attend a minimum of two self-help support group meetings each week (e.g., AA or NA).[3] Duration of treatment lasts from 6 to 12 months depending on the needs of the recovering teenager and his or her family, with the goal for each recovering teenager to learn how to apply daily a set of principles that will enable him or her to remain free of mind-altering chemicals and continue to develop skills in achieving maximum physical, emotional, and spiritual well-being. The recovering teenager continues to develop newly learned skills that enable him or her to manage anger, anxiety, and depression more effectively and significantly improve effectiveness in the areas of family, school, work, and peer interactions. The recovering teenager also continues to develop skills that result in encouraging drug-free friendships, constructive use of leisure time, and sharing and giving back to others.[4]

Treatment Environment: Intensive Day Treatment

The treatment conducted at the intensive day treatment program fosters a therapeutic climate that initially assumes complete responsibility for the care of the adolescent to ensure that access to alcohol, other mind-altering chemicals, and tobacco products are removed for a minimum of 45 and in some cases up to 90 days. The Model Treatment Program addresses the physical needs of the client including adequate food, clothing, shelter, and medical needs. The treatment climate is free of all tobacco products, encourages minimal use of sugar products, and provides for a sound nutritional program.

The staff is comprised of professionals and paraprofessionals who exemplify warmth, empathy, and discipline and a positive mental attitude; as well as a life style free of alcohol, other mind-altering drugs, and tobacco products. The treatment programs provide direct access to positive peer influence, are free of any physical abuse or threat, but carefully provide for reasonable rules and regulations. The treatment program's rules are consistently and fairly enforced and are derived from clearly defined expectations. The staff takes care to ensure that the treatment climate does not become either too laisse faire or too authoritarian—either extreme is detrimental to treatment outcomes.

Treatment includes individual and group therapy that openly and honestly discusses basic cultural values and consistently confronts irrational and dysfunctional patterns of thinking. Programs provide opportunities to practice newly learned skills within a supportive environment and provide opportunities to make mistakes and learn from them. Individual treatment plans are maintained with guidelines for periodic review and recommendations for ongoing follow-up treatment.

The program's clinical staffing incorporates a careful blending of professionals and paraprofessionals and includes psychiatrists, family practitioners specializing, in adolescent medicine, psychiatric nurses, psychologists, social workers, mental health counselors, recreation and art therapists, and clergy. Each have been trained in the principles and practices of chemical dependency and cognitive-behavioral counseling.

The staff also includes a group of peer counselors consisting of well-trained adolescents who have been in recovery for a minimum of one year. Carefully trained, supervised, and directed by adult professionals, this peer staff forms the cornerstone of the treatment approach.

Model Treatment Program's intensive day treatment program with a temporary host home as well as its other outpatient and inpatient programs provide a full array of support services including medical and psychiatric consultation, educational training and remediation, art and recreational therapy, career and job counseling, nutritional counseling, and, spiritual counseling. In addition, its treatment programs are designed to handle issues of special concern including (1) dual diagnosis; (2) sexual issues such as pregnancy, abortion, homosexuality, rape, masturbation, and sexual promiscuity; (3) AIDS; (4) child abuse and neglect; (5) alcoholic or drug-abusing parent(s); (6) youth where one or both of the parents are deceased, have experienced a divorce, or the child has been adopted; (7) physical impairments; (8) court-ordered teenagers; (9) spiritual issues; and (10) the use of self-help support groups and twelve-step programs.

Treatment Strategies: Intensive Day Treatment

For many drug-abusing teenagers entering the intensive day treatment program, the first recovery plateau, admitting, may take months to reach, and unfortunately, for a percentage of teenage substance abusers, is never achieved. Goals that must be completed in order to reach the first plateau focus on identifying, examining, and confronting the denial mechanisms that maintain dishonesty and keep teenagers from honestly admitting their drug problem. The therapeutic challenge is to break through a well-rehearsed cognitive structure that maintains the two outer layers of the emerging personality of the teenage substance abuser: psychological/physiological addiction and denial of feelings and actions.[5]

These two layers of the personality contain a distinct self-talk that includes an erroneous belief that "getting high on drugs is the only way to be happy and manage one's life." In addition, the self-talk includes a myriad of excuses justifying the drug usage (rationalizations), a constant blaming of others for current and previous unpleasant circumstances (projection), unrealistic expectations about the present and the future (wishful and magical thinking), and a continual self-deception or lying to oneself and others about present and past realities (denial). These deeply entrenched elements of a distorted cognitive structure must first be shattered before the drug-abusing teenager can admit that he or she has a drug problem.

Shattering these two deeply entrenched layers of self-destructive thinking requires a well-planned therapeutic approach utilizing cognitive-behavioral, gestalt, and reality therapies. This approach must initially focuses on the teenager's feelings and behavior while restricting the teenager's access to any mind-altering drugs. Then a process can begin that challenges the erroneous a posteriori belief, the obsession, that "I must get high to have fun or manage my life."

Each day that the chemically dependent teenager avoids getting high provides experiential evidence that contradicts the obsession and diminishes the physiological effects of the drugs. Therefore, the first step in providing an effective treatment intervention is to place the drug-abusing teenager in a structured drug-free environment where medical needs can be addressed and processing of emotional and behavioral experiences can begin.

Experience has taught the staff that treatment approaches depending heavily on antipsychotic and antidepressant medications, especially during this early admitting stage of treatment, usually are ineffective in the treatment of chemically dependent adolescents and are therefore seldom used. The staff has also learned to remain objective with clients, being careful not to side with the adolescent by blaming his or her parents for their chemical abuse. They also understand that, initially, they will be disliked by both the drug-abusing teenagers and their parents.

Reaching this first plateau is arduous and time consuming. Complicating matters is the length of time required for the effects of the mind-altering chemicals on the brain to disintegrate. For example, chronic users of marijuana may require four to seven months before the final traces of the marijuana will be eliminated from their bodies and their minds be totally free of the drug's influence.

In the meantime, recovery is enhanced by engaging the teenage substance abuser in a group process utilizing cognitive-behavioral, gestalt, and reality therapies. The teenager's current and past feelings and behaviors are repeatedly confronted. The reality is reinforced that much of the pain and misery experienced both in the past and now was and is a direct result of a drug habit and a faulty belief structure.

For many teenagers in treatment, eventually admitting that they have a drug problem is commonplace. Getting them to submit to a process of recovery, however, is a different matter. This is the challenge that must be overcome in order to reach the second plateau.

A major obstacle is refusal. The barriers of refusal are quite impenetrable at times and usually reinforce denial patterns. The "I don't care" (indifference), "I can get off drugs by myself" (self-sufficiency), "I already know how to get off drugs" (self-righteous), "I'm not worth it" (rejection), "You can't make me" (defiant), " It's my life and no one is going to tell me what I can and cannot do" (belligerent) attitudes are powerful forces to combat.

Individual cognitive-behavioral therapy or other kinds of individual therapy usually prove ineffective at this stage of treatment. Model Program uses a well-structured cognitive-behavioral group process that consistently challenges the teenager's irrational beliefs, points out the inconsistency of these beliefs, and graphically reminds the teenager of the realities resulting from adhering to such beliefs. It uses the experience of other teenagers who are more advanced in their recovery and have already successfully worked through the challenges that this plateau presents. Progress begins when the teenager starts to honestly admit that he or she has a drug problem, does not know how to solve it, and asks the group for help with it. Until this admission and submission takes place, the teenager's denial and refusal layers are continuing to dictate and control the teenager's future. Submission, occurs when the teenager is willing to hold himself or herself accountable to the group and the group therapist(s).

Several treatment strategies to help recovering teenage drug abusers reach the admitting and submitting plateaus of recovery are used. These techniques are effective in helping teenage substance abusers overcome the barriers of psychological/physiological addiction, denial, and refusal by enhancing awareness, providing an alternative means to manage feelings and fostering hope by explaining how change is possible.

Techniques used that enhance awareness include (1) the awareness wheel, (2) feeling log, (3) ABCDEs of emotion and behavior, (4) daily moral inventories, (5) developing a life plan, (6) rebel without a cause syndrome, (7) steps one, two, three, (8) styles of manipulation and actualization, and (9) searching and fearless moral inventory.

Techniques used that introduce alternative means to manage feelings include the three signs, the serenity prayer, and the fallible and correctable human being concept.

Techniques used that explain how change is possible include five steps to change, law of the harvest, and getting straight.[6]

Developing a healthy cognitive structure is paramount for teenage substance abusers to overcome chemical dependency. Awareness is the first step in helping teenage substance abusers develop a healthier cognitive structure. Learning alternative means to manage feelings is the second step in helping teenage substance abusers develop a healthier cognitive structure. Explaining the change process is the third step in helping teenage substance abusers develop a healthier cognitive structure.

Reaching the third plateau of treatment, committing, requires the teenage substance abuser to begin acting on a new set of beliefs and to struggle with the ambivalence and dissonance that accompanies any change. As the teenager begins to develop a new, positive, more rational, functional self-talk and begins to experience the emotional and behavioral responses that result from it, ambivalence and dissonance begin to emerge. This new self-talk and the previously well-rehearsed old "druggie" thinking patterns compete for the heart and soul of the recovering teenager. Unfortunately, the drug-abusing teenager will not give up old "druggie" thinking patterns without a battle and, often, without a long and arduous struggle. In addition, the teenager will feel awkward or ambivalent as he or she attempts to address life's challenges sober.

The experience of ambivalence and dissonance is similar to asking people to tie their shoes starting with their left hands when they had been used to tying their shoes by starting with their right hands. At first, they will feel very awkward and uncomfortable when performing the task and will have a strong inclination to resort back to their old way of tying their shoes. However, with ample time and correct practice, the new way of tying their shoes would become more comfortable and the old inclination would become less favorable.

Critical to reaching the committing plateau is helping the teenager stay focused on the benefits of adhering to and enacting new thinking patterns and continually reminding the teenager of the consequences of choosing to pay attention to their old "druggie" style of thinking. The development of a healthy fear of one's past, positive realistic expectations about one's future, and a willingness to act on one's new found beliefs are tantamount in developing a commitment to reach the third plateau and in making a solid commitment to live a drug-free life style.

Reaching the fourth and final plateau, transmitting, requires the recovering teenage to realize that in order to continue to receive the benefits that accompany a drug-free life style, the new thinking patterns need constant rehearsal and must be implemented on a daily basis. Many recovering teenagers have referred to this challenge as the acceptance hurdle.

To reach the transmitting plateau, the recovering teenager must learn how to manage and effectively minimize the impact of strong self-destructive attitudes that resulted from and/or occurred prior to drug usage. Damnation of self and others, the tyranny of shoulds, awfulizing, and I can't stand it-itis thinking patterns are still quite prevalent, as are the accompanying emotions of anger, resentment, self-pity, guilt, worry, and apprehension. Transmitting requires the acceptance that continuing to practice new formed habits are essential for sustained recovery.

For most recovering teenage substance abusers, reaching the transmitting plateau takes several years (usually five) to achieve and a lifetime to perfect. Recovering teenagers striving to reach this final plateau benefit immensely from individual cognitive-behavioral counseling and group processes that provide opportunities for teenagers to share accomplishments, continue to challenge distorted thinking patterns, and assist each other in recognizing and eliminating self-defeating thinking. Reaching out and assisting other teenagers new to recovery is also important. Such activity reinforces one's commitment, helps reduce selfishness and self-centeredness, and reminds the teenager that he or she could still be engaged in a self-destructive "druggie" life style.

Several treatment strategies are used to help the recovering teenage drug abuser reach the committing and transmitting plateaus of recovery and directly confront the self-destructive attitudes of damnation of self, damnation of others, tyranny of shoulds, awfulizing, and I can't stand it-itis. These techniques are also effective in helping to identify other self-defeating self-talk, changing it, and preventing the return of denial and refusal thinking patterns (i.e., relapse prevention).

Techniques used that identify self-defeating self-talk include (1) the five criteria, (2) styles of thinking, (3) self-downing and self-acceptance cycles, (4) language of anger and resentment, and (5) secondary virginity.

Techniques used that illustrate how to change self-talk include (1) steps five, six, and seven, (2) seven steps to a happy (F)ACE, (3) recovery scripts, (4) changing dislike behaviors, and (5) the Lord's Prayer.

Relapse prevention techniques include (1) steps eight and nine, (2) steps eleven and twelve, (3) ten most common causes of failure, (4) relapse signs and symptoms, and (5) goal setting.[7]

The development of a healthy cognitive structure is paramount for recovery. Recognizing self-defeating self-talk is the fourth step in helping teenage substance abusers develop a healthier cognitive structure. Changing self-talk is the fifth step in helping teenage substance abusers develop a healthier cognitive structure. Relapse prevention is the final step in helping teenage substance abusers develop a healthier cognitive structure.

Family Involvement: Intensive Day Treatment

As a chemically dependent adolescent becomes psychologically and/or physiologically addicted to drugs, the parents become psychologically addicted to their child. The parents begin to believe erroneously that their worth as human beings is dependent solely on the success or failure, the happiness or unhappiness, of their child. And just as damaging, the parents begin to believe that they are responsible totally for the welfare of their child and have caused their child's current drug problem. For just as chemical dependency can be viewed as a disease of attitudes that results in physiological, emotional and spiritual difficulties, so can co-dependency.

Parents of chemically dependent adolescents develop a toxic relationship with their drug-abusing teenagers. Maintaining this state of co-dependency is a faulty cognitive structure similar to the cognitive structure of the chemically dependent adolescent.[8]

Model Program uses several treatment strategies to help co-dependent enabling parents learn how to confront their child's disease of chemically dependency more openly and honestly. They include general, introductory, intermediate, and advanced strategies.

General treatment strategies used include (1) the awareness wheel, (2) ABCDEs of emotion and behavior, (3) overcoming denial and refusal, (4) moral inventories, (5) fallible and correctable human being (FHB/CHB), (6) five steps to change, (7) four key words to recovery, (8) serenity prayer, (9) the three signs, (10) five criteria for rational thinking, (11) the Lord's Prayer, and (12) parent weekend.

Introductory treatment strategies used include (1) co-dependency and the primary enabler, (2) sympathy kills: learning how to effectively express your feelings to your child, (3) consistency and commitment, (4) emotional ignorance and the importance of self-talk, (5) powerlessness over our kids the challenge of accepting step one, and (6) reaching out to others.

Intermediate treatment strategies used include (1) overcoming enabling behavior, (2) seven steps to a happy (F)ACE, (3) self-defeating styles of thinking, (4) script writing, (5) assertiveness training, (6) rule setting, negotiating, and the effective use of motivators, and (7) stress reduction techniques.

Advanced treatment strategies used include (1) couples communication, (2) signs of relapse, (3) family relationships, (4) relationships with the opposite sex, and (5) overcoming fears and insecurities.[9]

Each of these four types of treatment strategies, general, introductory, intermediate, and advanced, are introduced over a 9- to 14-month period of time, preferably in group counseling sessions. This time frame gives parents an ample opportunity to digest, practice, and fully incorporate newly learned patterns of thinking into their daily lives. To be successful with the parents, it is necessary to change their cognitive structure, and that takes time.

Parents with severe emotional problems and/or chemical dependency problems receive individual counseling in addition to the group counseling and, in some cases, may require temporary hospitalization. Appropriate screening procedures to determine the mental state of the parents: slightly dysfunctional, marginally dysfunctional, dysfunctional due to mental illness, or dysfunctional due to chemical dependence (refer to & chapter 3, Mental State: Parents).

The program also treats other family members including siblings, grandparents, and other relatives. The same treatment strategies outlined for the parents are used, with adaptations made to adjust for the age level of the person being treated. It is only necessary to involve grandparents or other relatives directly if they are providing a parental role for the recovering teenager or they have developed a co-dependent enabling relationship with the drug-abusing adolescent.

Siblings of the chemically dependent adolescent can benefit by reading, reviewing, and discussing Sharon Wegscheider-Cruse's booklet, *The Family Trap,* and identifying what role they were playing in the family: the family hero, scapegoat, lost child, or family mascot. It is also important to interview siblings to determine whether they have had any involvement in drug usage and to what extent. It is not uncommon for other siblings to be involved in drug usage. It is also important to provide avenues for the siblings to express openly and honestly the feelings they experienced while living with their chemically dependent brother or sister. Often, siblings have been physically, emotionally, and/or sexually abused by their older drug-abusing teenage brother or sister.

Staff Training

An ongoing staff training program is in operation at Model Treatment Program. The continuing education program is designed to improve and upgrade the program's clinical staff in the areas of basic and chemical dependency counseling skills including a working knowledge of the steps and principles of Alcoholics Anonymous (AA). In addition, an in-service program provides ongoing training in one-on-one and group cognitive-behavioral counseling. An ongoing review is also provided of a working knowledge of the principles of (1) cognitive-behavioral therapy; (2) related therapies, especially gestalt, reality, and actualizing therapies; (3) developmental theories; (4) family system theories; and (5) theories of chemical dependency counseling. Special seminars are provided to help the clinical staff improve their character strengths and further develop their skills of (1) confidentiality, (2) timing and tact, (3) listernership, (4) objectivity and discernment, (5) empathy and understanding, (6) honesty, (7) genuine interest and love, and (8) patience and perseverance.

Overall, Model Treatment's staff training program is dedicated to developing a clinical staff competent in state-of-the-art theory, practice, and technique.

Efficacy and Efficiency of Treatment Programs

Model Treatment Program employs a full-time evaluation staff for delineating, obtaining, and providing useful information to the programs executive committee which is charged with the responsibility of determining the ongoing efficacy and efficiency of treatment programs. Context, input, process, and product information is routinely collected and analyzed in an effort to improve and upgrade the quality of care being provided by the program's treatment facilities.

Currently, the evaluation staff is conducting a needs assessment to determine which sectors in the community are in most need of adolescent chemical dependency treatment. In addition, they are researching cost-containment strategies proven useful by other treatment agencies. They also recently implemented a new quality assurance plan in each of Model Treatment's treatment programs that utilizes state-of-the-art computer technology. The staff is anxiously awaiting the results of a 5-year follow-up study of families who completed the intensive day treatment program.

Summary

In this chapter, a model program for treating adolescent substance abuse was presented within the context of the eight fundamental elements of treatment.

Endnotes

1. The information presented in this chapter constitutes an integration of the elements of an ongoing treatment program developed and implemented by the author, with what the author considers as an ideal program for the treatment of adolescent substance abuse.
2. Refer also to the objectives for the admitting and submitting stages of recovery outlined in the rationale section of this chapter.
3. It has been my experience that recovering teenagers benefit more from self-help support groups such as AA and NA after they have completed several months of structured individual and group cognitive-behavioral therapy. Consequently, the recovering teenager enters an AA or a NA group with a willingness and readiness to continue to grow and change.
4. Refer also to the objectives for the committing and transmitting stages of recovery outlined in the rationale section of this chapter.
5. Refer to chapter 2 for a complete explanation of the layers of an emerging personality and cognitive structure of a teenage substance abuser.
6. Refer to chapter 5 for a complete explanation of the strategies used for reaching the admitting and submitting plateaus of recovery.
7. Refer to chapter 6 for a complete explanation of the strategies used for reaching the committing and transmitting plateaus of recovery.

8. Refer to chapter 7 for a complete explanation of the emerging personality and cognitive structure of a co-dependent enabling parent.
9. Refer to chapter 7 for an explanation of strategies useful in helping parents confront their co-dependent enabling tendencies.

Epilogue

In the previous 10 chapters, a description and illustration of the eight fundamental elements of an effective program for treating adolescent substance abuse was presented. Chapter 1 outlined the eight fundamental elements. They included (1) a sound rationale for diagnosis and treatment, (2) screening, assessment, and diagnostic procedures, (3) a continuum of care, (4) a healthy treatment environment, (5) effective treatment strategies, (6) active family involvement, (7) competent staff, and (8) efficacy and efficiency of treatment.

In chapter 2, *chemical dependency* was defined as a disease of attitudes leading to the use and abuse of mind-altering substances (e.g., alcohol, marijuana, cocaine) culminating in the physical deterioration of the body, emotional instability, and spiritual bankruptcy. *Attitudes* were viewed as "a relatively enduring organization of beliefs around an object or situation predisposing one to respond in some preferential manner." A nomological network explaining the formation of attitudes was depicted. A person's *cognitive structure* was viewed as containing two types of attitudes, a priori and a posteriori. *Personality* was described as the habitual application of a set of a priori and a posteriori cognitions that create and maintain a set of predictable emotional and behavioral responses across situations.

The emerging personality of an adolescent substance abuser was portrayed as a cognitive structure that contained four distinct interrelated layers: (1) psychological/physiological, (2) denial of feelings and actions, (3) refusal, and (4) self-destructive attitudes. At the core of the emerging personality was a caldron of emotional pain.

In chapter 3, a multi-method approach to assessment was introduced that included (1) drug screening, (2) signs and symptoms checklist, (3) psychosocial assessment and family interviews, (4) parental evaluation, (5) interviewing the teenage substance abuser, (6) medical examination, (7) psychological/psychiatric evaluation, and (8) clinical observations.

Three diagnostic dimensions used to formulate a diagnosis of an adolescent substance abuser were also explained. These three dimensions included degree of dependency, mental state of the teenager, and mental state of the parents.

In chapter 4, treatment options and the treatment environment were discussed. Treatment options ranged from outpatient treatment to hospitalization. Three important aspects of a healthy treatment environment were also discussed: treatment climate, staffing patterns, and supportive services.

In chapter 5, four plateaus of recovery were introduced: (1) admitting, (2) submitting, (3) committing, and (4) transmitting. Treatment objectives for reaching the admitting and transmitting plateaus of recovery were outlined. In addition, 15 techniques found useful in enhancing awareness, providing alternative means to manage feelings, and explaining how change was possible were introduced.

In chapter 6, treatment objectives for the committing and transmitting plateaus of recovery were outlined. Fifteen techniques were introduced that help recovering teenage substance abusers identify self-defeating self-talk, change it, and avoid relapse.

In chapter 7, strategies for treating the family members of adolescent substance abusers were introduced. General, introductory, intermediate, and advanced strategies for treating co-dependent enabling parents were outlined and discussed. The importance of treating other family members including siblings and grandparents was emphasized.

In chapter 8, the attributes and skills of a chemical dependency counselor were outlined and discussed. Attributes included (1) character strengths, (2) confidentiality, (3) timing and tact, (4) listernership, (5) objectivity and discernment, (6) empathy and understanding, (7) honesty, (8) genuine interest and love, and (9) patience and perseverance. Skills included (1) basic counseling skills, (2) cognitive-behavioral therapy skills, (3) chemical dependency counseling skills, (4) knowledge of developmental theories, (5) knowledge of family systems theories, (6) knowledge of other counseling theories, (7) cognitive-behavioral one-on-one counseling, and (8) cognitive-behavioral group counseling.

In chapter 9, issues of efficacy and efficiency of treatment were examined. The current state-of-the-art of adolescent treatment programs and the adequacy of methodologies available to assess their effectiveness was reviewed. In addition, four types of evaluation were introduced: context, input, process, and product. Measurable outcome variables for adolescent treatment programs were also discussed.

In chapter 10, the eight fundamental elements of a chemical dependency treatment program for adolescents were presented in the context of a model program for treating adolescent substance abuse.

Appendix A

Psychosocial Assessment

The psychosocial assessment is to be completed during the first 45 days of the client's treatment. It is a comprehensive document used to record an assortment of information gathered on the client from a variety of sources including (1) interviews with parents, (2) client interviews, (3) staff observations, and (4) testing results.

Intake Summary

School

lower grades	YES	NO	NA
negative attitude towards	YES	NO	NA
skipped classes	YES	NO	NA
suspended	YES	NO	NA
expelled	YES	NO	NA
dropout	YES	NO	NA

Family

avoided parents	YES	NO	NA
avoided siblings	YES	NO	NA

avoided family gatherings	YES	NO	NA
avoided chores	YES	NO	NA
and responsibilities	YES	NO	NA
accused parents of hassling or mistrusting	YES	NO	NA
attempted to create conflict between parents	YES	NO	NA
physically abusive with parents	YES	NO	NA
verbally abusive with parents	YES	NO	NA
physically abusive with siblings	YES	NO	NA
verbally abusive with siblings	YES	NO	NA

Sexual Behavior

sexual intercourse	YES	NO	NA
pregnant	YES	NO	NA
abortion	YES	NO	NA
miscarriages	YES	NO	NA
birth control pills	YES	NO	NA
homosexual behavior	YES	NO	NA

other ____

____

Law Breaking/Dishonesty

traffic violations	YES	NO	NA
driving under the influence	YES	NO	NA
vandalism	YES	NO	NA
breaking and entering	YES	NO	NA
selling drugs	YES	NO	NA
burglary	YES	NO	NA
carried a concealed weapon	YES	NO	NA
forged checks	YES	NO	NA

unauthorized credit card use	YES	NO	NA
concealed drug usage	YES	NO	NA
lied about friends	YES	NO	NA
cheated in school	YES	NO	NA
forged school excuses	YES	NO	NA
lied about whereabouts	YES	NO	NA
stole money from parents	YES	NO	NA
stole money from employer	YES	NO	NA
arrested	YES	NO	NA
spent time in jail	YES	NO	NA

other ____

____

Physical Health

frequent colds	YES	NO	NA
extreme fatigue	YES	NO	NA
menstrual problems	YES	NO	NA
kidney infection	YES	NO	NA
gonorrhea	YES	NO	NA
seizures	YES	NO	NA
syphilis	YES	NO	NA
herpes	YES	NO	NA
HIV-positive	YES	NO	NA

other ____

____

Emotional Health

easily irritated	YES	NO	NA
fits of anger or rage	YES	NO	NA

depressed	YES	NO	NA
run away from home	YES	NO	NA
suicidal depression	YES	NO	NA
suicidal attempts	YES	NO	NA
anxious	YES	NO	NA
black outs	YES	NO	NA
resentful	YES	NO	NA

other ______________________________

____

Spiritual Health

never believed in God	YES	NO	NA
stopped believing in God	YES	NO	NA
angry with God	YES	NO	NA
violated God's laws	YES	NO	NA
suicidal	YES	NO	NA
used a lot of profanity	YES	NO	NA

Work/Finances

difficulty in holding job	YES	NO	NA
fired from job	YES	NO	NA
verbally abusive to employer	YES	NO	NA
verbally abusive to customer	YES	NO	NA
verbally abusive to co-worker	YES	NO	NA
physically abusive to employer	YES	NO	NA
physically abusive to customer	YES	NO	NA
physically abusive to co-worker	YES	NO	NA
spent most of money on drugs	YES	NO	NA
no savings account	YES	NO	NA

bounced checks	YES	NO	NA
always borrowing money	YES	NO	NA
constantly asking for money	YES	NO	NA

Friends/Leisure Time

physically abusive to friends	YES	NO	NA
verbally abusive to friends	YES	NO	NA
lied to friends	YES	NO	NA
stole from friends	YES	NO	NA
used drugs with friends	YES	NO	NA
started friends on drugs	YES	NO	NA
manipulated friends	YES	NO	NA
stopped playing sports	YES	NO	NA
gave up hobbies	YES	NO	NA
majority of time getting high	YES	NO	NA

Previous Treatment

mental hospital (drugs)	YES	NO	NA
outpatient drug counseling	YES	NO	NA
day treatment program (drugs)	YES	NO	NA
psychiatric inpatient	YES	NO	NA
psychiatric outpatient	YES	NO	NA
psychologist	YES	NO	NA
mental health counselor	YES	NO	NA
pastoral counselor/clergy	YES	NO	NA
social worker	YES	NO	NA
psychotropic medication	YES	NO	NA

LIST ALL TREATMENT, MEDICATIONS PRESCRIBED AND DATES OF TREATMENT:

NAME OF PROVIDER	MEDICATIONS	DATE
1. ________________	______________	_____
2. ________________	______________	_____
3. ________________	______________	_____
4. ________________	______________	_____
5. ________________	______________	_____

Family Members	*Drug Usuage*		*Mental Illness*	
mother	YES	NO	YES	NO
father	YES	NO	YES	NO
stepmother	YES	NO	YES	NO
stepfather	YES	NO	YES	NO
brother	YES	NO	YES	NO
sister	YES	NO	YES	NO
grandparents	YES	NO	YES	NO
aunts	YES	NO	YES	NO
uncles	YES	NO	YES	NO
cousins	YES	NO	YES	NO
chemical dependency in family			YES	NO

IF DRUG USAGE, IDENTIFY PERSON, TYPE, FREQUENCY

1. ____
2. ____
3. ____
4. ____

IF MENTAL ILLNESS, IDENTIFY PERSON AND TYPE

1. ______________________________

2. ______________________________

3. ______________________________

4. ______________________________

IF CHEMICAL DEPENDENCY, IDENTIFY FAMILY MEMBER(S)

1. ______________________________

2. ______________________________

3. ______________________________

4. ______________________________

Parental Co-Dependent Enabling Questionnaire

1.	Do you and your spouse frequently disagree or argue about your child's behavior?	YES	NO
2.	Do you often worry about your child's problems?	YES	NO
3.	Do you find yourself trying to cover up or make excuses for your child's behavior?	YES	NO
4.	Do you feel frustrated because no matter how hard you try, nothing seems to change your child's behavior?	YES	NO
5.	Do you feel relieved when your child leaves the house?	YES	NO
6.	Do you feel angry with or have a general dislike for your child?	YES	NO
7.	Are you afraid that you may have become a failure as a parent?	YES	NO
8.	Have you tried to change your behavior in hopes that it would cause a change in your child's behavior?	YES	NO
9.	Do you give money to your child without your spouse's knowledge?	YES	NO

10. Do you have a growing fear that your child has become out of control? YES NO

11. Do you have a fear that your child might injure himself or herself or others? YES NO

12. Do you find yourself frequently bargaining with your child in an attempt to change his or her behavior? YES NO

13. Do you feel heart-sick because you have had to compromise your own values or lower your expectations concerning your child? YES NO

14. Do you find yourself desiring to spend less time at home to avoid conflicts with your child? YES NO

Evidence of Drug Usage

length of suspected drug usage ______________________

known drugs currently using ______________________

____

____

____

____

other evidence ______________________

____

____

Legal History

_____ currently in trouble with law

_____ past arrest record

_____ currently on probation

_____ on probation in past

NAME OF PROBATION OFFICER ______________________

NAME OF COURT-DESIGNATED WORKER ______________________

NAME OF SOCIAL WORKER ______________________

NAME OF LAWYER ______________________

IF IN TROUBLE WITH THE LAW, PRESENT OR PAST, PLEASE ______________________

DESCRIBE: ______________________

____

____

____

____

Developmental History

Infancy (health, home environment, behavior)

____

____

____

____

____

____

Childhood (health, home environment, behavior)

____

____

____

____

____

____

Adolescent (health, home environment, behavior)

____

____

____

____

____

____

Siblings Relationship Age

1. ____
2. ____
3. ____
4. ____
5. ____
6. ____
7. ____

Quality of Relationship with Siblings

____

____

____

____

____

____

Parental Status

_____ natural parents

_____ natural father, stepmother

_____ natural mother, stepfather

_____ single mother (father deceased)

_____ single father (mother deceased)

_____ single parent (separated)

_____ single parent (divorced)

_____ adoptive parent(s)

______ legal guardian (both parents deceased)

______ legal guardian (parental abandonment)

______ other

Quality of Relationship with Parents

____

____

____

____

____

____

Grandparents

______ maternal grandfather still living

______ maternal grandmother still living

______ grandfather (father's side) still living

______ grandmother (father's side) still living

Quality of Relationship with Grandparents

____

____

____

____

____

Quality of Peer Relationship

____

____

____

____

____

Education

Highest grade completed	____________________
Educational testing scores	
general learning ability	____________________
reading comprehension	____________________
math comprehension	____________________
writing skills	____________________
other	____________________
learning disabilities	____________________

Pyschosexual

pregnancy	YES	NO
abortion	YES	NO
pre-marital sex	YES	NO
homosexual behavior	YES	NO
incest	YES	NO
sexual abuse	YES	NO
rape	YES	NO
masturbation	YES	NO
pornography	YES	NO
sexual addiction	YES	NO
sex with animals	YES	NO

Significant Past Experiences

From your knowledge of your client, briefly describe two or three experiences that best illustrate the developmental history of the client (e.g., family experiences, school experiences, peer experiences). Complete these summaries of significant past experiences on a separate sheet an attach to the psychosocial assessment.

Clinical Observations

Addiction, Denial, and Refusal Attitudes

After 45 days of treatment, check if the client is still showing signs of any of the following attitudes.

______ psychological addiction (obsession)

______ magical thinking

______ wishful thinking

______ denial

______ rationalization

______ projection

______ belligerence

______ indifference

______ self-sufficient

______ self-righteous

______ defiance

______ rejection

After 45 days, check if the client is still experiencing difficulty with any of the following:

______ participation and motivation in group raps

______ following group rules

______ accepting responsibility for drug problem

______ openness to new ideas

______ admitting powerlessness and unmanagability

______ completes daily moral inventories

______ honesty about past drug usage and behaviors

______ speech content disorganized or unclear

______ speech content weird or bizarre

______ speech too rapid or too slow

_____ suicidal ideations

_____ suicidal attempts

_____ delusional thinking

_____ auditory hallucinations

_____ visual hallucinations

_____ olfactory hallucinations

_____ dissociation

_____ paranoid thinking

_____ explosive behavior

_____ attempts to injure self or others

_____ jerky movements

_____ sluggishness, lethargy

_____ sleeplessness

_____ poor appetite

Drug Usage

List of drug usage in the past as reported by client after 45 days in treatment.

Drug	*# × Used*	*# Months Used*	*Age of Onset*
Alcohol			
beer	_____	_____	_____
wine	_____	_____	_____
hard liquor	_____	_____	_____
Cocaine			
crack	_____	_____	_____
rock	_____	_____	_____
coke	_____	_____	_____
base (free)	_____	_____	_____

Drug	*# × Used*	*# Months Used*	*Age of Onset*
Marijuana			
pot	________	________	________
hash	________	________	________
hash oil	________	________	________
Hallucinogens			
LSD	________	________	________
PCP	________	________	________
MDMA	________	________	________
ecstasy	________	________	________
psilocybin	________	________	________
mushrooms	________	________	________
peyote	________	________	________
Inhalants			
gas	________	________	________
aerosols	________	________	________
glue	________	________	________
nitrates	________	________	________
rush	________	________	________
white out	________	________	________
Narcotics			
heroin	________	________	________
demerol	________	________	________
dilaudid	________	________	________
morphine	________	________	________
codeine	________	________	________

Drug	*# × Used*	*# Months Used*	*Age of Onset*
Stimulants			
amphetamines	________	________	________
nicotine	________	________	________
caffeine	________	________	________
Depressants			
barbiturates	________	________	________
sedatives	________	________	________
valium	________	________	________
tranquilizers	________	________	________

Clients Strengths

Based on your clinical observations, list the client's strengths.

____

____

____

____

Client Challenges

Based on your clinical observations, list the client's current challenges.

____

____

____

____

Overall Summary

Psychological

Attach a summary of any and all psychological testing and mental status examinations.

Health History

Attach a summary of all pertinent health history.

Diagnostic Sumary (DSM-III-R)

Axis I.

Axis II.

Axis III.

Axis IV.

Axis V.

Recommendations and Follow-Up Treatment

____

____

____

____

____

____

____

____

____

____

____

____

____

____

Recommendations and Follow-Up Treatment (continued)

____

____

____

____

____

____

____

____

Appendix B

Twelve Steps of Alcoholics Anonymous[1]

1. We admitted we were powerless over alcohol—that our lives had become unmangeable.
2. Came to believe that a Power greater than ourselves could restore us to sanity.
3. Made a decision to turn our will and our lives over to the care of God as we understood Him.
4. Made a searching and fearless moral inventory of ourselves.
5. Admitted to God, to ourselves, and to another human being the exact nature of our wrongs.
6. Were entirely ready to have God remove all these defects of character.
7. Humbly asked Him to remove our shortcomings.
8. Made a list of all persons we had harmed, and became willing to make amends to them all.
9. Made direct amends to such people wherever possible, except when to do so would injure them or others.
10. Continued to take personal inventory and when we were wrong, promptly admitted it.
11. Sought through prayer and meditation to improve our conscious contact with God as we understood Him, praying only for knowledge of His will for us and the power to carry that out.
12. Having had a spiritual awakening as the result of these steps, we tried to carry this message to alcoholics, and to practice these principles in all our affairs.

Endnote

1. The Twelve Steps and other AA excerpts appearing in this publication are reprinted with permission of Alcoholics Anonymous World Services, Inc. Permission to reprint this material does not mean that AA has reviewed or approved the contents of this publication, nor that AA agrees with the views expressed herein. AA is a program of recovery from alcoholism *only*—use of the Twelve Steps and other excerpts in connection with programs and activites which are patterened after AA, but which address other problems, does not imply otherwise.

References

American Medical Society on Alcoholism and Other Drug Dependencies. (1988). *Guidelines for facilities treating chemically dependent patients at risk for AIDS or infected by HIV virus* [Pamphlet]. Ft. Lauderdale, FL: AMSAODD.

American Psychiatric Association. (1987). *Diagnostic and statistical manual of mental disorders* (3rd ed. revised). Washington DC: American Psychiatric Association.

Anglin, T. M. (1987). Interviewing guidelines for the clinical evaluation of adolescent substance abuse. In P. D. Rogers (Ed.), *The pediatric clinics of North America: Chemical dependency* (Vol. 34:2, pp. 381–398). Philadelphia: W. B. Saunders.

Anonymous. (1970). *The little red book.* Center City, MN: Hazelden.

Anonymous. (1980a). *Alcoholics anonymous* (3rd ed.). New York: Alcoholics Anonymous World Services.

Anonymous. (1980b). *Big book study guide.* Little Rock, AR: Kelly Foundation.

Anonymous. (1982). *Each day a new beginning: Daily, meditations for women.* New York: Harper & Row.

Anonymous. (1986). *Twelve steps and twelve traditions* (thirty-second printing). New York: Alcoholics Anonymous World Services.

Arnold, M. B. (1970). *Feelings and emotions.* New York: Academic Press.

Bassin, A. (1971). *Developing a life plan* [Unpublished handout]. Tallahassee, FL.

Beck, A. T. (1976). *Cognitive therapy and emotional disorders.* New York: International University Press.

Beck, A. T., & Emery, G. (1977). *Cognitive therapy of substance abuse.* Philadelphia, PA: Center for Cognitive Therapy.

Beschner, G. M., & Friedman, A. S. (1985). Treatment of adolescent drug abusers. *The International Journal of the Addictions, 20*(6&7), 971–993.

Binstock, L. (1982). How to conquer the ten most common causes of failure. In O. Mandino (Ed.), *University of success.* New York: Bantam.

Brammer, M. B. (1979). *The helping relationship: Process and skills.* Englewood Cliffs, NJ: Prentice-Hall.

Burnett, R. D., Kulhavy, R. W., & Krug, S. E. (1983). *Individualized stress management: Program coordinator's manual.* Champaign, IL: IPAT.

Carpenter, L. (1979). *Are you an unhappy parent? Maybe you have fallen into the good parent trap.* Lexington, KY: Rational Behavior Therapy Center.

Carpenter, L. (1982). *Watch your language* [Unpublished handout] Lexington, KY.

Cassidy, F. S. (1992). *Second chance* [Promotion literature]. Memphis, TN: Second Chance Ministry.

Cavaiola, A. A., & Kane-Cavaiola, C. (1989). Basics of adolescent development for the chemical dependency professional. In P. B. Henry (Ed.), *Practical approaches in treating adolescent chemical dependency: A guide to clinical assessment and intervention* (pp. 11–24). New York: Haworth.

Clark, H. W. (1987). On professional therapists and alcoholics anonymous. *Journal of Psychoactive Drugs, 19*(3), 233–242.

Covert, J., & Wangberg, D. (1992). Peer Counseling: Positive Peer Pressure. In G. W. Lawson & A. W. Lawson (Eds.), *Adolescent substance abuse: Etiology, treatment, and prevention* (pp. 131–140). Gaithersburg, MD: Aspen.

Donovan, D. M., & Marlatt, G. A. (Eds.). (1988). *Assessment of addictive behaviors.* New York: Guilford.

Dupont, R. L. (1984). *Getting tough on gateway drugs: A guide for the family.* Washington, DC: American Psychiatric Press.

Ehrlich, P. (1987). 12 step principles and adolescent chemical dependence treatment. *Journal of Psychoactive Drugs, 19*(3), 311–317.

Ellis, A. (1962). *Reason and emotion in psychotherapy.* New York: Lyle Stuart.

Ellis, A., McInerney, J. F., DiGiuseppe, R., & Yeager, R. J. (1988). *Rational-emotive therapy with alcoholics and substance abusers.* New York: Pergamon Press.

Fowles, D. C. (1988, May). Models of addiction [Special issue]. *Journal of Abnormal Psychology, 97*(2), 1–136.

Friedman, A. S., & Glichman, N. W. (1986). Program characteristics for successful treatment of adolescent drug abuse. *Journal of Nervous and Mental Disease, 174*(11), 669–679.

Friedman, A. S., Schwartz, R., & Utada, A. (1989). Outcome of a unique youth drug abuse program: A follow-up study of the clients of Straight, Inc. *Journal of Substance Abuse Treatment, 6,* 259–268.

Gabe, J. (1989). *A professional's guide to adolescent substance abuse.* Springfield, IL: Academy of Addictions Treatment Professionals.

Galanter, M., Gleaton, T., Marcus, C. E., & McMillen, J. (1984). Self-help groups for parents of young drug and alcohol abusers. *American Journal Psychiatry, 141*(7), 889–891.

George, R. L. (1990). *Counseling the chemically dependent.* Engelwood Cliffs, NJ: Prentice Hall.

Glasser, W. (1965). *Reality therapy: A new approach to psychiatry.* New York: Harper & Row.

Glasser, W. (1972). *The helper must be.* [Unpublished lecture notes]. Los Angeles.

Glasser, W. (1984). *Control theory: A new explanation of how we control our lives.* New York: Harper & Row.

Goldstein, M. S., Surber, M., & Wilner, D. M. (1984). Outcome evaluations in substance abuse: A comparison of alcoholism, drug abuse, and other mental health interventions. *The International Journal of theAddictions, 19*(5), 479–502.

Gorski, T. T., & Miller, M. (1982). *Counseling for relapse prevention*. Independence, MO: Independence.

Henry, P. B. (Ed.). (1989). *Practical approaches in treating adolescent chemical dependency: A guide to clinical assessment and intervention*. Binghampton, NY: Haworth.

Hoffmann, N. G., Sonis, W. A., & Halikas, J. A. (1987). Issues in the evaluation of chemical dependency treatment programs for adolescents. *Pediatric Clinics of North America, 34*(2), 449–459.

Hoogerman, D., Huntley, D., Griffith, B., Petermann, H., & Koch, C. (1984). Effective intervention for adolescents harmfully involved in alcohol and drugs. *The Journal of the Florida Medical Association, 71*(4), 227–232.

Isralowitz, R., & Singer, M. (Eds.). (1983). *Adolescent substance abuse: A guide to prevention and treatment*. New York: Haworth.

Kelly, G. (1955). *The psychology of personality constructs* (Vols. 1 & 2). New York: Norton.

Kentucky Chemical Dependency Counselors' Professional Certification Board. (1987). *Certification manual*. Lexington, KY: KCDC Professional Certification Board.

Kids Helping Kids. (1990). *Evaluation of treatment program* [Unpublished results of a follow-up survey of teenagers in treatment]. Hebron, KY.

King, P. (1988). Treatment for chemically dependent adolescents. *Professional Counselor, 2*(4), 46–48.

Knudtson, F. (1980). *Developmental psychology*. Berkeley, CA: Association for Advanced Training in the Behavioral Sciences. (In preparatory course for the national and state licensing examinations in psychology, twelfth series, vol. 2, 1982)

Korb, M. P., Gorrell, J., & Van De Riet, V. (1989). *Gestalt therapy: Practice and theory*. New York: Pergamon Press.

Lach, E. (1991). *A checklist for teenage behavior* [Pamphlet]. Lexington, KY: Possibilities Unlimited.

Lange, A. J., & Jakubowski, P. (1977). *Responsible assertiveness behavior: Cognitive-behavioral procedures for trainers*. Champaign, IL: Research Press.

Lawson, G. W., & Lawson, A. W. (Eds.). (1992). *Adolescent substance abuse: Etiology, treatment, and prevention*. Gaithersburg, MD: Aspen.

Lawson, G. W., Ellis, D. C., & Rivers, P. C. (1984). *Essentials of chemical dependency counseling*. Rockville, MD: Aspen.

Lazarus, R. (1966). *Psychological stress and the coping process*. New York: McGraw-Hill.

MacKenzie, R. G., Cheng, M., & Haftel, A. J. (1987). The clinical utility and evaluation of drug screening techniques. In P. D. Rogers (Ed.), *The pediatric clinics of North America: Chemical dependency* (Vol. 34:2, pp. 423–436). Philadelphia: W. B. Saunders Company.

Marlatt, G. A., & Gordon, J. R. (1985). *Relapse prevention: Maintenance strategies in the treatment of addictive behaviors.* New York: Guilford.

Mast, C. K. (1986). *Sex respect: The option of true sexual freedom.* Bradley, IL: Respect.

Maultsby, M. C. (1975). *Help yourself to happiness.* New York: Institute for Rational Living.

Maultsby, M. C. (1978). *A million dollars for your hangover.* Lexington, KY: Rational Self-Help Books.

Maultsby, M. C. (1979, December). Behavioral diagnosis and treatment of the emotionally distressed adolescent. *Interaction,* p. 4.

Maultsby, M. C. (1980). *Rational rules for making rules* [Unpublished handout]. Lexington, KY.

Maultsby, M. C. (1981). *The professional's handbook for group rational behavioral therapy: The ideal cognitive-behavioral psychotherapy.* Lexington, KY: RSA. (Supplement to the professional self-training kit for group rational behavioral therapy.)

Maultsby, M. C. (1982a). *The rational use of should* [Unpublished handout]. Lexington, Ky.

Maultsby, M. C. (1982b). *Self-downing cycle, self-acceptance cycle.* [Unpublished handout]. Lexington, KY.

Maultsby, M. C. (1984). *Rational behavior therapy.* Englewood Cliffs, NJ: Prentice-Hall.

Maultsby, M. C. (1986). *Coping better: Anytime, anywhere.* New York: Prentice Hall.

Maultsby, M. C., & Hendricks, A. (1974). *You and your emotions.* Lexington, KY: Rational Behavioral Therapy.

McCourt, W., & Glantz, M. (1980). Cognitive behavior therapy in groups for alcoholics: A preliminary report. *Journal of Studies on Alcohol, 41*(3), 338–346.

Meichenbaum, D. (1977). *Cognitive-behavior modification: An intearated approach.* New York: Plenum Press.

Meichenbaum, D. (1985). *Stress inoculation training.* New York: Pergamon Press.

Meyer, R. G. (1983). *The clinician's handbook: The pyschopathology of adulthood and late adolescence.* Boston: Allyn & Bacon.

Miller, S., Nunnally, E. W., & Wackman, D. B. (1991). *Talking and Listening Together.* Littleton, CO: Interpersonal Communicatin Programs.

Miller, S., Nunnaly, E. W., & Wackman, D. B. (1979). Talking Together. Littleton, CO: Interpersonal Communication Programs.

Miller, W. R., & Hester, R. K. (1980). Treating the problem drinker: Modern approaches. In W. R. Miller (Ed.), *The addictive behaviors: Treatment of alcoholism, drug abuse, smoking, and obesity* (pp. 11–141). Oxford, England: Pergamon.

Mischel, W. (1973). Toward a cognitive social learning reconceptualization of personality. *Psychological Review, 80,* 252–283.

Monahan, B. (1985). Relapse: A process. *Recovery,* Sept.–Oct., 8.

Mowrer, H. (1960). *Learning theory and behavior.* New York: John Wiley & Sons.

Nakken, C. (1988). *The addictive personality: Roots, rituals, recovery*. Minneapolis: Hazelden.

National Institute on Drug Abuse. (1992). *User's guide: Assessment*. Alliance for the 21st century series (#271-90-2205). Rockville, Maryland: NIDA.

Nay, W. R. (1979). *Multimethod clinical assessment*. NY: Gardner Press, Inc.

Nay, W. R., & Ross, G. R. (1993). Cognitive-behavorial intervention for adolescent drug abuse. In A. J. Finch, W. M. Nelson, & S. O. Edith (Eds.), *Cognitive-behavioral procedures with children and adolescents* (pp. 315–342). Boston: Allyn & Bacon.

O'Connell, D. F. (1988). Counseling the dually diagnosed patient. *The Counselor, July/August*, 1–7.

Office for Treatment Improvement, United States Department of Health and Human Services. (1992). *Request for applications: HIV/AIDS and related diseases among substance abusers: Community based outreach and intervention demonstration program* (FDA # 93.949). Washington, DC: United States Government.

Okun, B. F., & Rappaport, L. J. (1980). *Working with families*. North Scituate, MA: Duxbury Press.

Peters, R. (1970). The education of emotion. In M. B. Arnold (Ed.), *Feelings and emotion*. New York: Academic Press.

Poppen, R. (1988). *Behavioral relaxation training and assessment*. New York: Pergamon Press.

Rencken, R. H. (1989). *Intervention strategies for sexual abuse*. Alexandria, VA: American Association for Counseling and Development.

Richeson, F. (1977). *Four dimensions in recovery* (cassettetape 1, side 1). St. Paul: Step One.

Ries, R., Batran, J., & Shuckit, M. A. (1980). Recognizing the drug abuser with psychiatric complaints. *Behavioral Medicine, 3*, 18–21.

Rokeach, M. (1970). *Beliefs, attitudes and values: A theory of organization and change*. San Francisco: Jossey-Bass.

Ross, G. R. (1978). *Development and validation of a scale of dysfunctional self regard* Unpublished doctoral dissertation, University of South Florida, Tampa, FL.

Ross, G. R. (1983a). *Application for six month follow-up conference* [Unpublished handout]. Lexington, KY.

Ross, G. R. (1983b). *Daily moral inventory* [Unpublished handout]. Lexington, KY.

Ross, G. R. (1983c). *FHB/CHB* [Lecture]. Lexington, KY.

Ross, G. R. (1983d). *Seven steps to a happy (F)ACE* [Unpublished handout]. Lexington, KY.

Ross, G. R. (1983e). *Were only as sick as the secrets we keep* [Lecture]. Lexington, KY.

Ross, G. R. (1985a). *Critiquing group sessions* [Unpublished handout]. Lexington, KY.

Ross, G. R. (1985b). *RSA groups*. Lexington, KY: unpublished paper.

Ross, G. R. (1988). *What is getting straight?* [Lecture]. Lexington, KY.

Ross, G. R. (1990a). *Language of anger and resentment* [Lecture]. Lexington, KY.
Ross, G. R. (1990b). Recognizing and treating the chemical dependent offender. *The Advocate, 13*(1), 52–55.
Ross, G. R. (1991). *Possibilities Unlimited Inc.: Policies and procedures manual.* Lexington, KY: unpublished.
Rothschild, B. H. (1986). The use of rational-emotive therapy techniques in the drug-free therapeutic community. *Journal of Psychoactive Drugs, 18*(3), 261–266.
Ryrie, C. C. (1978). *The Ryrie study bible.* Chicago: Moody Press.
Samenow, S. E. (1984). *Inside the criminal mind.* New York: Random House.
Samenow, S. E. (1987). *Errors in thinking* [Unpublished handout]. Alexandria, VA.
Satir, V. (1964). *Conjoint family therapy.* Palo Alto, CA: Science and Behavior Books.
Schacter, S. (1967). Cognitive effects of bodily functioning: Studies of obesity and eating. In E. D. Glass (Ed.), *Neurophysiology and emotion.* New York: Rockefeller University Press.
Schacter, S. (1971). *Emotion, obesity, and crime.* New York: Academic Press.
Schuckit, M. A. (1984). *Drug and alcohol abuse: A clinical guide to diagnosis and treatment* (2nd ed.). New York: Plenum Press.
Schuller, R. H. (1982). *Self esteem the new reformation.* Waco, TX: Word Books.
Selekman, M. D., & Todd, T. C. (1991). Critical issues in treatment of adolescent substance abusers and their families. In T. C. Todd & M. D. Selekman (Eds.), *Family therapy approaches with adolescent substance abusers* (pp. 3–28). Boston: Allyn & Bacon.
Shostrom, E. L. (1968). *Man the manipulator: The inner Journey from manipulation to actualization.* New York: Bantam Books.
Shostrom, E. L. (1977). *Actualizing therapy: Foundations for a scientific ethic.* San Diego: EdITS.
Shulman, G. (1985). Adolescent 'state of the art' humbling. *U.S. Journal of Drug and Alcohol Dependence, 9*(6), 15.
Siminov, P. (1970). The information theory of emotion. In M. Arnold (Ed.), *Feelings and emotion.* New York: Academic Press.
Snyder, W. (1993). Seeing the troubled adolescent in context: Family systems theory and practice. In Substance Abuse and Mental Health Services Administration, *Empowering families, helping adolescents: Family-centered treatment of adolescents with mental health and substance abuse problems* (pp. 13–40). Washington, DC: Department of Health & Human Services.
Sobell, M. B., Serge, B., Sobell, L. C., Roy, J., & Stevens, J. (1987). Alcohol treatment outcome evaluation methodology: State of the art 1980–1984. *Addictive Behaviors, 12,* 113–128.
Spielberger, C. (1970). Anxiety as an emotional state. In C. Spielberger (Ed.), *Anxiety: Current trends in theory and research* (Vol. 1). New York: Academic Press.
Stanton, M. (1979). Drugs and the family: A review of the literature. *Marriage and Family Review, 2*(1), 1–10.

Stufflebeam, D. L., Foley, W. J., Gephart, W. J., Guba, E. G., Hammond, R. L., Merriman, H. O., & Provus, M. M. (1971). *Educational evaluation and decision making* (PDK National Study Committee on Evaluation). Itasca, IL: F. E. Peacock.

Sunday Patriot News. (1979, October 21). Editorial. *Sunday Patriot News.* (Editorial)

Swindoll, C. R. (1987a). *Galatians: Letter of liberation.* Bible Study Guide. Waco, TX: Word Books.

Swindoll, C. R. (1987b). *The quest for character.* Portland: Multnomah.

Twerski, A. J. (1990). *Addictive thinking.* Center City, MN: Hazelden Foundation.

U.S. Journal of Drug and Alcohol Dependence. (1985). Editorial (trade publication). *The U.S. Journal of Drug and Alcohol Dependency, 9*(6), 1–2.

Vaillant, G. E. (1983). *The natural history of alcoholism: Causes patterns, and paths to recovery.* Cambridge, MA: Harvard University Press.

Voth, H. (1980). *How to get your kid off marijuana.* Los Angeles: Patient Care Publications.

Wegscheider-Cruse, S. (1983). *The family trap.* Rapid City, SD: Nuturing Networks.

Wegscheider-Cruse, S. (1988). *The co-dependency trap.* Rapid City, SD: Nuturing Networks.

Weinberg, J. R., & Kosloske, D. (1977). *Fourth step guide: Journey into growth.* Minneapolis, MN: Comp Care.

Wheeler, K., & Malmquist, J. (1987). Treatment approaches in adolescent chemical dependency. In P. D. Rogers (Ed.), *The pediatric clinics of North America: Chemical dependency* (Vol. 34, 2, pp. 437–448). Philadelphia: W.B. Saunders.

Whitfield, C. L. (1985). *Alcoholism and spirituality.* Rutherford, NJ: Perrin.

Wilford, B. B. (Ed.). (1990). *Syllabus for the review course in addiction medicine.* Washington, DC: American Society of Addiction Medicine.

Wilson, G. T. (1987). Cognitive processes in addiction. *British Journal of Addiction, 82,* 343–353.

Yochelson, S., & Samenow, S. E. (1976). *The criminal personality. Volume 1: A profile for change.* New York: Jason Aronson.

Ziglar, Z. (1985). *See you at the top.* [Cassette tape 5 & 6]. Chicago: Nightingale-Conant.

Author Index

Subject Index